Mary Heilmann

Works on Paper

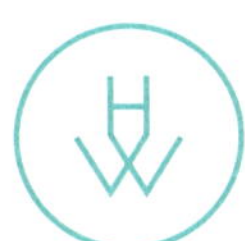

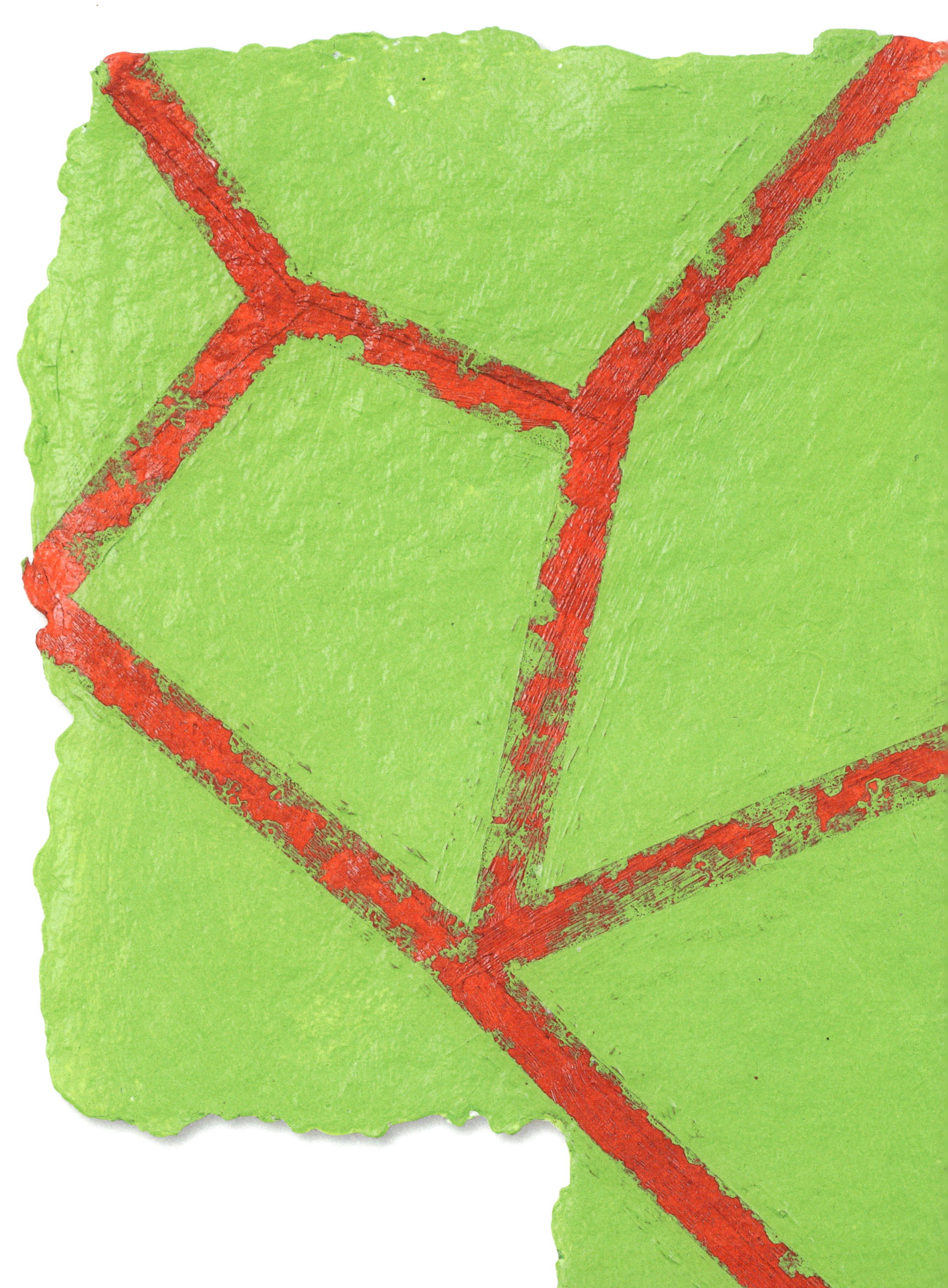

Mary Heilmann

Works on Paper
1973–2019

Hauser & Wirth Publishers

Contents

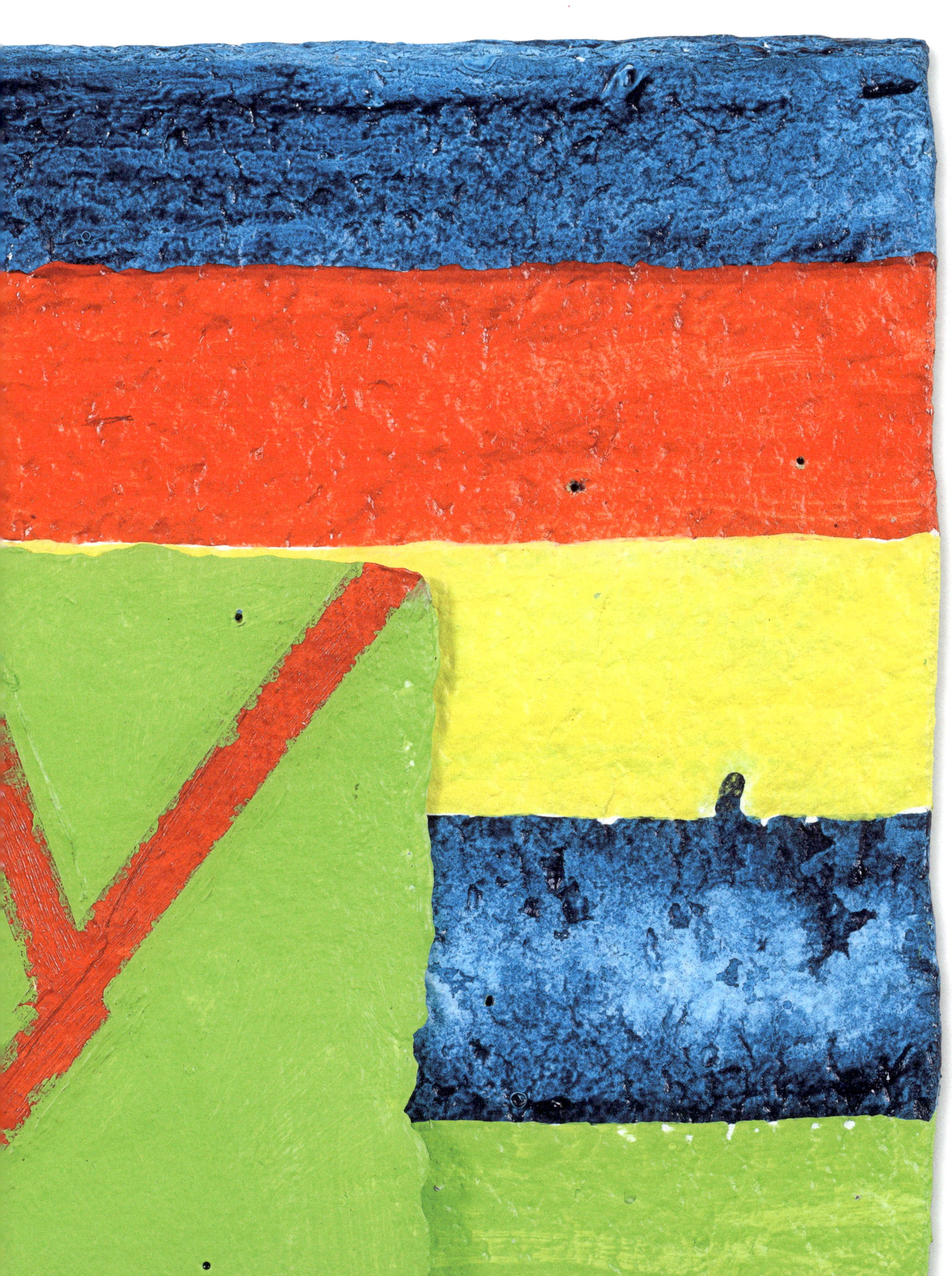

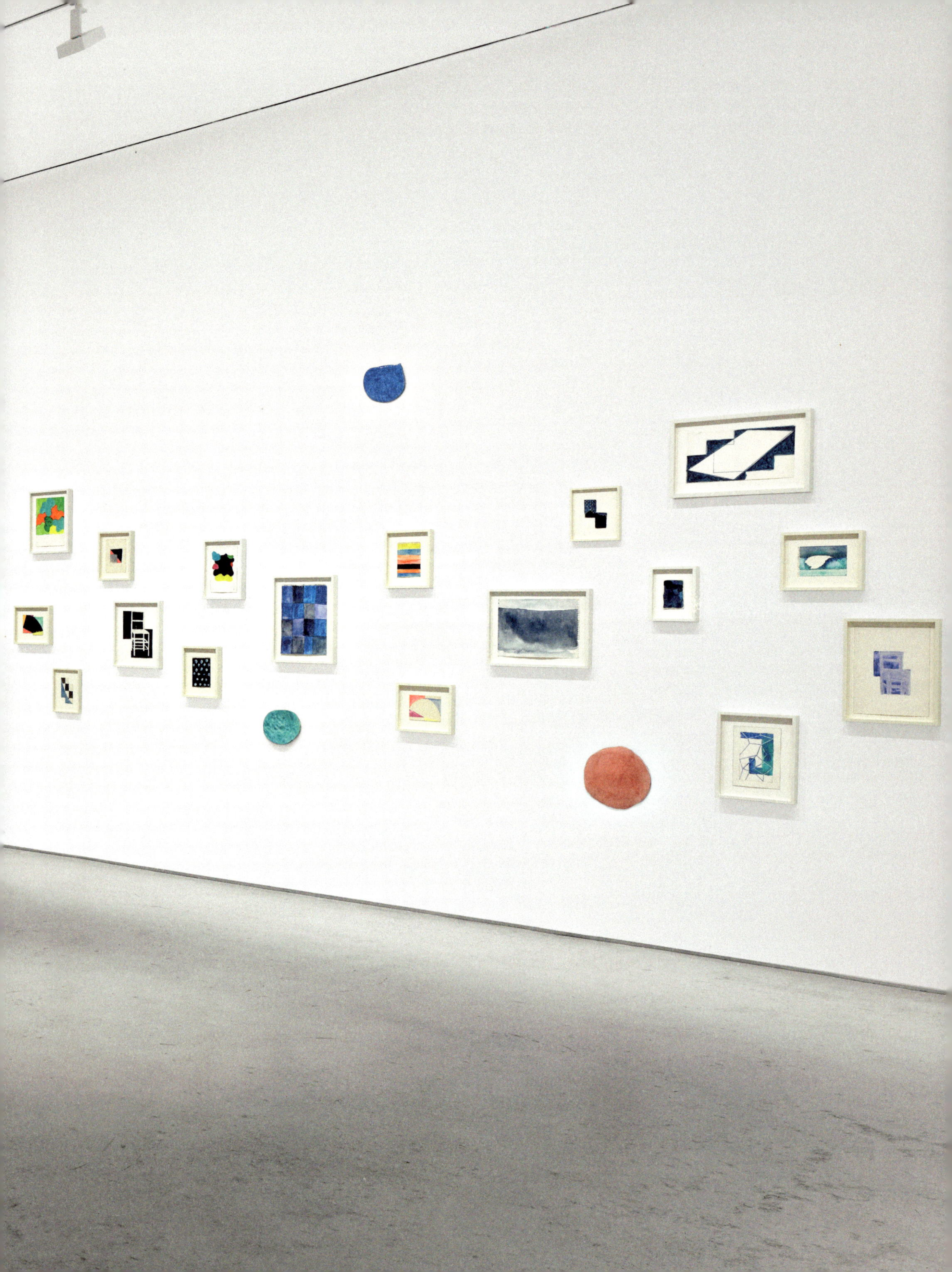

Vintage Gold

Alexis Lowry

"Vintage Gold." That's how Mary Heilmann described the trove of early drawings displayed across her Tribeca studio when Gary Simmons and I visited her in March of 2024. We were there to plan for an exhibition of Heilmann's works on paper that Simmons curated at Hauser & Wirth, *Daydream Nation*, and her description couldn't have felt more apt. Standing in front of this dynamic and rarely seen body of work, it felt like a door to understanding the artist's enigmatic career of more than fifty years was being unlocked.

Heilmann is celebrated for her evocative paintings that distill complex images and ideas into deceptively simple geometric forms and abstract gestural marks. In her own telling, her work begins with "daydreaming"—conjuring the sights, sounds, and events of her past or imagined future as color, shape, and line.[1] From this unique lexicon, she's developed a distinct visual language that is as informed by Minimalism's economy of means as it is by the Japanese aesthetic of *wabi-sabi* (the embrace of imperfection).

"Most of the time," Heilmann explains, "I start by writing, sketching, doodling, 'not serious drawing,' and I start by an idea I already have in my head."[2] "Serious," it should be said, is a relative term here. Throughout the 1970s and 1980s, Heilmann frequently captured her thoughts in pocket-sized sketchbooks that form a rich archival record of her process. Using small pads of paper, she jotted down ideas for paintings and tested compositional strategies at an intimate scale. These early sketchbooks reveal how drawing served as a crucial kind of memory notation for the artist—a way to capture and transpose into visual form the fleeting sense of a wave, a road, a chair, or a blanket. Yet these easy-going marks do more than give insight into Heilmann's larger paintings; many also exist as small works of art in their own right. They are, in this sense, truly vintage gold. In fact, drawing has always occupied a central, if lesser-known, place in Heilmann's practice. While she used paper to sketch out ideas for larger paintings until 1995—the year she acquired her first computer and began rendering those ideas on screen—she continues to paint on and with paper today.[3]

This publication presents the first survey in print of Heilmann's works on paper to date. It offers a lushly illustrated and comprehensive overview of her drawing practice and, through art historian Jo Applin's insightful essay and artist Ilana Savdie's compelling written reflection, extends consideration to many of the artist's core concerns through the particular lens of paper, memory, and process. It builds on the aforementioned exhibition, *Daydream Nation*, which featured a range of works from studies for larger paintings to fully realized paintings on paper, alongside a selection of Heilmann's chairs, ceramic sculptures, and a new wall drawing—her seventh— which was developed in conversation with Simmons.[4] (The latter frequently works with the embodied scale of wall drawings in his own work). The title of the exhibition—taken from the 1988 Sonic Youth album of the same name, beloved by both Heilmann and Simmons— situates Heilmann's work in relationship to the culture of youthful rebellion in New York City that remains so central to her, personally as well as professionally; it also evokes Heilmann's long-standing interest in daydreaming as a creative process and the importance of travel as a means of inducing this mode of thinking.

Heilmann often works in series, revisiting certain arrangements of form and color over time. Reviewing an exhibition of Heilmann's paintings on paper at Pat Hearn Gallery in 1995, the critic Roberta Smith observed, "the artist's work seems fueled by an almost Zenlike belief that nothing made by hand is ever made the same way twice."[5] With Heilmann, repetition begets difference, and it is in this multiplicity that some truth about the workings of memory emerges. It is also through this repetition, as Applin so insightfully argues in this publication, that the artist's work resists the easy structure of chronological categorization: Heilmann's "works shift back and forth, often across the years"—and, I would add, between media—"as opposed to moving inexorably forward, one leading to the other,"[6] each new iteration of a line, or a square, or a brush mark its own echo and distortion.

1.   See Mary Heilmann in "Fantasy," *Art in the Twenty-First Century*, season 5, episode 2, directed by Susan Sollins, aired October 13, 2009, PBS, television program; see also Heilmann, "Mary Heilmann," *Artforum* 54, no. 8 (April 2016).

2.   Heilmann in *Mary Heilmann: Waves, Roads, & Hallucinations*, directed by Matt Creed (New York: Tribeca, 2024), film.

3.   Lately Heilmann has been mixing paper pulp with acrylic to create dense and tactile surfaces on canvas.

4.   *Mary Heilmann: Daydream Nation* was on view at Hauser & Wirth New York, 22nd Street, from May 2 to June 26, 2024.

5.   Roberta Smith, "Heading West, with Canvases," *New York Times*, November 17, 1995.

6.   See Jo Applin, "Warm Up: Mary Heilmann's Works on Paper," in this publication, p. 15.

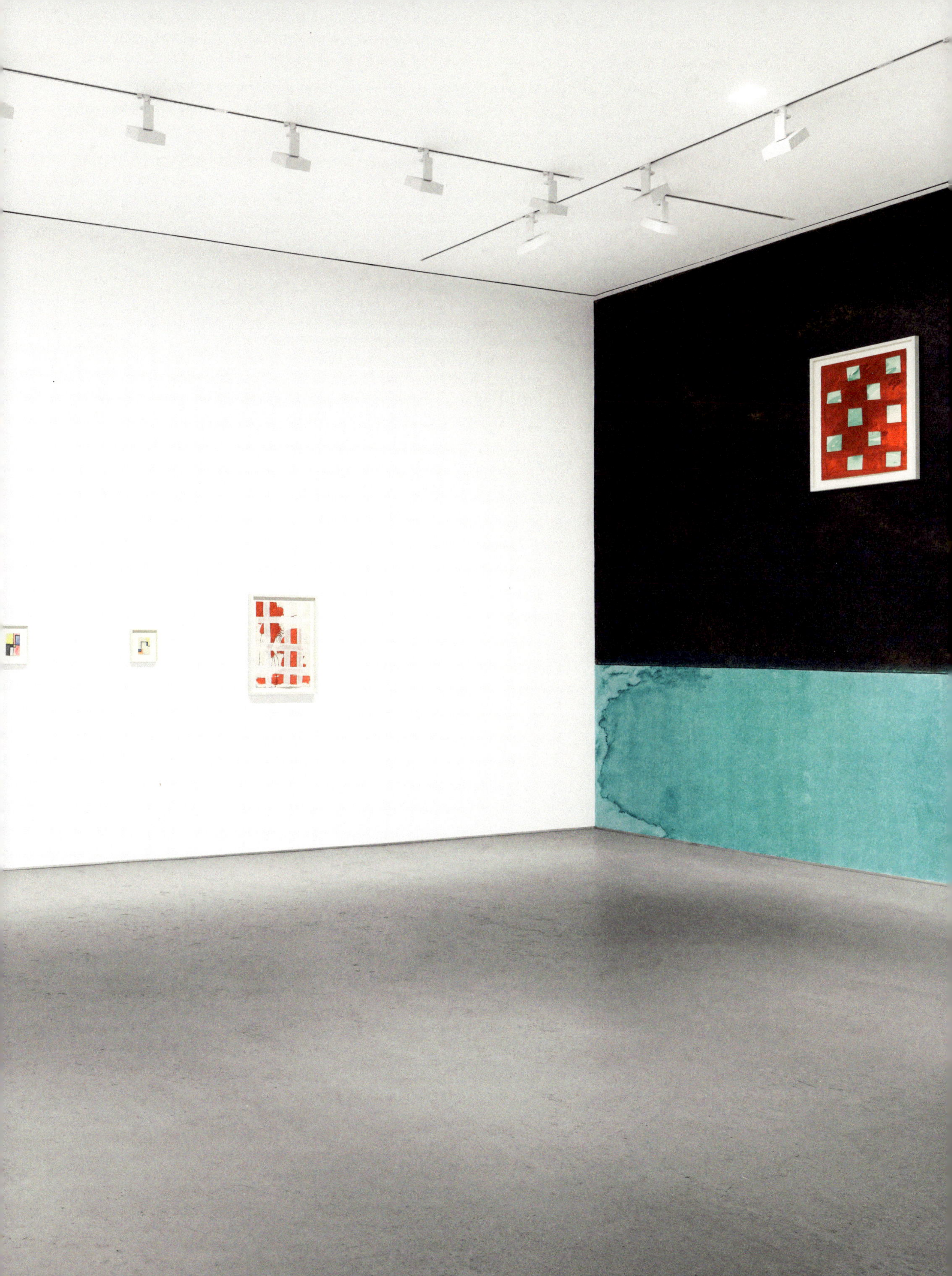

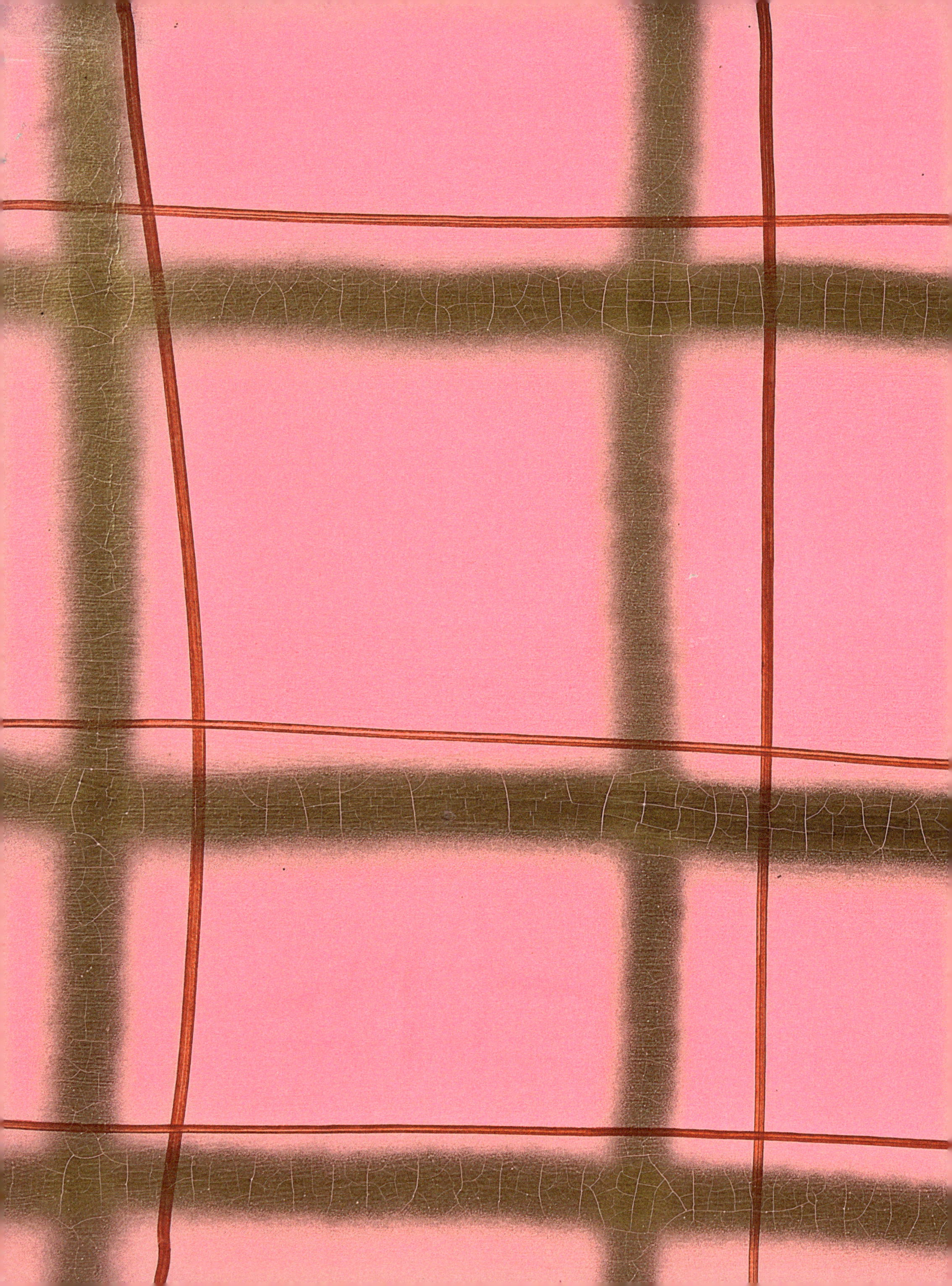

Warm Up: Mary Heilmann's Works on Paper

Jo Applin

Mary Heilmann is best known for the abstract paintings she has been making since the early 1970s. Less well-known, though no less numerous, are the extraordinary works on paper she has also made throughout her career, at some times more intensely than others. These include sketchbook drawings, large watercolor and acrylic "paintings on paper," and, since 1991, a group of smaller works on stiff sheets of handmade, textured paper.[1] Some exist in series, others are one-offs. Exploiting shifts in scale and different material supports, Heilmann incorporates a range of mediums into her paper-based practice. Over the years, these have included her preferred acrylic and watercolor paints, alongside oil paint, pastel, pencil, spray paint, colored pencil, and, on occasion, collaged elements pasted onto the surfaces of her works.

Pink Screen (detail), 1973. Acrylic and spray paint on paper
22 × 28 in. (55.9 × 71.1 cm)

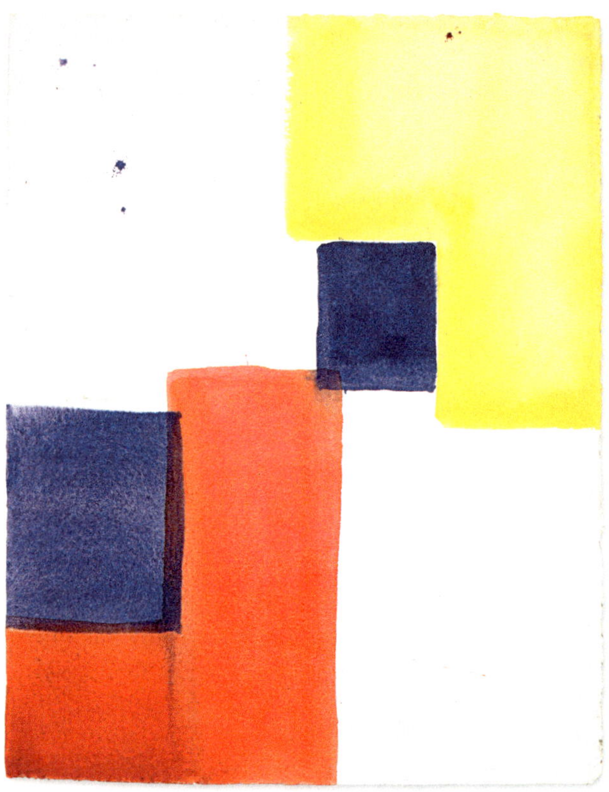

Works on paper tend to be coded as more "personal" than their large-scale painted counterparts, as though closer to "works in progress" or private "notes to self" than definitive public statements. I am not so sure this holds true for Heilmann, whose works on paper do something distinct from the paintings on canvas. The more intimate scale affords a less certain, more febrile form of expression. For instance, when Heilmann overlays an image with wonky geometric lines, patterns, and grids, it seems like a deliberately low-key modernist order has been imposed after the fact (fig. 1)— a playful, small-scale, and decidedly wobbly nod to her modernist predecessors, and at the same time a witty riposte.[2] Two of Heilmann's works on paper adopt this strategy vividly: the red spills and spatter of *Splash* (1982; p. 127) are pinned in place by a fat white grid, while in *Tea Garden* (1984; p. 103), a blocky checkerboard overlays a swirl of teal green, as though we are peering through a latticed window. That push and pull between the two registers of expressionism and geometric abstraction, modernist form and expressive expansiveness, lends the works their very particular, and often peculiar, charge.

Starting in the 1970s, and stopping sometime in the mid-1990s, Heilmann filled nearly forty mid-sized spiralbound sketchbooks with half-formed ideas and fully fleshed-out works (fig. 2). Watercolor paintings fill entire pages, while elsewhere penciled sketches and miniature iterations of the same idea repeat across the page in ink and pencil, as though she were trying to get the geometry and orientation right. One group of watercolors Heilmann made while on vacation in Hawaii is a rare example of the artist working in a figurative mode (pp. 74–77). In these, she captured palm trees and shorelines in naturalistic greens and blues applied in expressive, brushy strokes. They look like a set of homemade postcards, or scenes quickly captured for posterity. While they may seem an anomaly, the Hawaii sketches are, in fact, salient reminders that Heilmann frequently makes reference to personal memories and souvenirs; despite its ostensible abstraction, her work comes with its own autobiographical "backstory."[3]

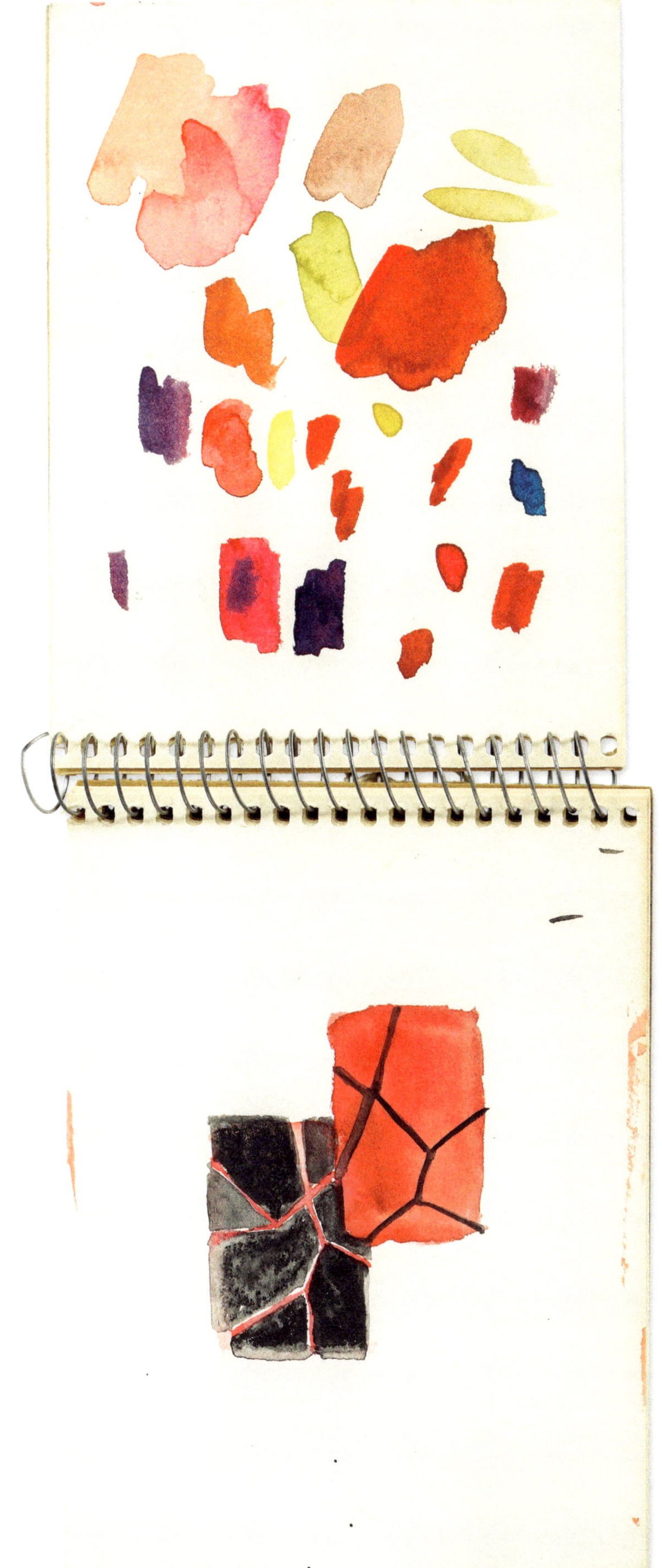

Fig. 2. Heilmann's sketchbook from ca. 1990

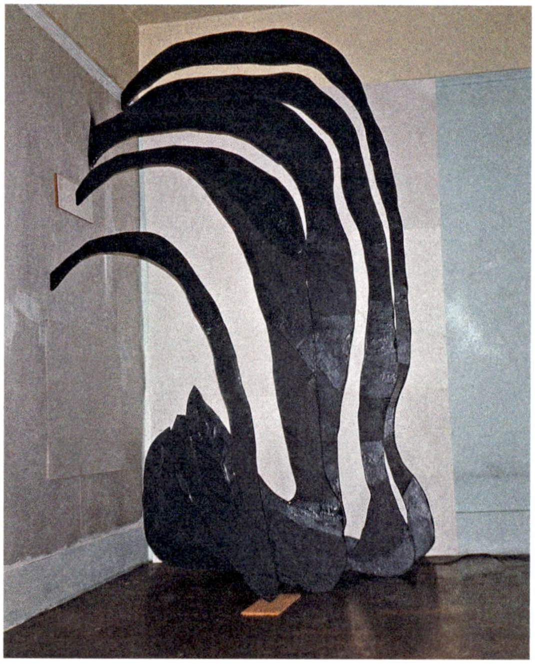

Heilmann trained in ceramics under Peter Voulkos at the University of California, Berkeley, between 1965 and 1967. Bucking against the conservativism there, where she always felt on the margins, Heilmann began to attend classes with William T. Wiley at the University of California, Davis, on the advice of her professor, Jim Melchert; there she first met and befriended Bruce Nauman.[4] These were formative years for Heilmann, and while she may have been "trying to be radical," she also recognized the subversive power of humor and how to bring that into the work.[5] It was an approach already familiar to the artists emerging on the West Coast art scene ("LA was funnier, more edgy than New York," she says).[6] During that period, Heilmann set about making ever-bigger sculptures, like *Ooze* (1967; fig. 3), inspired in part by photographs she had seen of Lucy Lippard's 1966 *Eccentric Abstraction* exhibition at Fischbach Gallery in New York, which featured contributions from eight artists including Eva Hesse, Louise Bourgeois, and Nauman. Heilmann's decision to start painting in 1970 was a deliberate ploy. She wanted to annoy her peers among whom she initially struggled to find a footing in New York. Painting—considered decidedly old hat by then—gave Heilmann an excuse to pick fights in bars with other artists, like Robert Smithson, establishing her difference within the art world.[7] Going "against the tide of art," as Briony Fer has put it, Heilmann's decision can be thought of as contrarian as well as in keeping with her long-standing interest in looking back and working in a retrospective mode—examining not just her own life, but longer histories of modernist painting, as well, repurposed for the punk era.[8]

By the time Heilmann arrived in New York, Lee Lozano—a decade older than Heilmann, who was not yet thirty—was making her own semi-geometric paintings and drawings. Lozano would sometimes clamp two or three canvases together, the image breaching the frame to stretch across the conjoined surfaces (fig. 4). This was an approach Heilmann adopted, too, for her paintings and later works on paper, gumming sheets together in awkward, offset formations. In 1970 both artists had solo shows just a few months apart, presenting their work in similarly dark, immersive environments. At the Whitney Museum Art Resource Center on the Lower East Side of Manhattan, Heilmann showed *The Book of Night* (1970; fig. 5),

Fig. 3. *Ooze*, 1967. Plywood with roofing tar, 86 × 48 × 24 in. (218.4 × 121.9 × 70 cm)

large, painted black sheets of folded canvas punctured with holes that reveal a series of silver stars painted on the final page, while at the Whitney Museum's building on Madison Avenue, Lozano showed her series of Wave paintings that, when spotlit, glowed against their black background (fig. 6).[9] Despite having much in common, to Heilmann's disappointment, the two women didn't hit it off. Lozano dismissed her work as "too much like Eva Hesse's stuff" (fig. 7)—a compliment as far as Heilmann, ever the contrarian, was concerned—and promptly left the younger artist's studio.[10]

The references with which Heilmann fills her works stem from everyday life: the artificial neon sights and sounds of New York City; ocean waves that recall her Californian childhood spent on the beach; contemporary film and fashion; and the music she has loved over the course of her life, from The Drifters to Sonic Youth. Hallucinatory colors and forms may refer to the drug-fueled years of the late sixties and seventies, including *Another Psychedelic Wave* (2005; fig. 8),

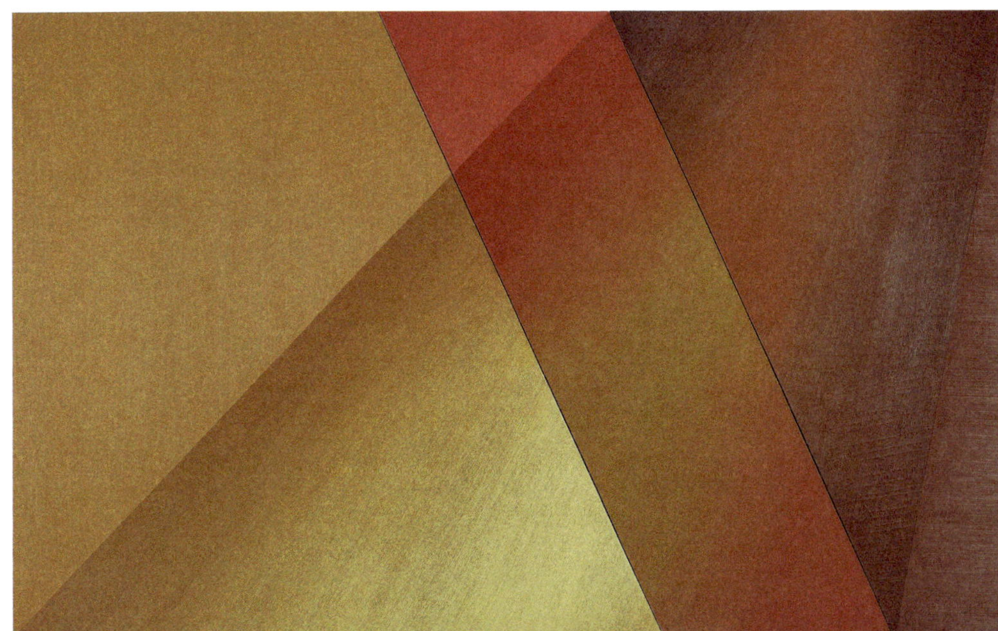

a small oil-on-paper work measuring just around four by six inches, in which fat bands of acid green, hot pink, and burnt orange span the sheet in vivid horizontal spills, one dripping into the other. Other works allude to the bi-coastal road trips Heilmann has made over the course of her career: in *Converge* (2007; fig. 9), an archival inkjet print of a photograph taken by Heilmann of the highway at dusk has been placed next to its abstraction, the road reconfigured as an aquatint checkerboard of bluish hues, the shift between abstraction and figuration registering as two sides of the same coin. Jutta Koether has described Heilmann's practice as a form of "open modernism," in which an abstract set of painted lines or bands refers to a modernist geometric grid or hallucinogenic vision and, at the same time, an air vent, a window, a horizon line, a wave, or a set of traffic markings.[11] We can think of this as an aleatory, dreamlike chain, where one thing, thought, or image sparks the memory of another: a sunset, a Mexican textile, a shoreline. Thinking in these terms suggests a

circular—rather than linear or chronological—ordering, in keeping with the artist's own claim that her works shift back and forth, often across the years, as opposed to moving inexorably forward, one leading to the other.[12]

When Heilmann purchased a computer in 1995, she quickly became enthralled by its possibilities, both in terms of remaking older works and plotting new ones. She mastered programs such as Photoshop, learning in the process how to draw "using light."[13] Working on a computer "completely reconfigured" how Heilmann thought about her artmaking, enabling her work to be, as she described, more "open, mobile, and free."[14] As opposed to the thick, tactile property of her paintings and works on paper, the works she made on screen were "edgeless, abstract" forms and colors.[15] With that shift to digital "drawing," Heilmann stopped making physical studies and sketches in her sketchbooks, and increasingly turned her attention to making paintings on paper.

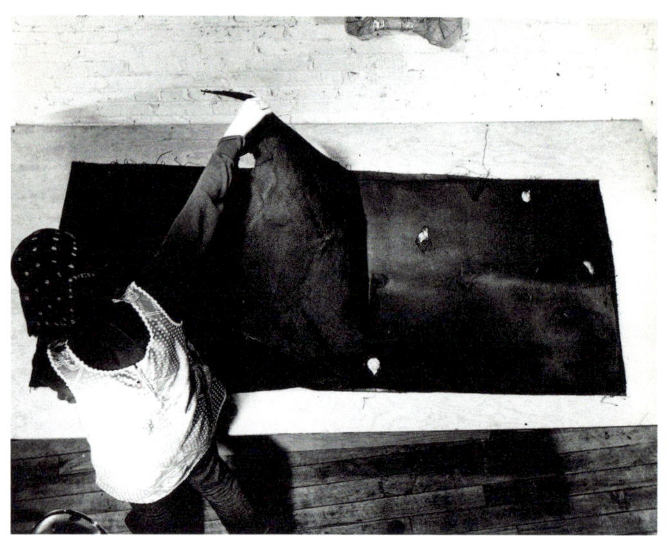

Fig. 5. Heilmann turning the pages of *The Book of Night* at the Whitney Museum Art Resource Center, New York, 1970

Fig. 6. Installation view of Lee Lozano's Wave paintings, Whitney Museum of American Art, New York, 1970

Heilmann's turn to working on a computer coincided with her move out of the city into a new home and studio in Long Island. The relocation also returned Heilmann to her earliest love, the ocean. That same year, she made her "indigo" series of works in oil on gessoed paper, painted in rich hues of blue and white (pp. 61–66). While she named the group after surfing terms, such as *Close Out* (1995; p. 64), they also conjure more urban images: a dark night glimpsed from a car window, the distant horizon barely visible in a relay between sights seen and memories recalled, between representation and abstraction. Some are painted in fat horizontal swipes, others with intimate gestural marks in a thin, sheer watery wash. Drips are clearly visible, revealing that the work was completed on a vertical axis, not flat on a table. They also reveal the order in which the layers of paint were applied. These details matter because Heilmann is fiercely private about her process and has always worked alone, leaving it for viewers to work things out.

A small group of watercolors from around 1989 capture the artist's silhouette against a black-and-white motif, an unusually literal insertion of Heilmann's self into her work (p. 99). The two included in this publication measure over sixteen inches in height: far from intimate, they feel like a statement of authorial intent. We meet the same impulse to both foreground and evade biographical interpretation in a work she made nearly twenty years later, *Her Life* (2006): a thirteen-minute slide presentation complete with a musical soundtrack accompanies a series of dreamlike pairings of photographs—buildings, roads, neon shop signage, and so on— alongside their painted abstractions, a strategy Heilmann described as "notating abstract imagery from the past."[16] And yet, of course, the slideshow both reveals nothing and everything at the same time; on offer here is obfuscation as much as information: a series of disconnected dots that refuse to join. Less, perhaps, a statement of intent than of evasion.

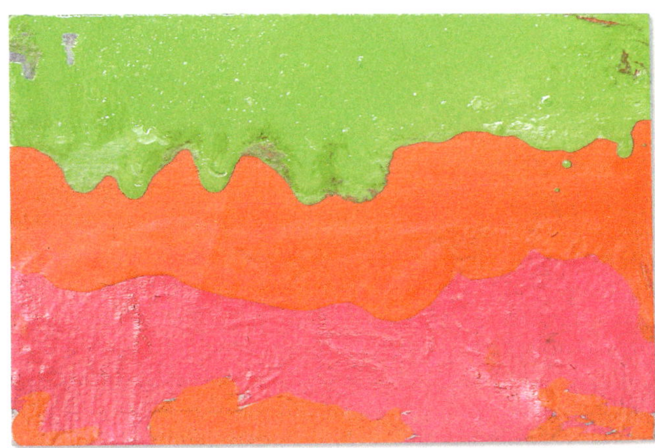

Fig. 8. *Another Psychedelic Wave*, 2005. Oil on paper,
4 × 6 in. (10.2 × 15.2 cm)

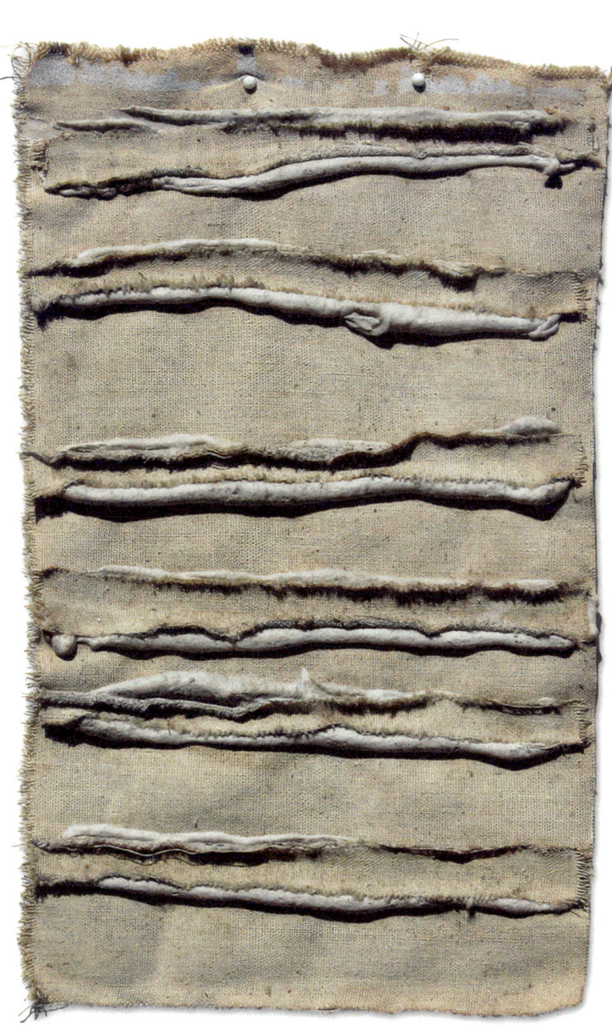

Fig. 7. Untitled, ca. 1968. Glue and canvas,
14 ½ × 9 in. (36.8 × 22.9 cm)

CALL AND RESPONSE

Shared motifs boomerang back and forth between Heilmann's
paintings, her works on paper, and the drawings and watercolors in
her sketchbooks. The relationship between them is not so much a
"before" and an "after" as a "call" and "response": one image finds
itself echoed, mirrored, or repeated back in a same-but-different form
or medium. Heilmann refers to these works as "warm-up studies,"
seemingly confirming their provisional quality as intermediary
works, the "before" to the "after" of the subsequent painting
or work on paper.[17] The temporal lag between the call and the
response—between the initial "warm-up study" and later finished
work or, perhaps, between one version of an idea and another—is
one of Heilmann's more idiosyncratic traits. It can be several years
before an earlier refrain is picked up. For instance, there is a forty-year
gap between an untitled watercolor study (1982—84; p. 28) and its

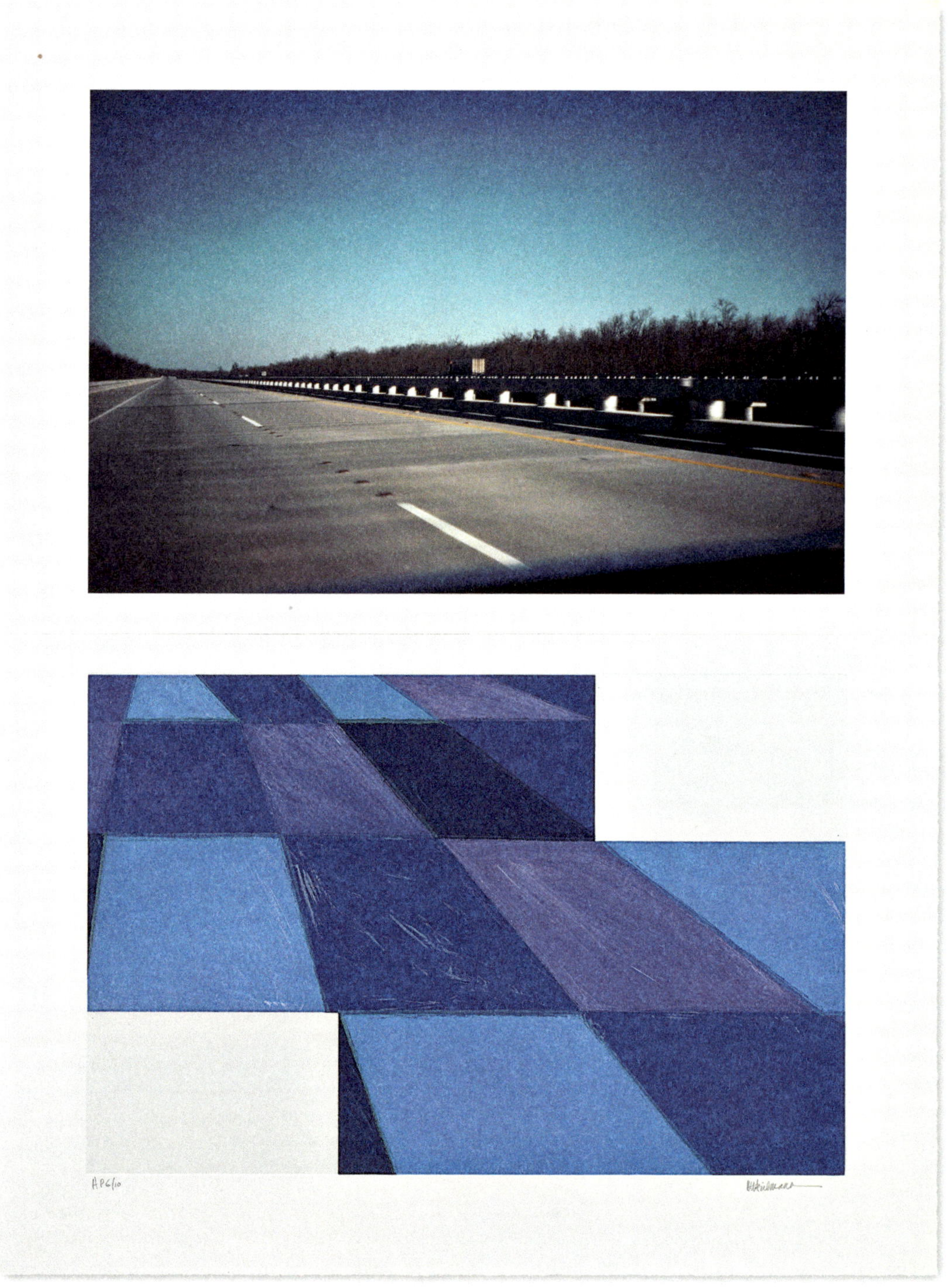

Fig. 9. *Converge*, 2007. Aquatint and archival pigment inkjet print,
38 ⅝ × 28 ½ in. (98.1 × 72.4 cm)

reemergence as the acrylic wall drawing *A Long Lost Soul* (2024; see p. 9, right wall). The long time lag between the earlier study and later drawing in this instance serves as a potent reminder that an artist's career rarely follows a neat linear order or progressive development and may just as readily encompass a circular process of back and forth.

Memory matters to Heilmann. She describes her work as an "autobiographical marker, a cue, by which I evoke a moment from my past, or my projected future, each a charm to conjure a mental reality, and to give it physical form."[18] She often starts her working day sitting quietly with already completed paintings and drawings. The aim is not to arrive at something brand new and fresh, but to return and rethink earlier works. This forms a key part of her process—another kind of "warm up"—as she looks back to move forwards. She says, "pieces are often made by recycling, combining previous paintings with new paintings, or two previous paintings superimposed, one on top of the other."[19] Heilmann describes her magpielike tendency to retrospectively repurpose material

from her own life in her work as a form of "obsessive-compulsive daydreaming."[20] While daydreaming might be considered a playful, or wasteful, activity, for Heilmann it is the cornerstone of her working practice, a kind of "meditation."[21] Freud had something to say about daydreaming, too, describing it as a form of artistic creativity akin to childhood play. Both activities, he writes, are deeply serious and creative forms of worldbuilding, as past, present, and future events are reordered and "strung together" to accommodate "the subject's shifting impressions of life."[22] This recalls what, in another context, Johanna Burton has described as Heilmann's series of "poetic pings based on color and shape."[23]

In Heilmann's larger acrylic paintings on paper, she presses the paint out and over the edges. She employs the same practice with her paintings on canvas, where the edges are as central to the work as the main surface. In fact, Heilmann often has her canvases mounted over stretcher bars that are deeper than the standard—about two inches, as opposed to the more usual three-fourths to one and a half inches—as if to assert their status as objects in the world, as *things.* It is another reason she likes to paint on paper with acrylic: not only because of the speed with which it dries, but also for the density with which the paint can be built up—quickly—so that even a flat surface can feel "dimensional."[24] That sense of her works as tactile objects continues in the much smaller, yet no less physically present, pieces of handmade paper with which she began working in the 1990s and returned to around 2014. These works hold their own as objects in ways wholly distinct from the paintings on canvas. Since 2021, Heilmann has mixed extra paper pulp with paint, producing effects that she considers "almost sculptural" as she sets about "building with color."[25]

The choice to hang the small paper pieces unframed on the wall lends weight to their status as objects, as does Heilmann's decision to sometimes glue them together into assembled, offset shapes. Examples include *Red Fall Encore* (2018; fig. 10) as well as *Negative Space One* and *Negative Space Two* (both 2014; both p. 125)—with these, Heilmann's choice of paper takes on a starring role. *6 Hot and Glassy* and *Mighty Right* (both 2019; both p. 72) may evoke waves lapping at the shoreline, the crust of paint-soaked paper pulp substituting ocean spray. But, like that famous nineteenth-century duck-rabbit illusion, just as the image comes into focus, it flips back to a gestural, painterly abstraction, refusing to settle as either one or the other. Traces of self and memories seep back into the work like watercolor pigments into the page, layered one on top of another. Because paper, Heilmann says, "has always been there."[26] Even though she has never made a habit of drawing in pencil, Heilmann can't remember a time when she wasn't surrounded by paper and sketchbooks, from the "big, beautiful" sheets of paper in school to her most recent handmade paper pieces, the sculptural surfaces of which she literally builds up from wet paper pulp.[27]

When Heilmann published her memoir, *The All Night Movie,* in 1999, it was as though she had released a key to understanding her works. It takes the form of an illustrated scrapbook, with text interspersed with photographic fragments and reproductions of her work alongside quotes and references to "the music heard at each phase in my life, from the '40s to the '90s."[28] In the accompanying text, Heilmann writes about her life and career, from her adolescence spent at the beach to her training in ceramics and subsequent move into large, abstract sculpture. In the chapter titled, "1968:

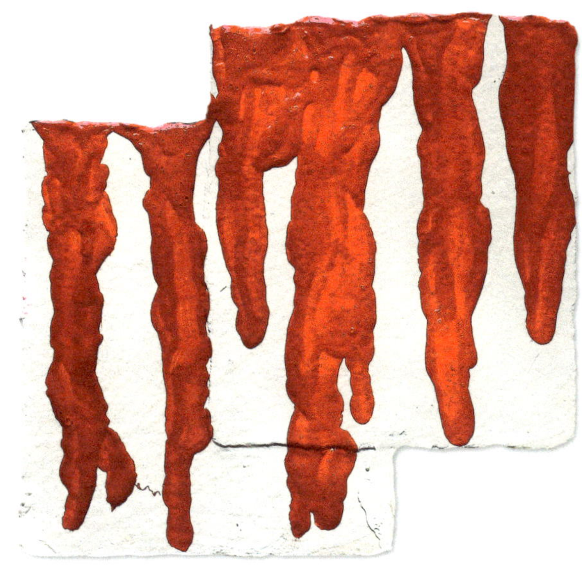

Fig. 10. *Red Fall Encore*, 2018. Acrylic and gesso on paper, 6 ¼ × 6 in. (15.9 × 15.2. cm)

NEW YORK," Heilmann describes her move to the city and her decision to jettison sculpture for painting. With *The All Night Movie,* Heilmann makes a claim for thinking about her work in retrospective terms, cueing readers to the contingencies of recollection and memory, and the creative, piecemeal means by which the past can be reconstructed, one thing—a color, a sound, a flash of remembrance— leading us to another. The act of turning the page or flicking back and forth through the book makes an object of *The All Night Movie,* its papery contents both a printed repository of her past, and physically present work in its own right.

Freud describes how writers use their daydreams as material sources, "softening" overtly personal aspects by "altering and disguising" them in a less biographically recognizable manner. He explains this process as one in which the writer uses the page as a lure of sorts and "bribes us" via "the purely formal—that is, aesthetic—yield of pleasure" that the work produces, offered up as what he calls an "incentive bonus, or a fore-pleasure" in lieu of full biographical disclosure.[29] While Heilmann tends to use daydreaming as preparation for, rather than source material for her work, her own act of "softening"—the incorporation of sly nods and humorous asides to modernism's past, for instance—can also be thought of as "bonuses" of a sort, tempering the more anecdotal, personal references that also surface from time to time. We can think of this not just as an act of "altering and disguising," but also as a more generous, generative form of call and response. In musical terms, a "call and response" describes a conversation between artist and audience, a playful invitation to join in with the making of a work's meaning. Heilmann's act of daydreaming—that softening of the contours between self and work, between abstraction and biography—does not so much "bribe" her viewers with the "purely formal" as gleefully welcome them in.

Many thanks to Mary Heilmann, Liane Thatcher, Alexis Lowry, and Jake Brodsky for their conversations and assistance in the preparation of this essay.

1. Heilmann's first paintings on handmade paper were made with leftover sheets from a group of prints she published with Pace Gallery in 1990.

2. Briony Fer has discussed Heilmann's relationship to Ellsworth Kelly and Piet Mondrian in Fer, "Mary Heilmann Painting, Her Way," in *Mary Heilmann: Looking at Pictures*, ed. Lydia Yee with Habda Rashid (London: Whitechapel Gallery, 2016), 70–81.

3. Heilmann has said, "Every piece of abstract art that I make has a backstory," in "Mary Heilmann: Every Piece has a Backstory," *Art21*, 2009, http://www.art21.org/texts/mary-heilmann/interview-mary-heilmann-every-piece-has-a-backstory, quoted in Yee, "Looking at Pictures," in *Mary Heilmann: Looking at Pictures*, 14.

4. Mary Heilmann, in conversation with the author, September 18, 2024.

5. Heilmann, in conversation.

6. Heilmann, in conversation.

7. Heilmann, interview by Ross Bleckner, "Mary Heilmann," in *BOMB* 67 (Spring 1999): 59.

8. Fer, "Mary Heilmann, Painting Her Way," 70.

9. On this encounter between Heilmann and Lozano, see Jo Applin, "Abrupt Terminations," in *Lee Lozano: Not Working* (New Haven: Yale University Press, 2018), 67–100.

10. Heilmann, in conversation with the author, July 17, 2015.

11. Jutta Koether, "Painting and All That. . . in Flight," in *The All Night Movie*, by Mary Heilmann (Zurich: Hauser & Wirth and Offizin Verlag, 1999), 78.

12. Heilmann, in conversation, 2024.

13. Heilmann, interview by Bleckner, 56.

14. Heilmann, quoted in Elizabeth Armstrong, "To Be Someone," in *Mary Heilmann: To Be Someone*, ed. Elizabeth Armstrong (Costa Mesa, California: Orange County Museum of Art, 2007), 11.

15. Heilmann, interview by Bleckner, 63.

16. Heilmann, interview by Bleckner, 58.

17. Heilmann, in conversation, 2024.

18. Heilmann, "Looking at Pictures," in *The All Night Movie*, 7.

19. Heilmann, interview by Bleckner, 62.

20. See Heilmann, "Obsessive-Compulsive Daydreaming," *Art Journal* 70, no. 2 (Summer 2011): 42–49.

21. Heilmann, in conversation, 2024.

22. Sigmund Freud, "Creative Writers and Day-Dreaming" in *Art and Literature*, Penguin Freud Library vol. 14 (London: Penguin, 1990), 135.

23. Johanna Burton, "Mountain Wave: Mary Heilmann's 'Mary Heilmann Phase,'" in *Mary Heilmann: To Be Someone*, 51.

24. Heilmann, in conversation, 2024.

25. Heilmann, in conversation, 2024.

26. Heilmann, in conversation, 2024.

27. Heilmann, in conversation, 2024.

28. Heilmann, interview by Bleckner, 63.

29. Freud, "Creative Writers and Day-Dreaming," 141.

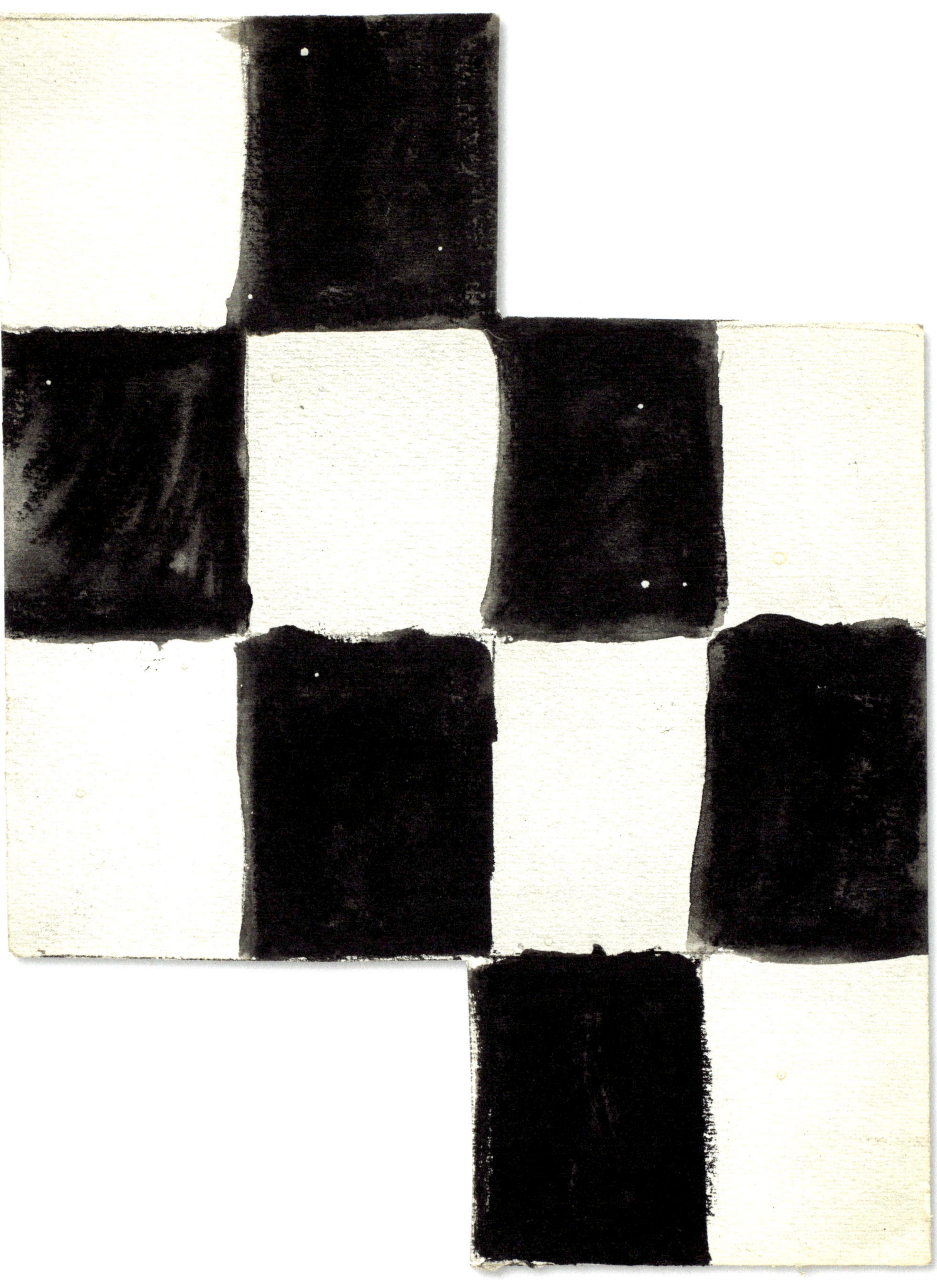

Fake Drips

Ilana Savdie

I remember Mary Heilmann once describing her work as "fake-shaped"—a term I found funny in the moment but that has continued to echo with sincerity in my mind. It struck me that listening to her speak and standing in front of her paintings is often a similar experience. Her words, like her work, can be casual and light, yet remain selective and direct. They are whimsical yet non-ornamental, purposely unbothered and highly self-aware. The register is mischievous and cheeky. It is this quality in her and her work that I find the most irresistible.

When I stand before a Mary Heilmann painting, I do what I often do in front of work that holds me: I pull it apart into material, tool, and time, and slowly try to put it back together, describing each step to myself so I can momentarily wear the hand of its maker. The experience of Heilmann's work can make it feel deceptively casual, fluid, and playful. It is when you trace the steps that made them that their schema begins to materialize before your eyes. Her work reveals, through this process, a sharp, matter-of-fact, and often even self-deprecating sense of humor that comes through in her hand. It is as though she is inviting you to forget that she is a formalist while every move before you is intentional and direct. Incidence is targeted. "Here's a drip, now here's a fake drip," she describes as she paints during a 2009 interview with *Art21*.

Heilmann often claims to have become a painter "to piss off the sculptors." She has a way of suggestively prodding at the ideological turf wars of art history. In their whimsy, her paintings uncrown, yet never abandon, those deeply theoretical modes of artmaking that dominated the spaces she came up in. Exploiting a tension between the serious and unserious is how she has managed, over the course of her multi-decade career, to infiltrate the spaces that initially attempted to exclude her.

It is in her drawings, mostly watercolors labeled as "studies," that I am able to fully grasp the thoughtful strategy of each gesture. In her off-register mark making (often due to what I read as an intentionally comedic choice of brush), she holds on to that youthful doubt we all contend with as painters and funnels it into undiluted resolve. In her hand, doubt is clever, laid bare in every gesture, as if channeled into a new raw material.

Heilmann's wizardry lies in a sensory intelligence and intuition that allows her to walk the tightrope of sincerity and play. Memory and emotion are pared down to elementary forms and colors, yet the nuance is always there. In one small watercolor study from 1989 (opposite), the fluid lines of a simple black-and-white grid, cropped by the shaped paper into square duets, allow for the forms to glide into each other, almost suggestive of a ballet. In another study from the same year (p. 102), the grid dissects a deep red ground, like blood samples pressed together between plexi slides. A small watercolor she made while on a trip to Hawaii (p. 76, left) appears as a collapsing landscape of blues dissolving into greens, brushed around a scoop of empty space, like a boulder of gravity pressing down and distorting the scene. I start to see her drawings as a sort of membrane of nostalgia.

It is in her seemingly incongruous color combinations, humorously fluid marks, or that "fake-shaped"-ness in her work that I locate the playful. Yet almost subcutaneous in these matter-of-fact simplifications are hints of the familiar. She seems to always be giving me some kind of permission for that nostalgia. I can recall a pool I never swam in, a punk, feminist movement I wasn't alive for, an art-historical argument I never had at a bar I never went to. The drawings riff on memories and allow me to riff along with them, as if rewarding me for knowing—about her, about art history, about being somewhere sometime that I never really was.

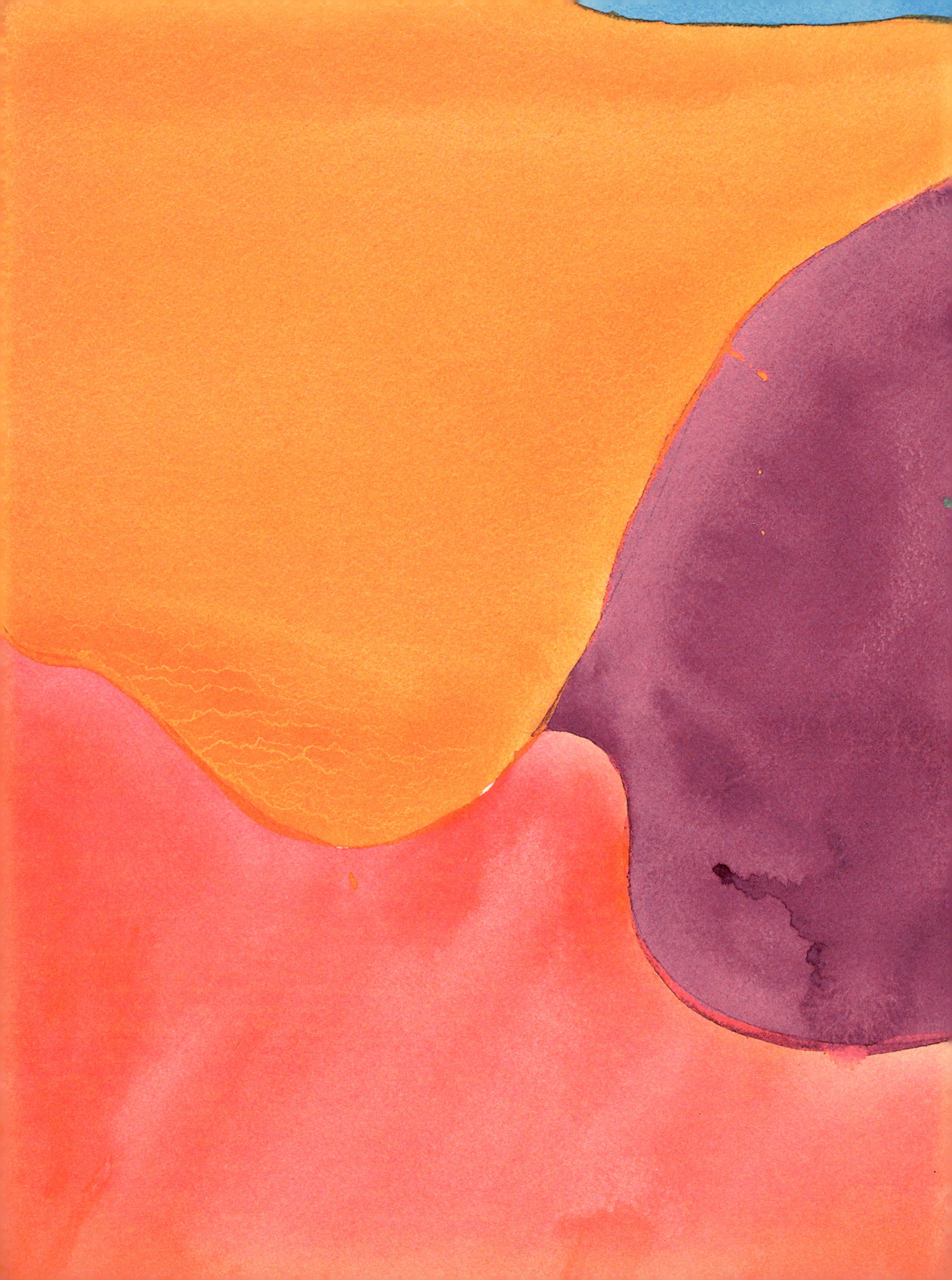

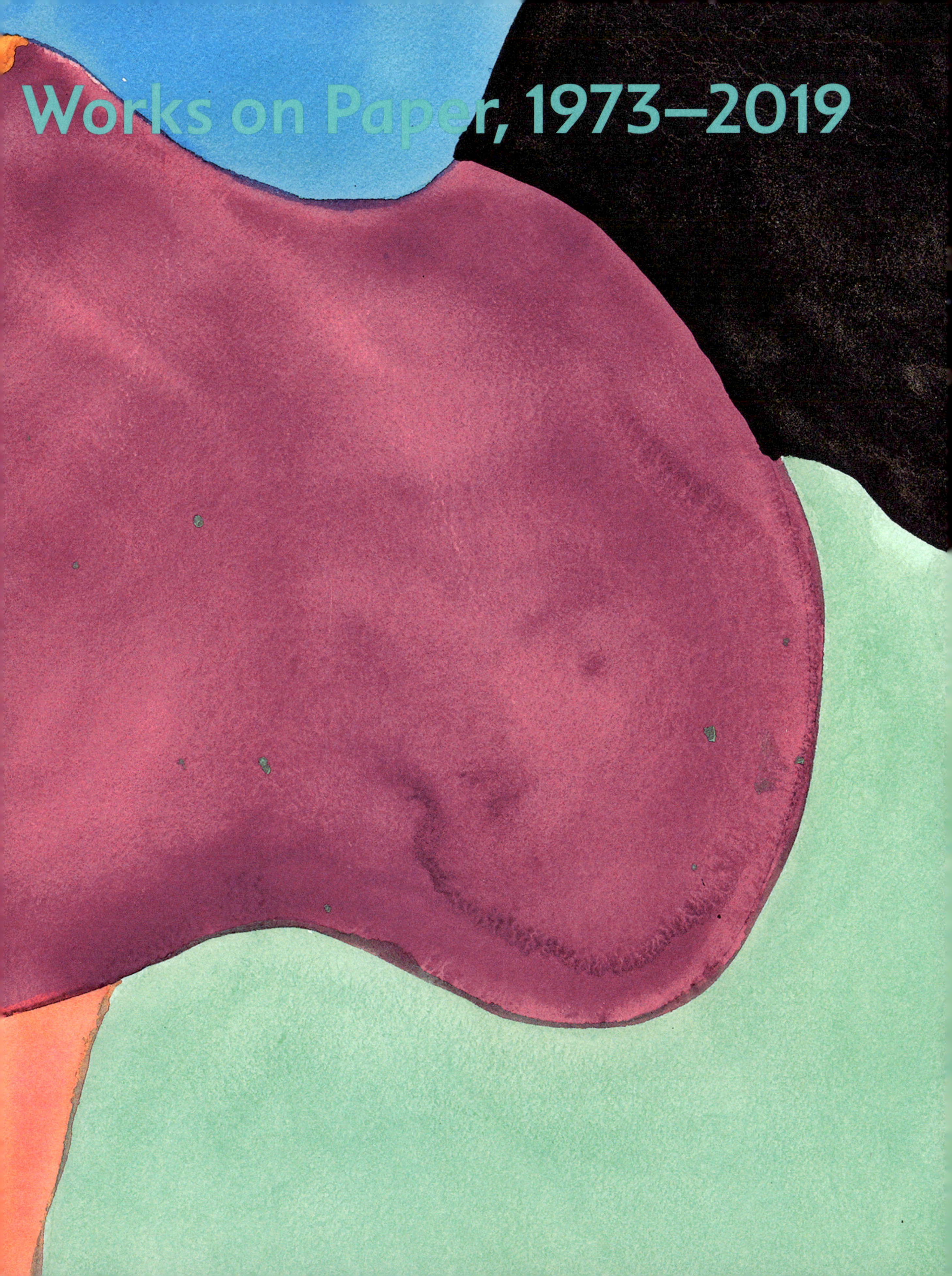
Works on Paper, 1973–2019

Mondrian, 1985. Watercolor on paper, 30 × 22 ½ in. (76.2 × 57.2 cm)

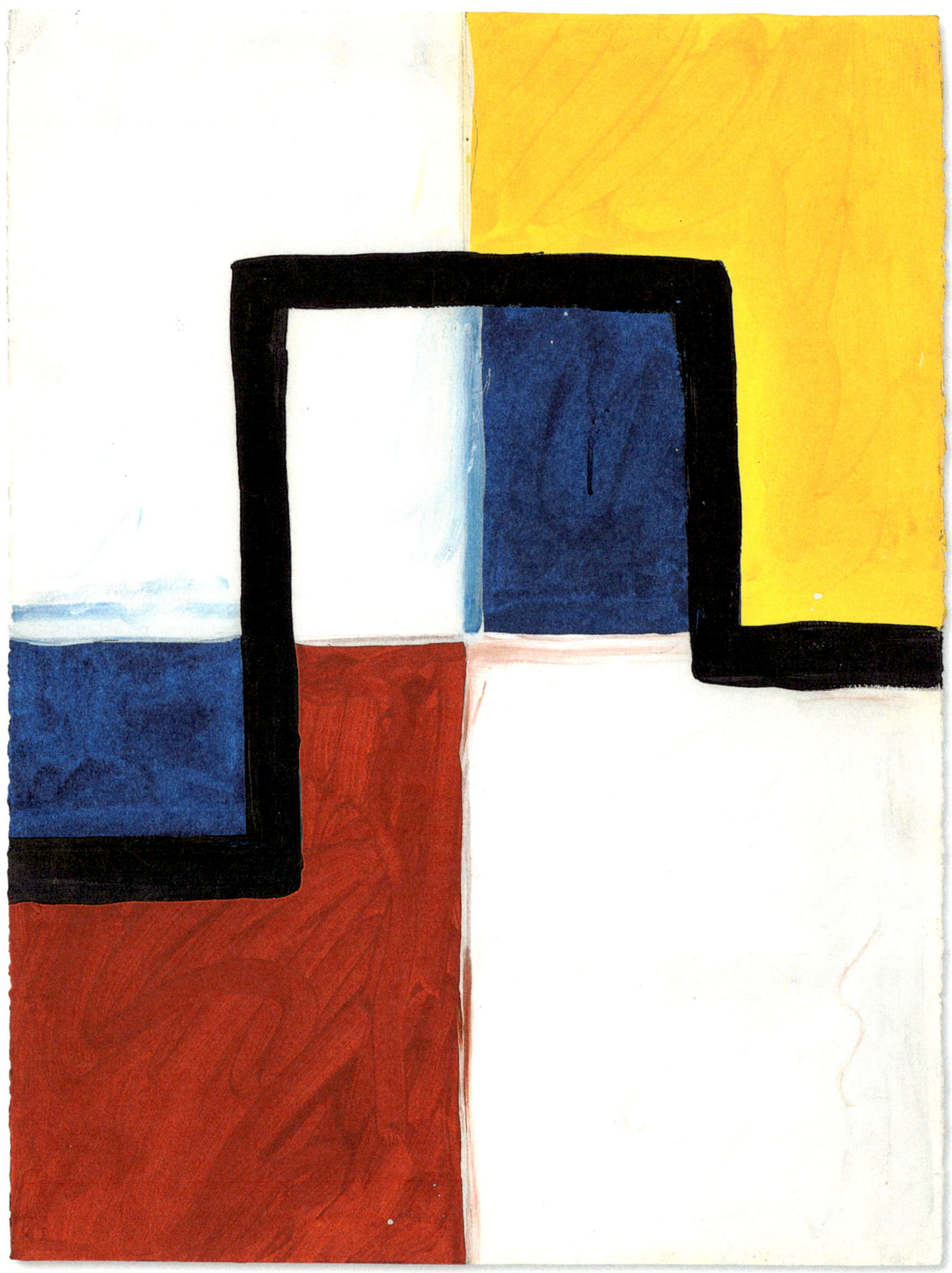

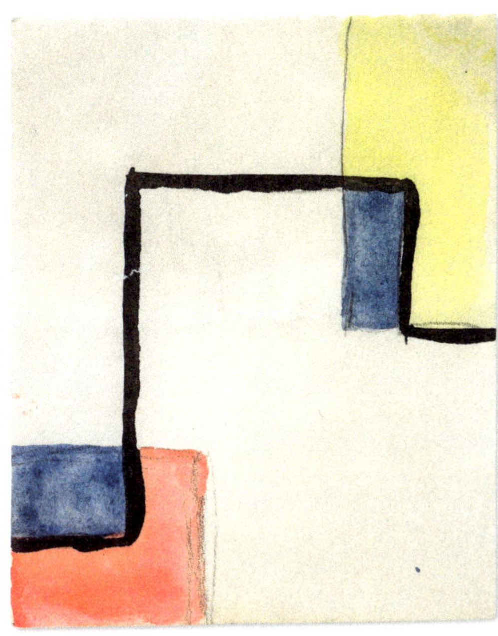

Untitled Watercolor Study, ca. 1983–86. Watercolor and pencil on paper, 4 ½ × 3 ½ in. (11.4 × 8.9 cm)

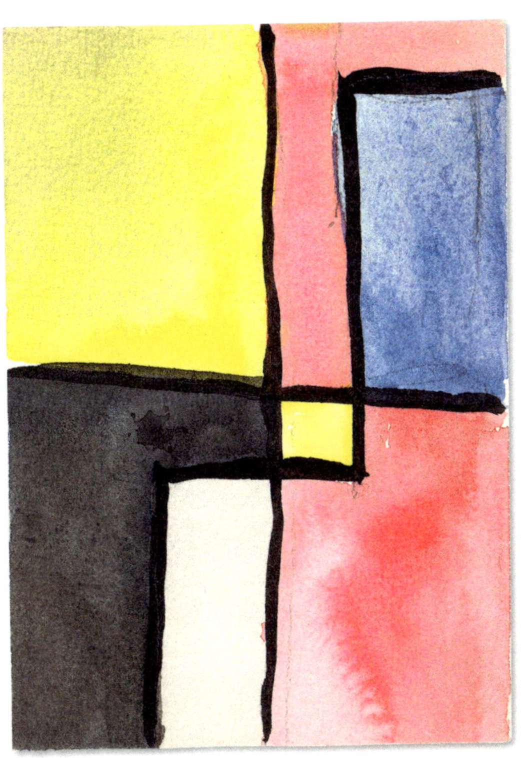

Untitled Watercolor Study, ca. 1983–86. Watercolor on paper, 5 ⅝ × 3 ⅞ in. (14.3 × 9.8 cm)

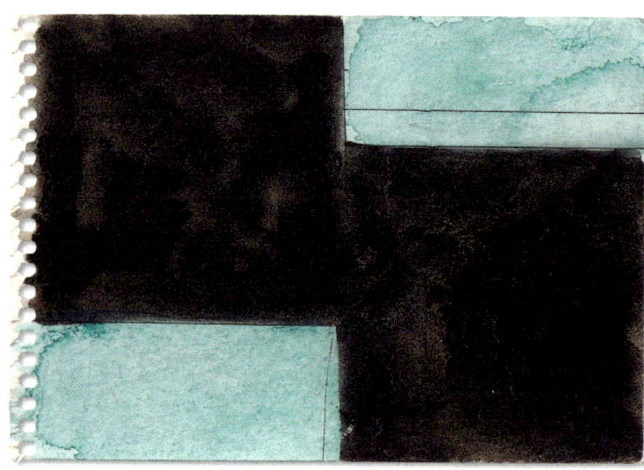

Untitled Watercolor Study, ca. 1982–84. Watercolor and pencil on paper, 5 × 7 in. (12.7 × 17.8 cm)

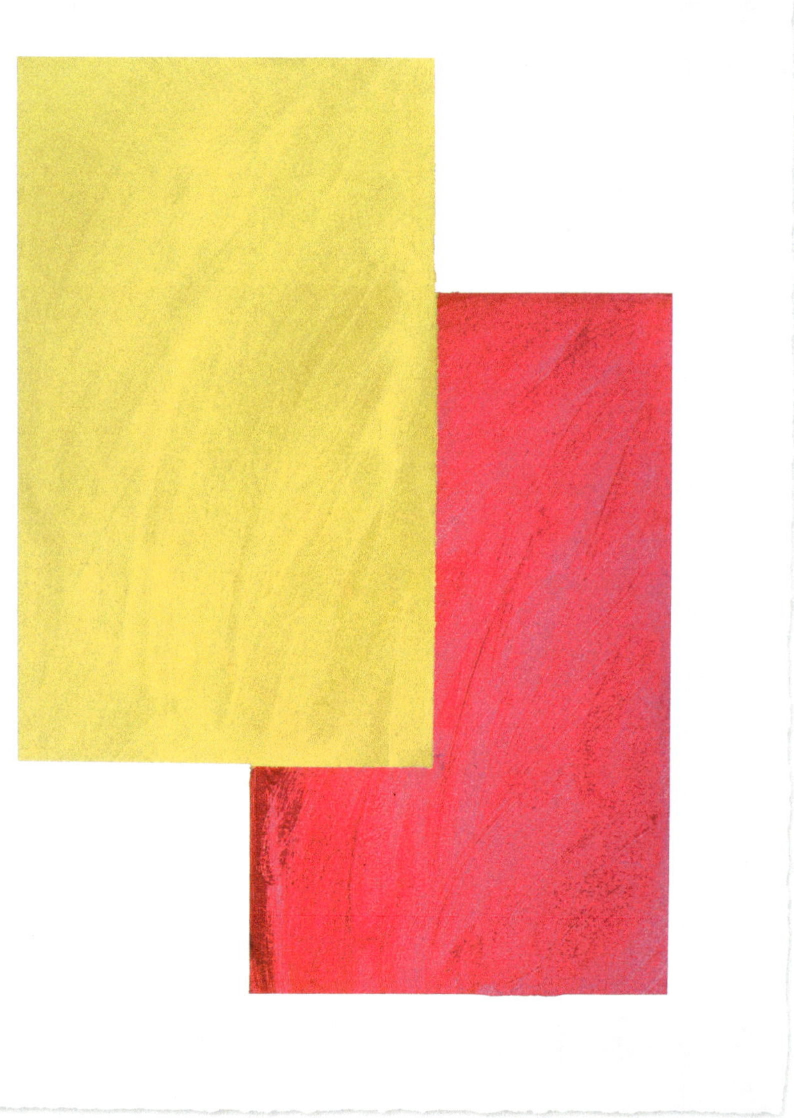

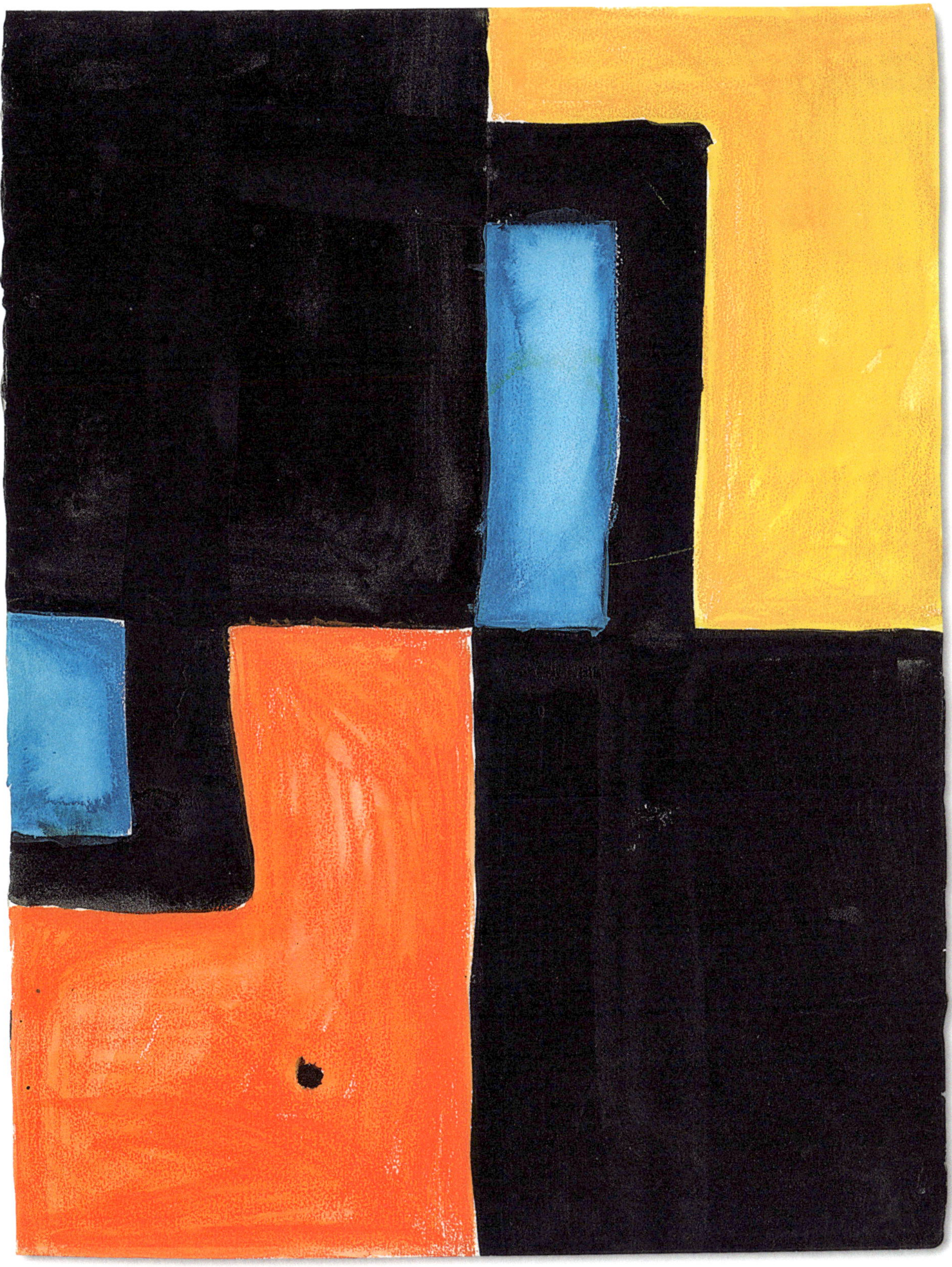

Aztec, 1985. Watercolor on paper, 30 × 22 ¼ in. (76.2 × 56.5 cm)

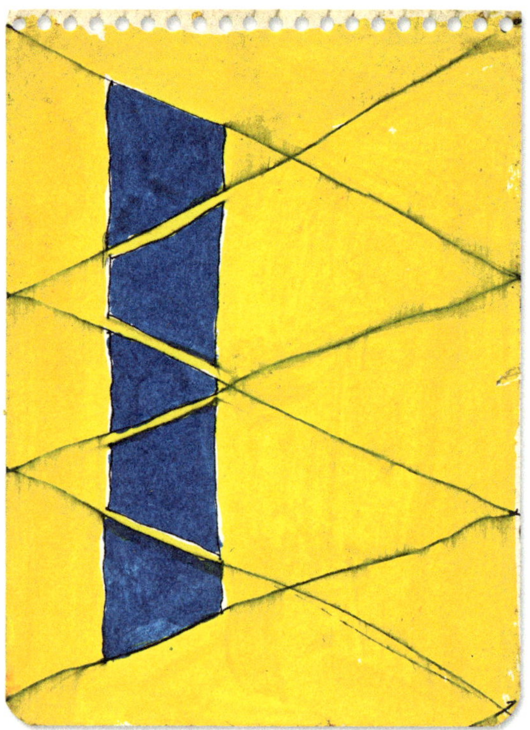

Red, Yellow, Blue Drawing, 1976. Acrylic on paper, 30 × 22 in. (76.2 × 55.9 cm)

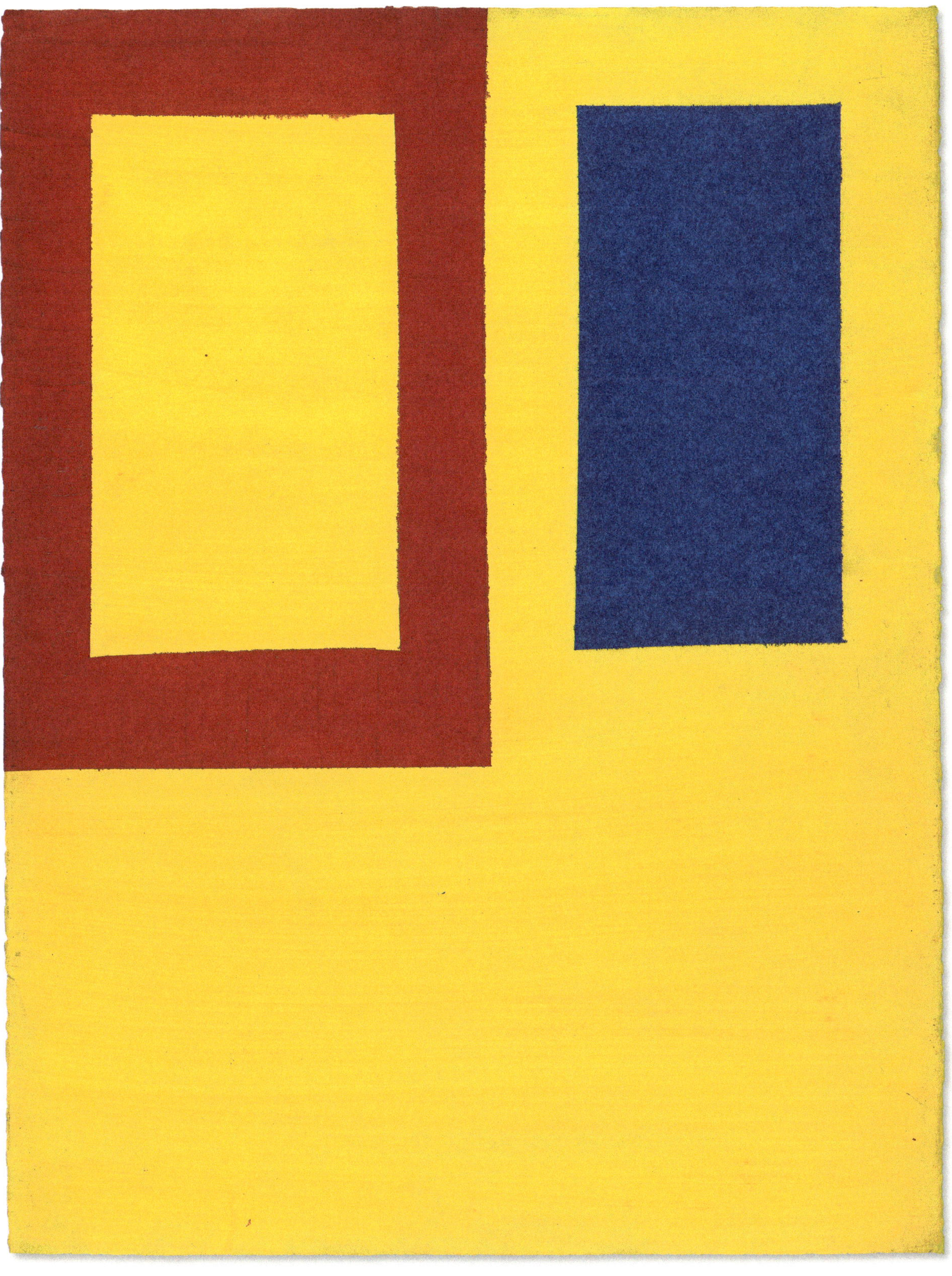

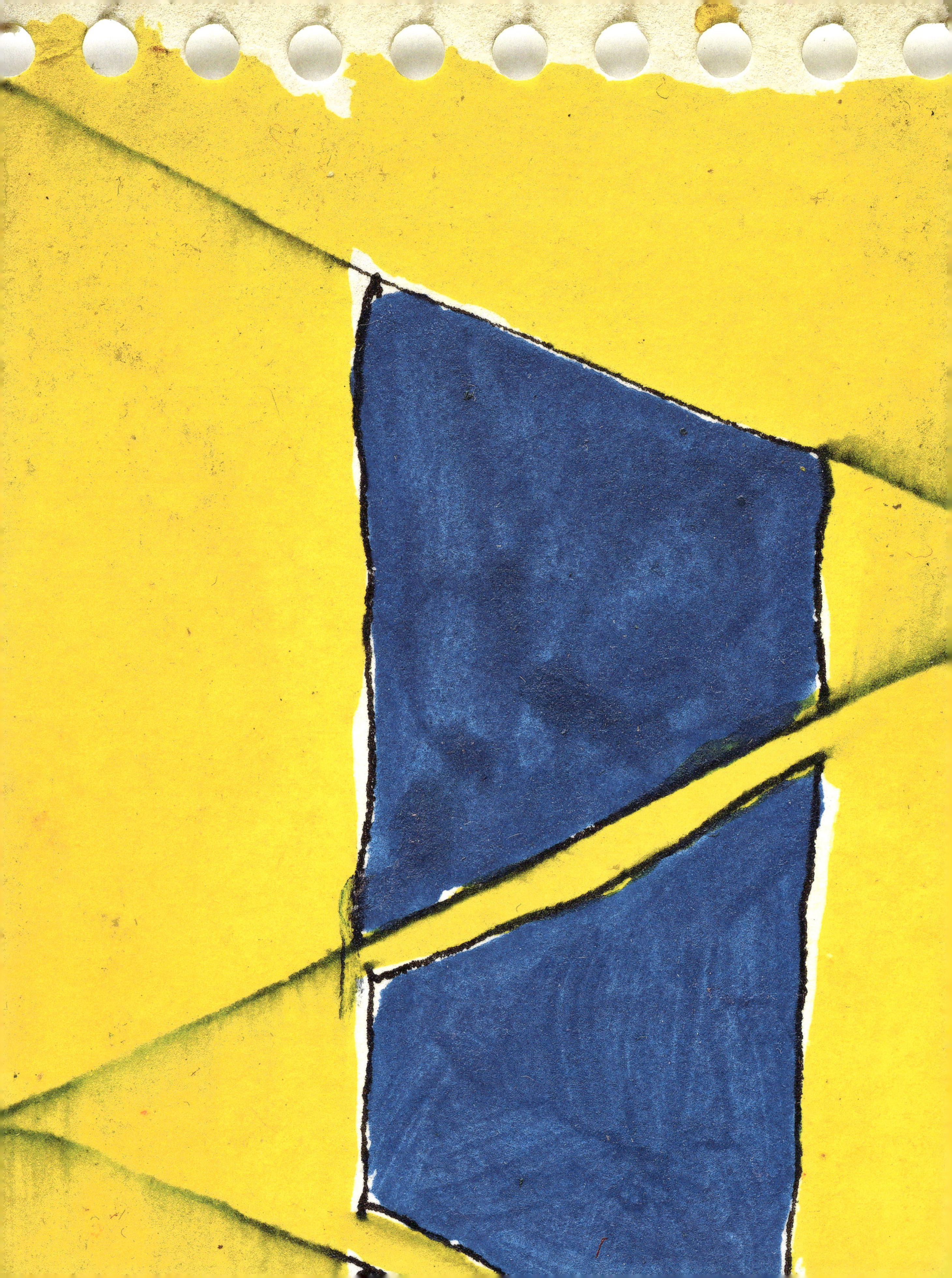

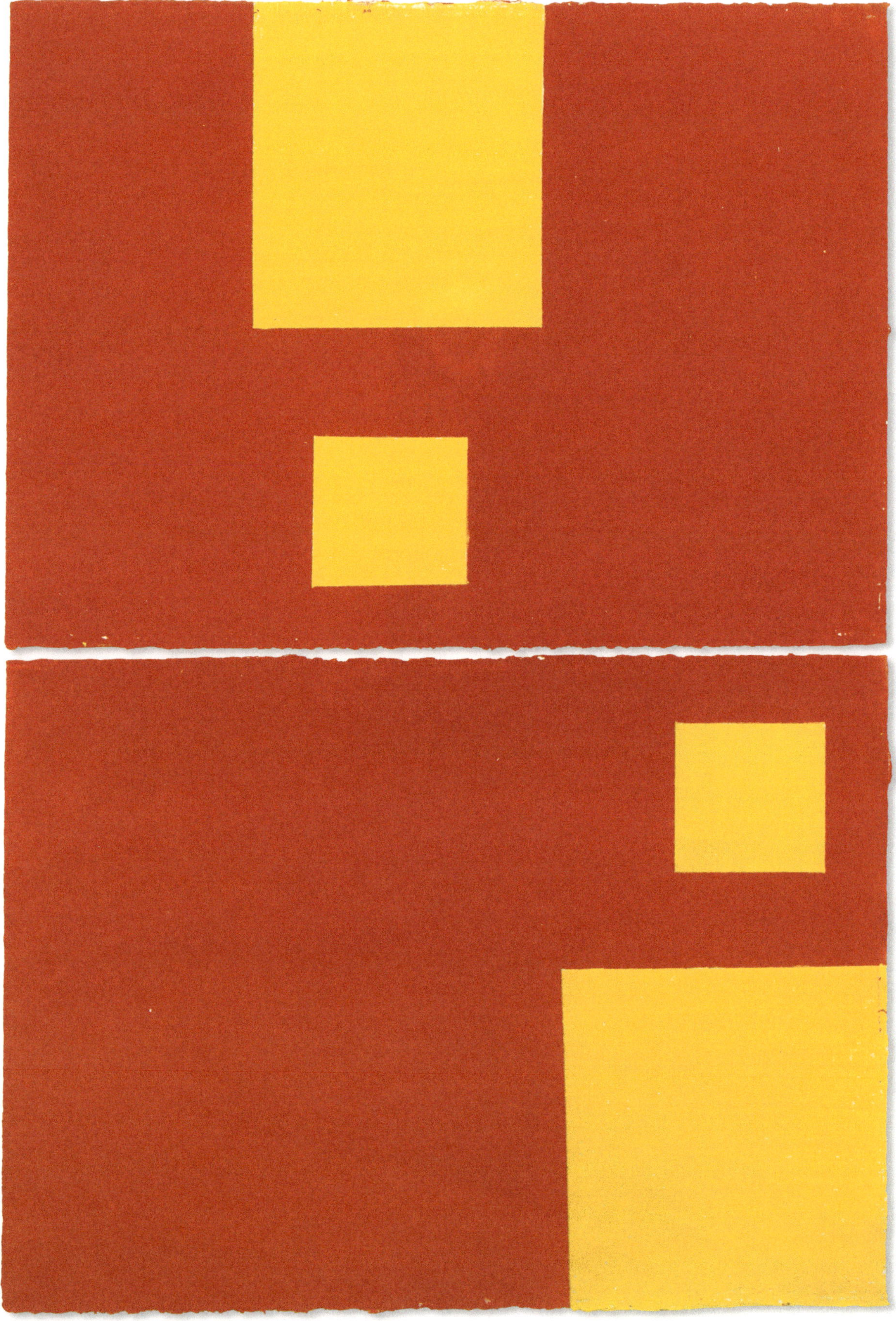

Untitled, 1978. Acrylic on paper, 44 × 29 in. (111.8 × 73.7 cm)

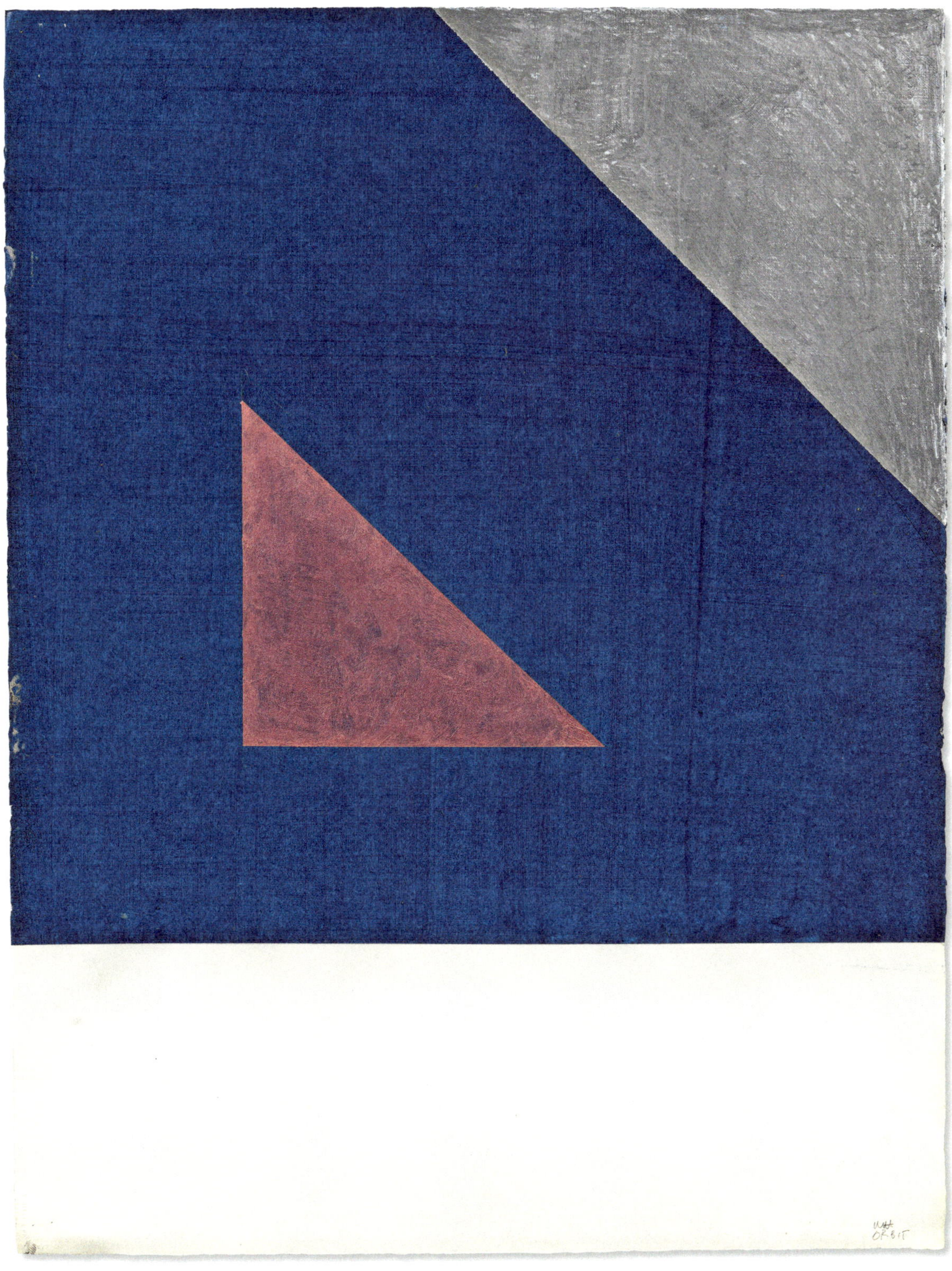

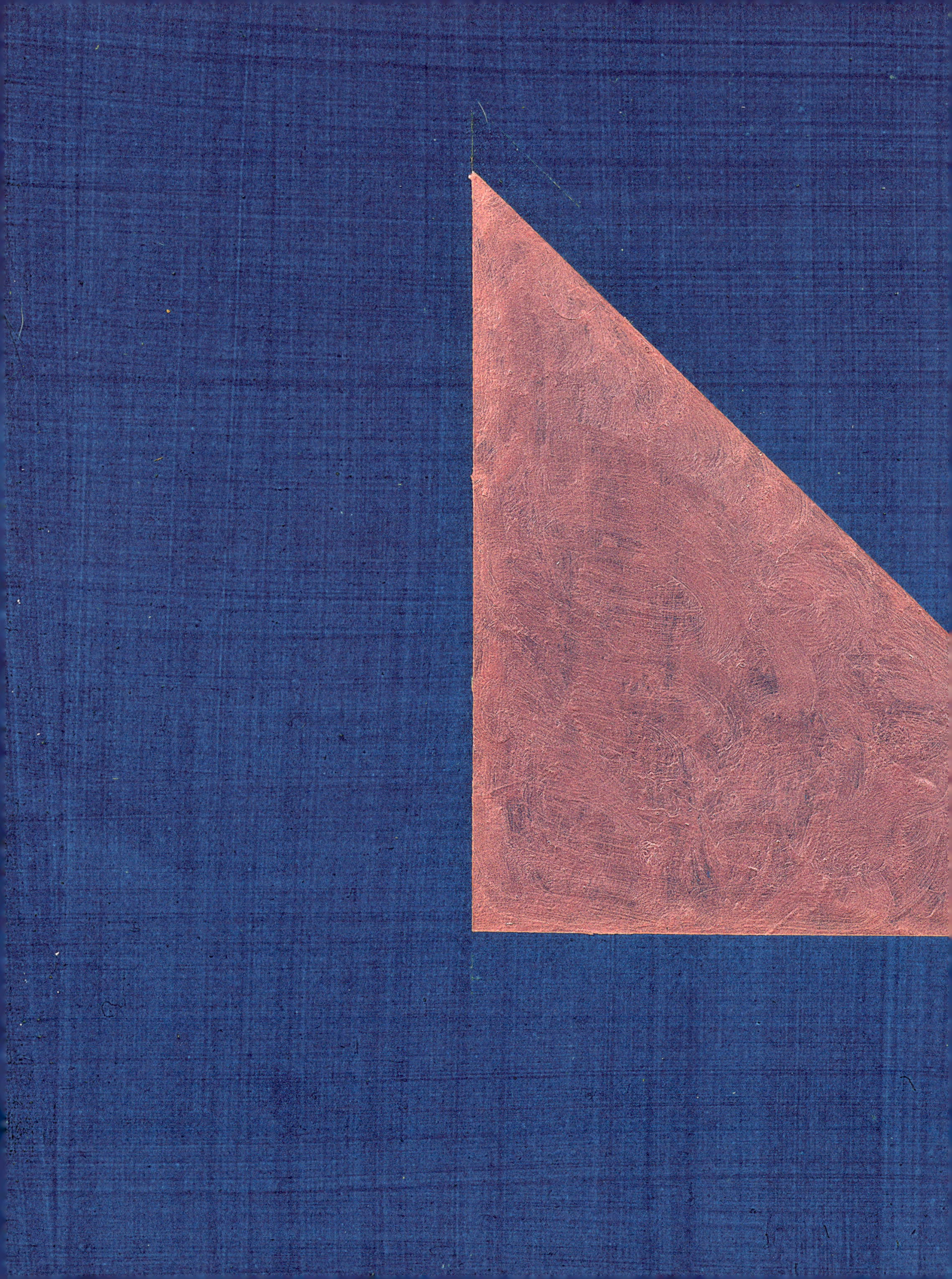

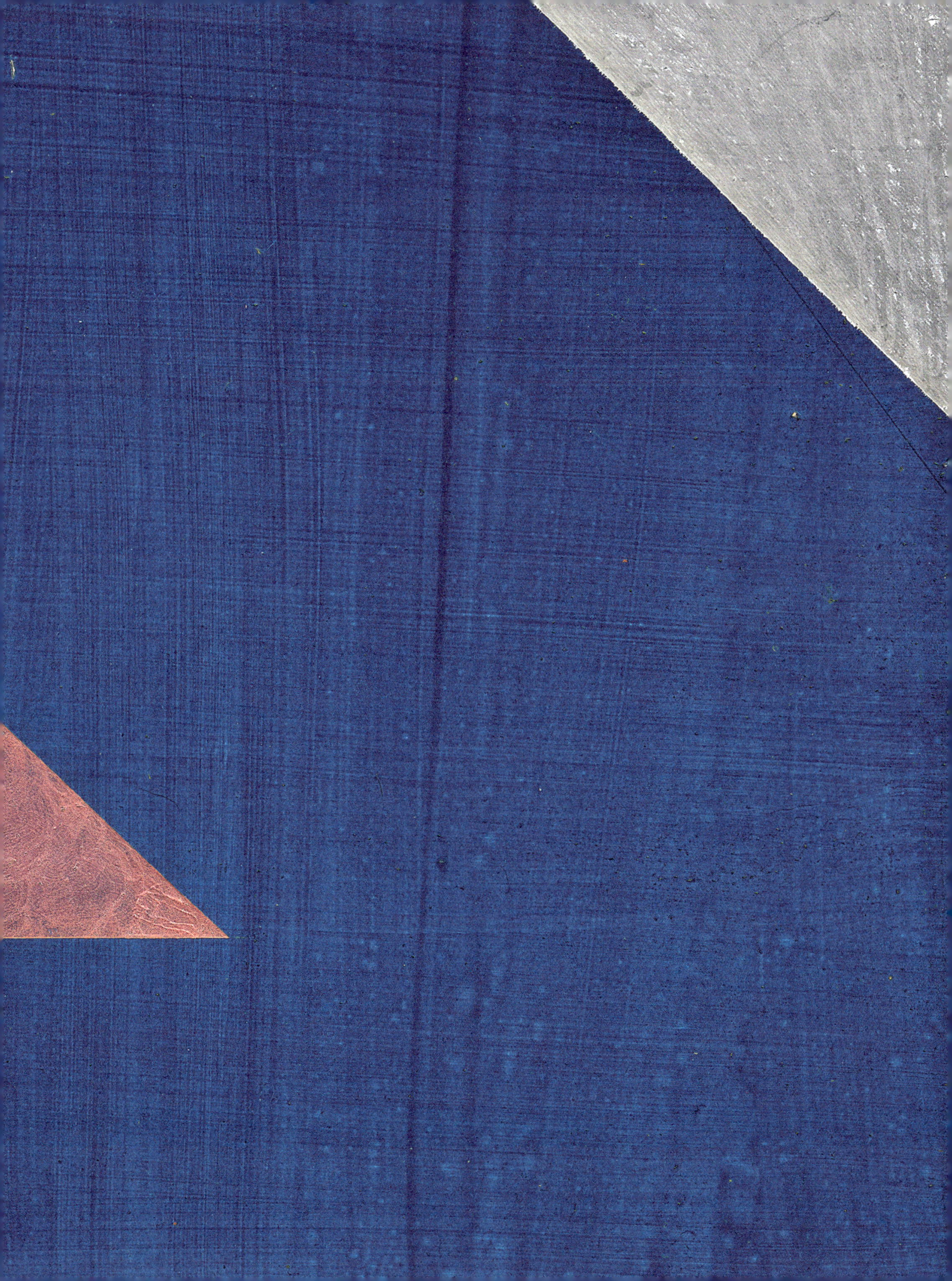

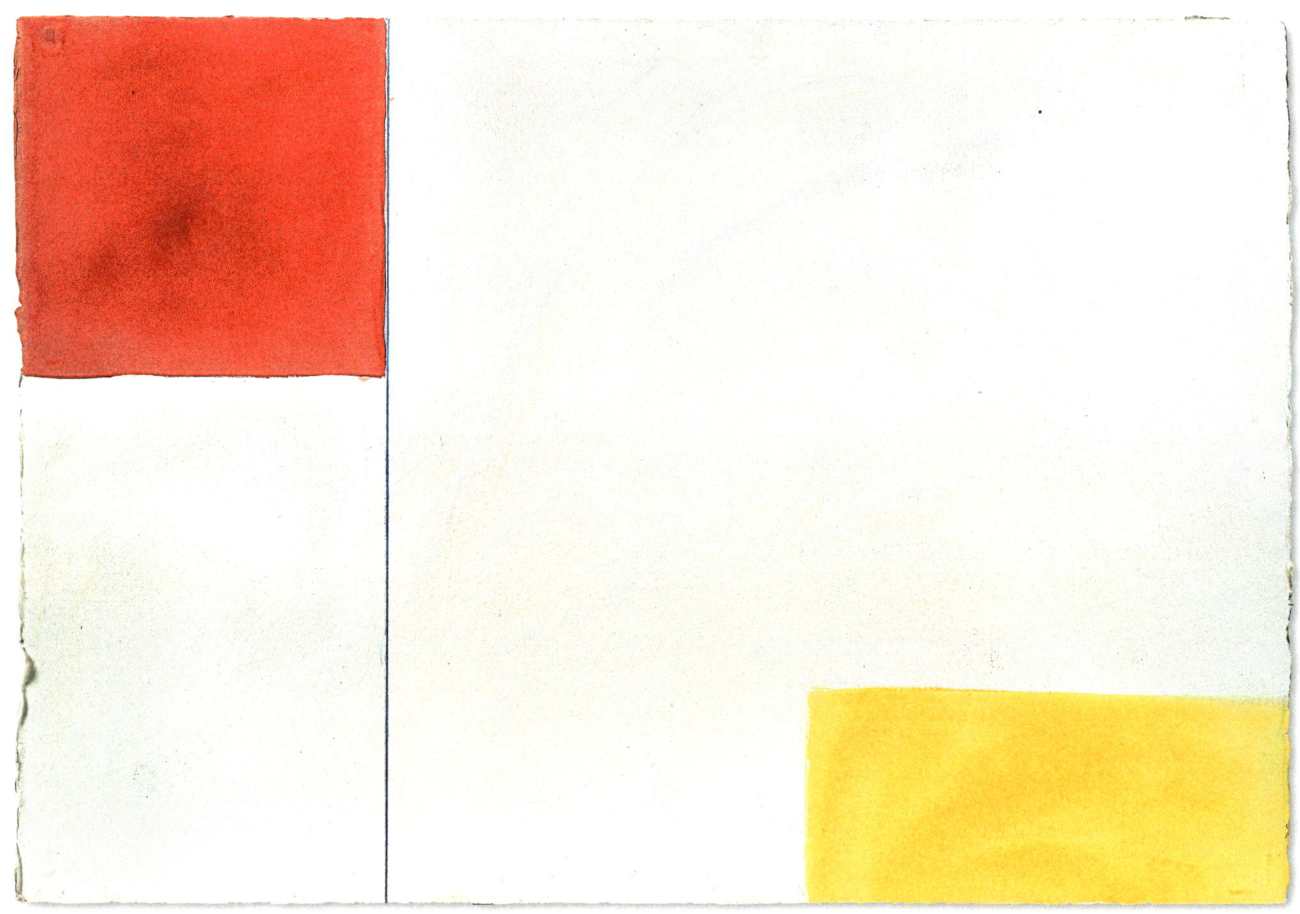

Islands, 1999. Acrylic and watercolor on paper, 29 ½ × 41 ½ in. (74.9 × 105.4 cm)

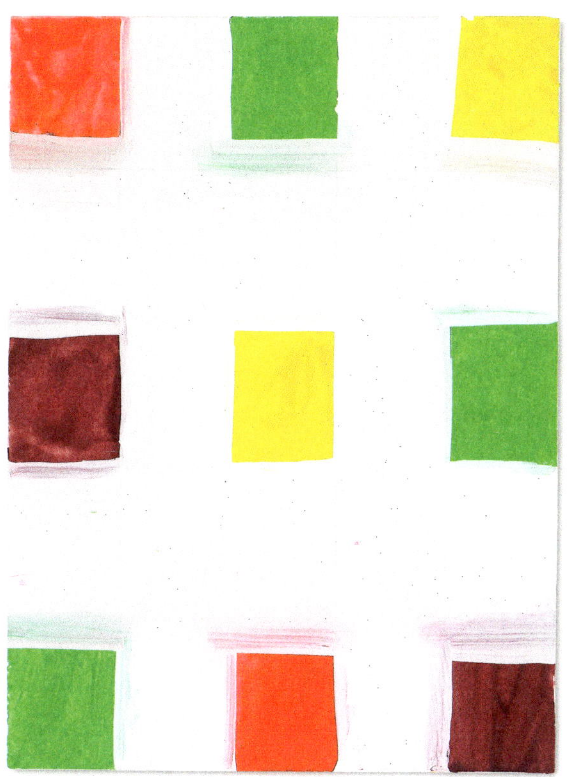

Joe's Greens, 1996. Oil on gessoed paper, 14 × 10 in. (35.6 × 25.4 cm)

Lovebird, 1997. Acrylic on paper, 10 ³/₈ × 10 in. (26.4 × 25.4 cm)

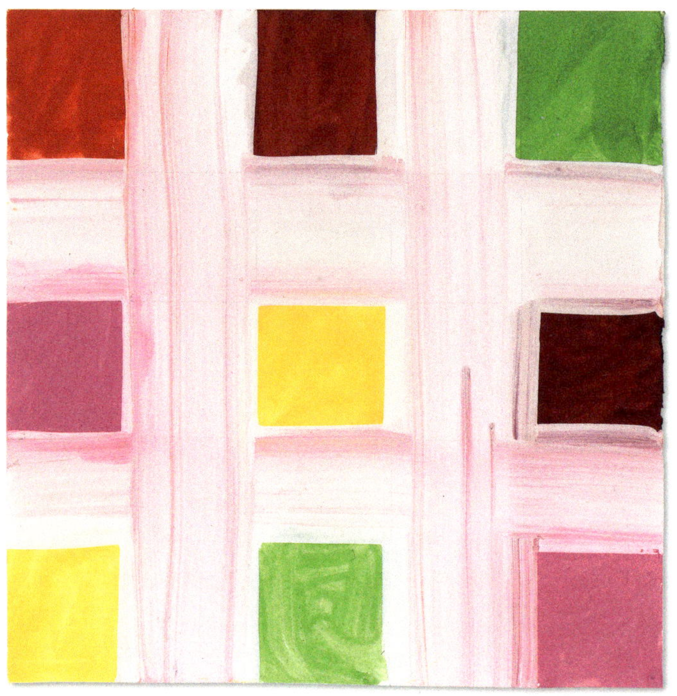

Richie, 1997. Oil on gessoed paper, 41 × 29 ½ in. (104.1 × 74.9 cm)

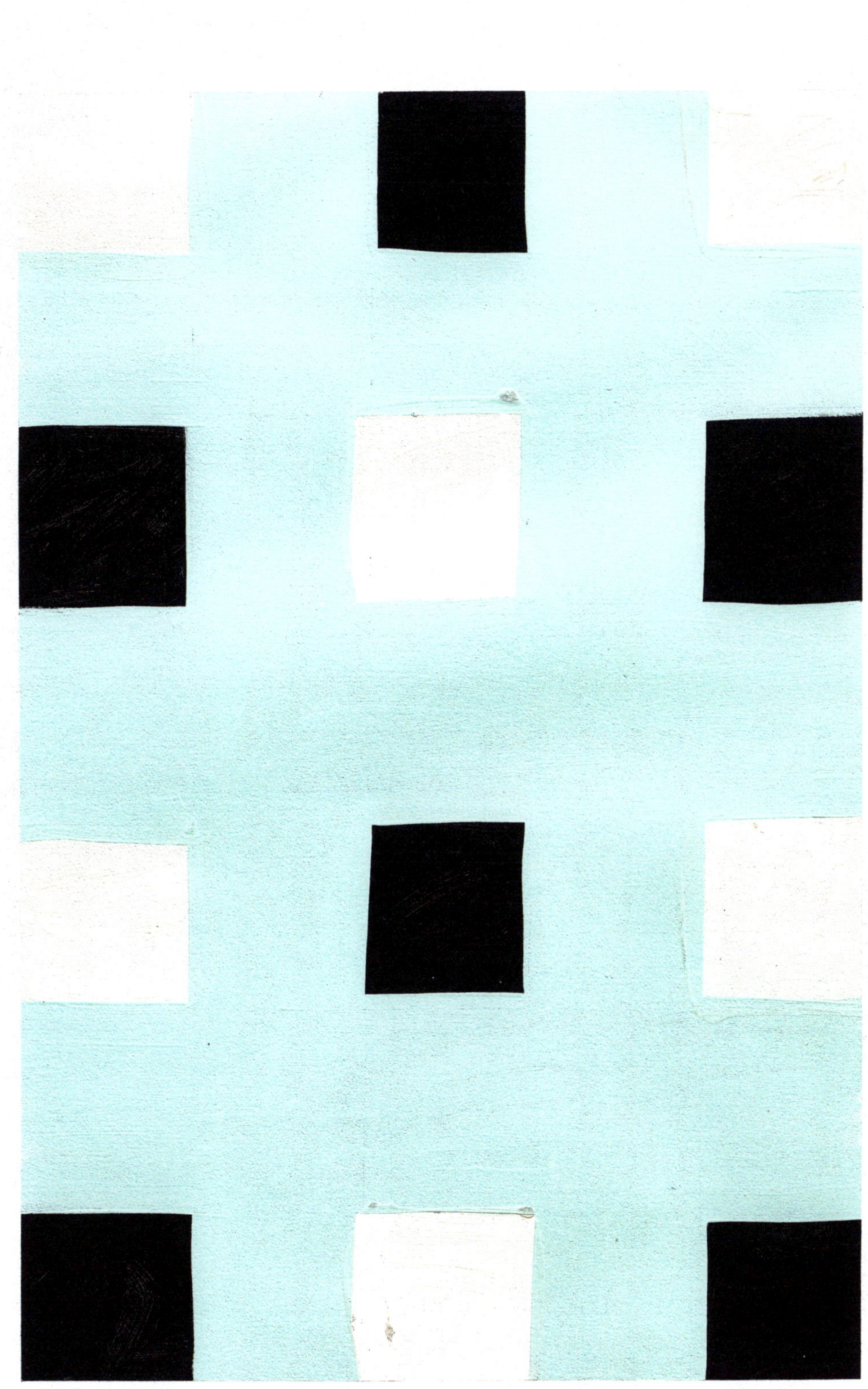

Pink Screen, 1973. Acrylic and spray paint on paper, 22 × 28 in. (55.9 × 71.1 cm)

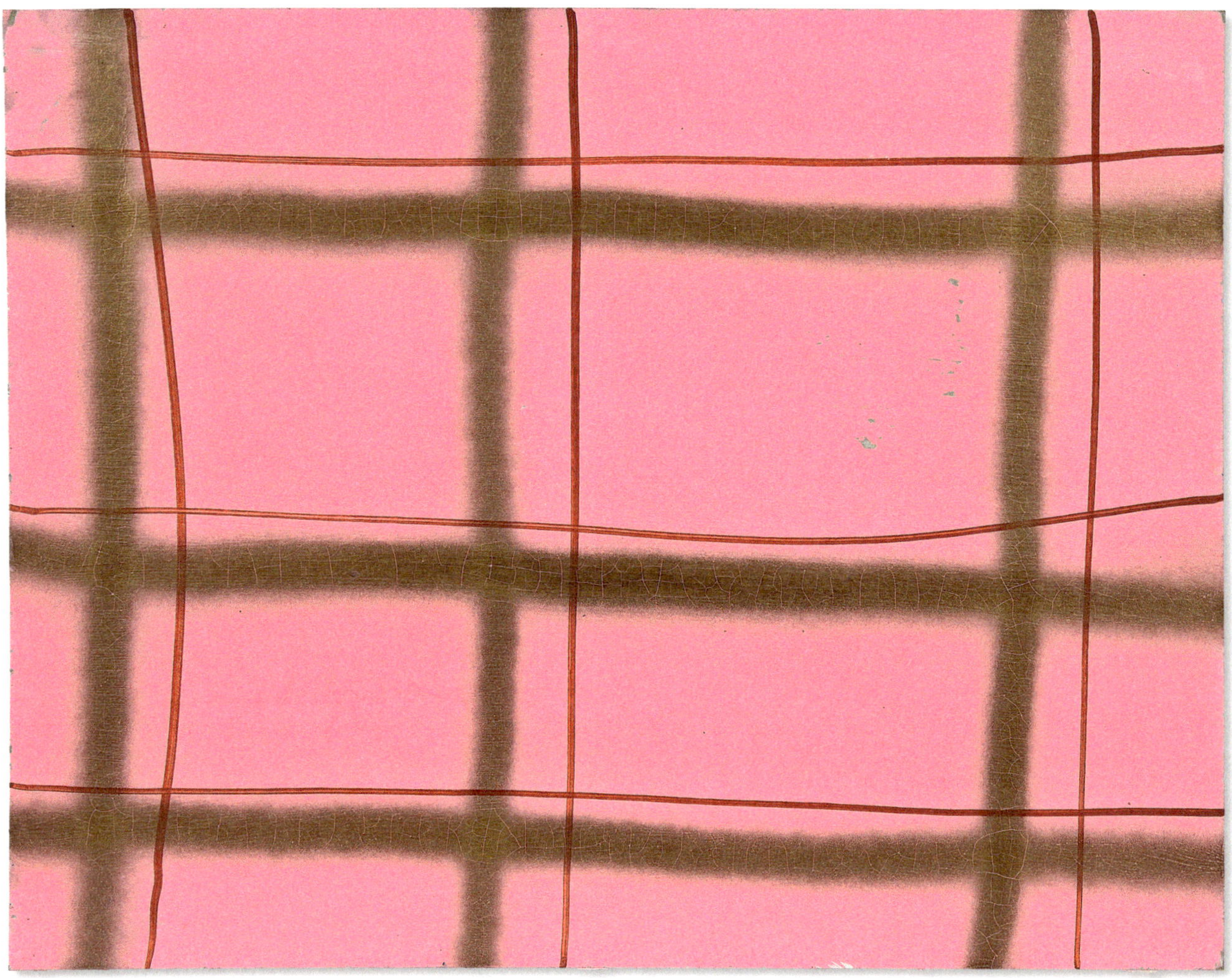

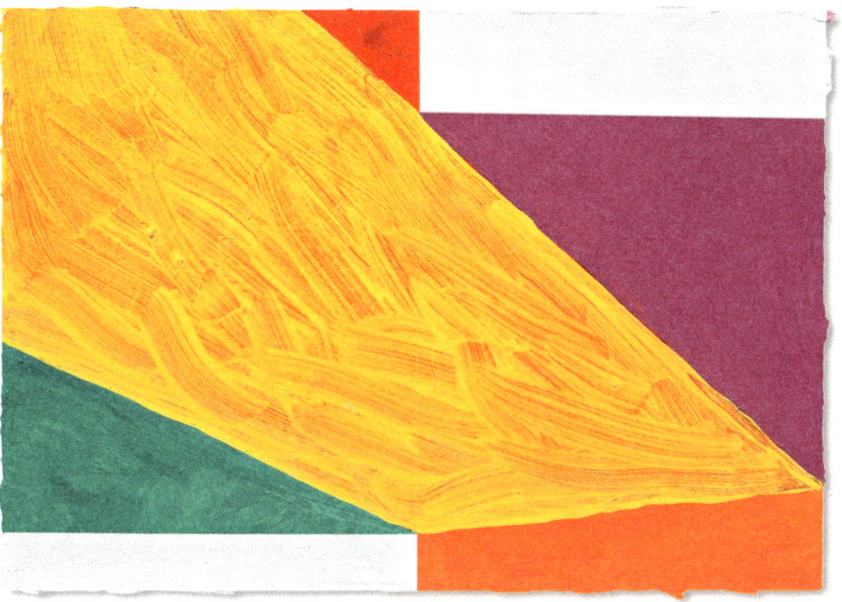

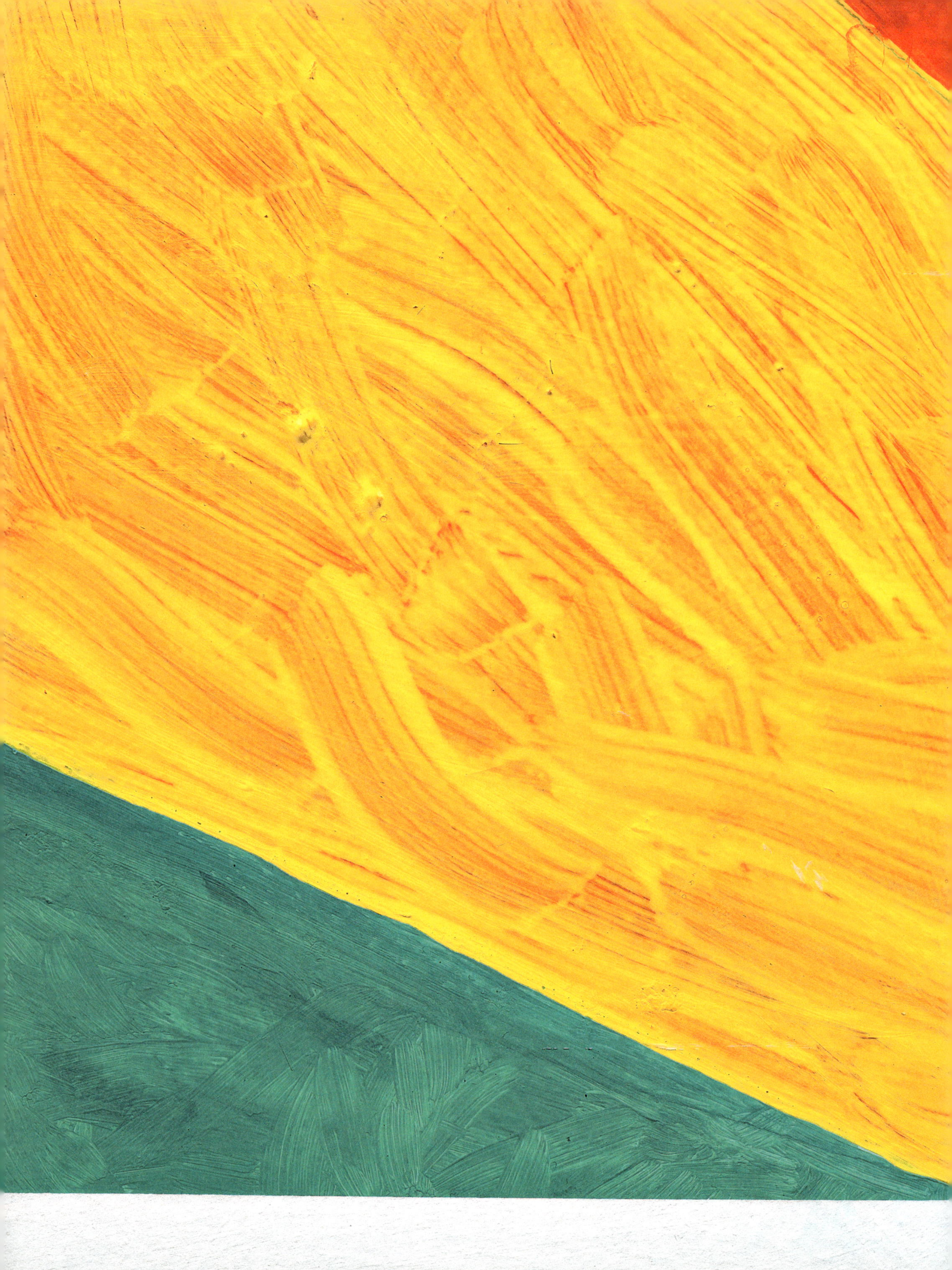

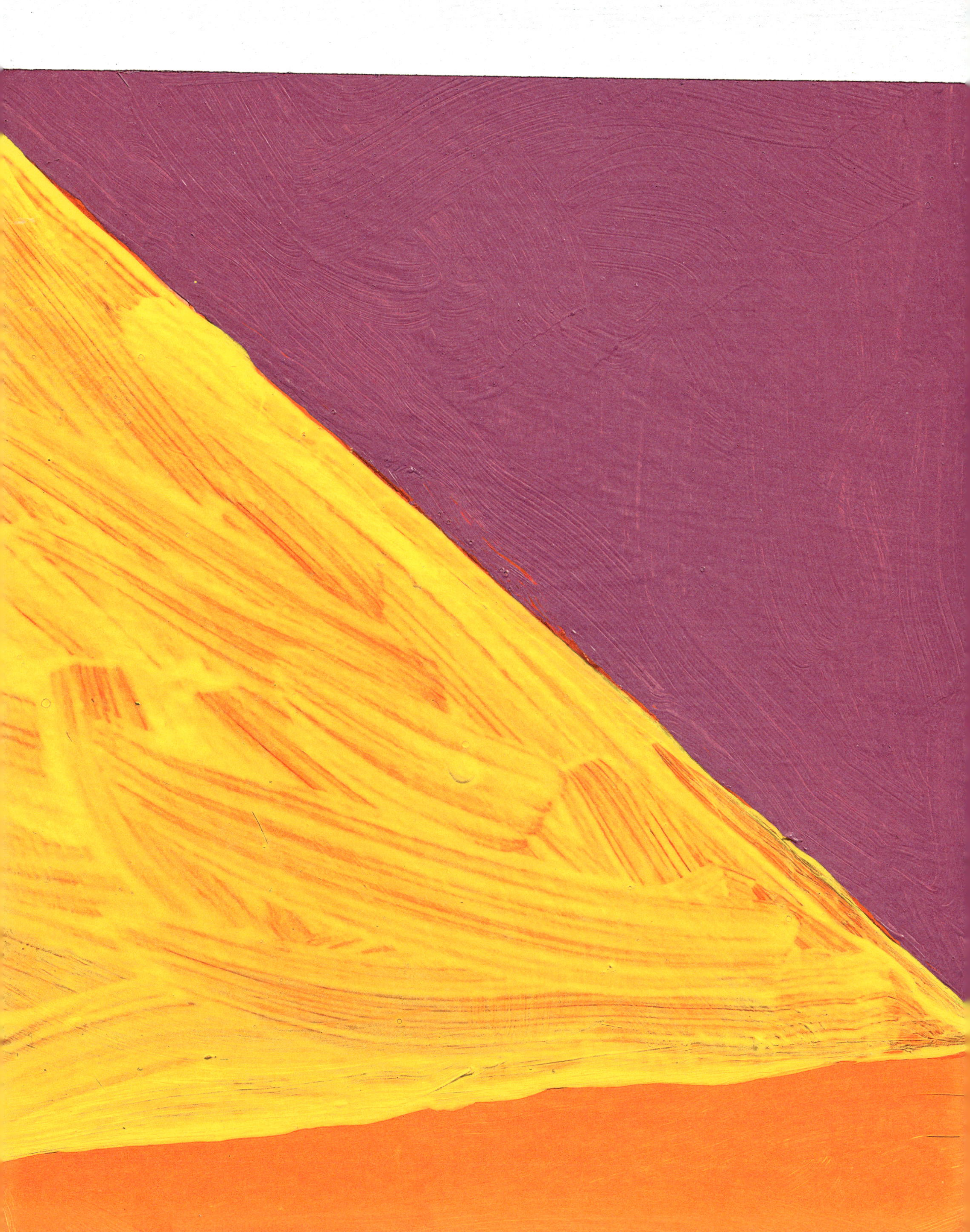

The Diamond, 1982. Pastel and watercolor on paper, 30 × 22 in. (76.2 × 55.9 cm)

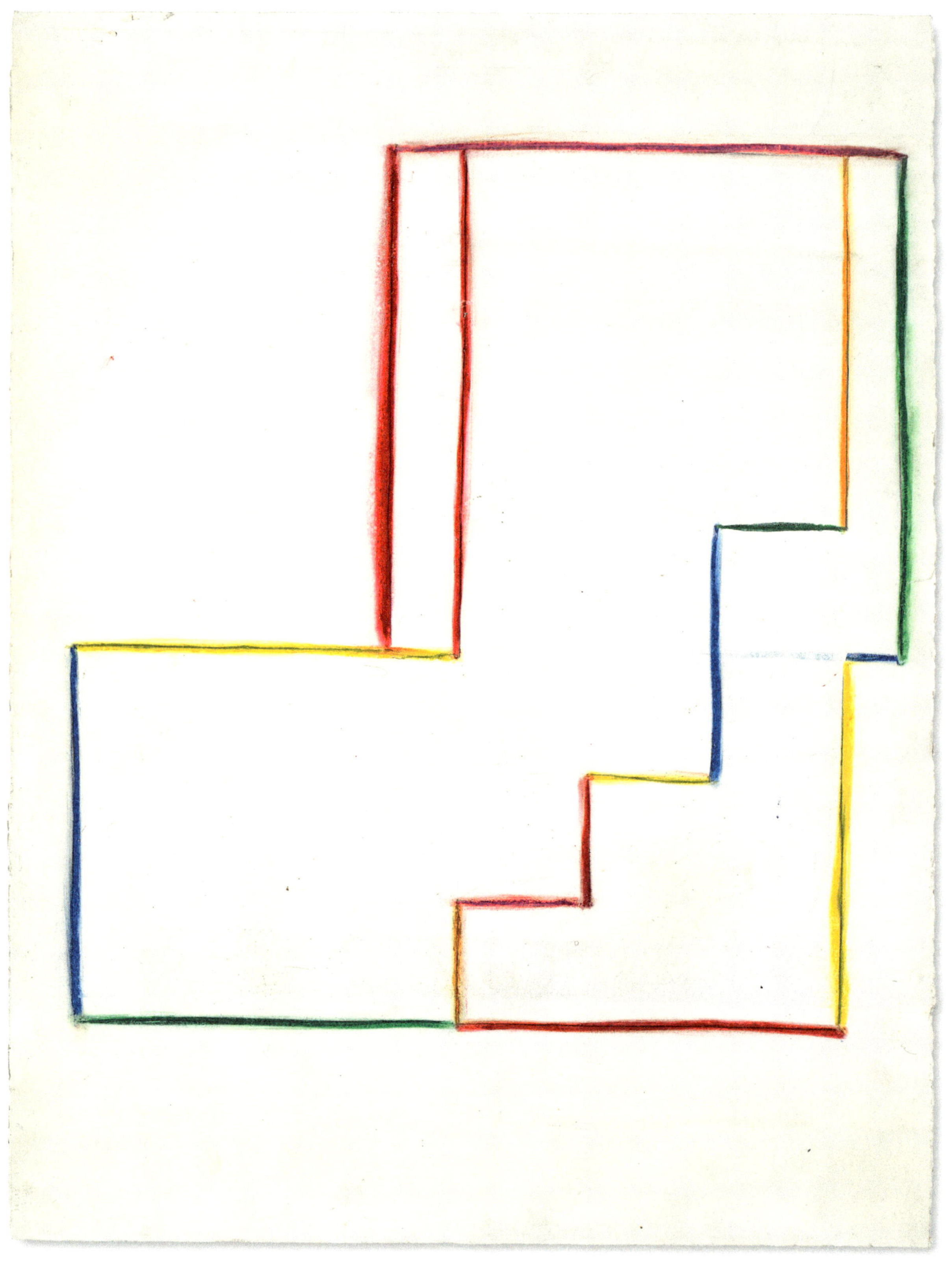

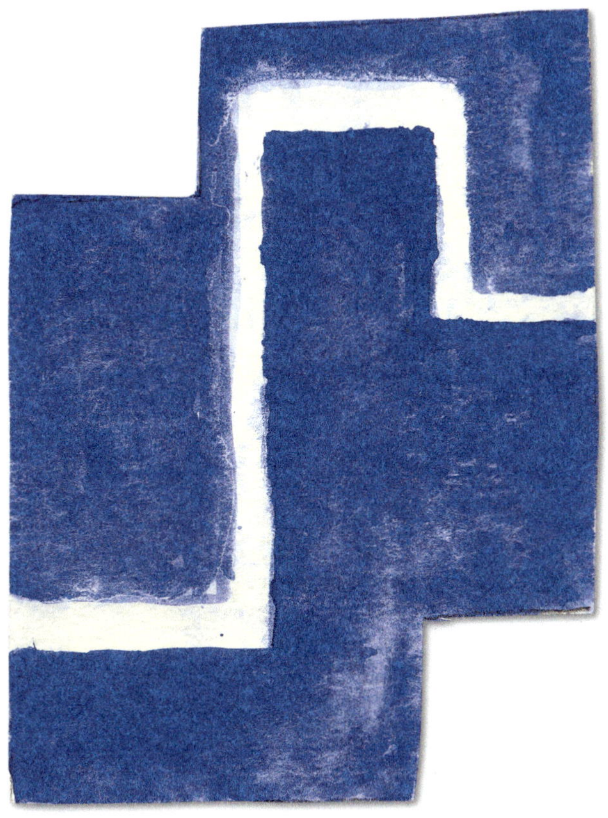

Little Chartreuse, 1993. Oil on gessoed handmade paper, 27 ½ × 23 ¼ in. (69.9 × 59.1 cm)

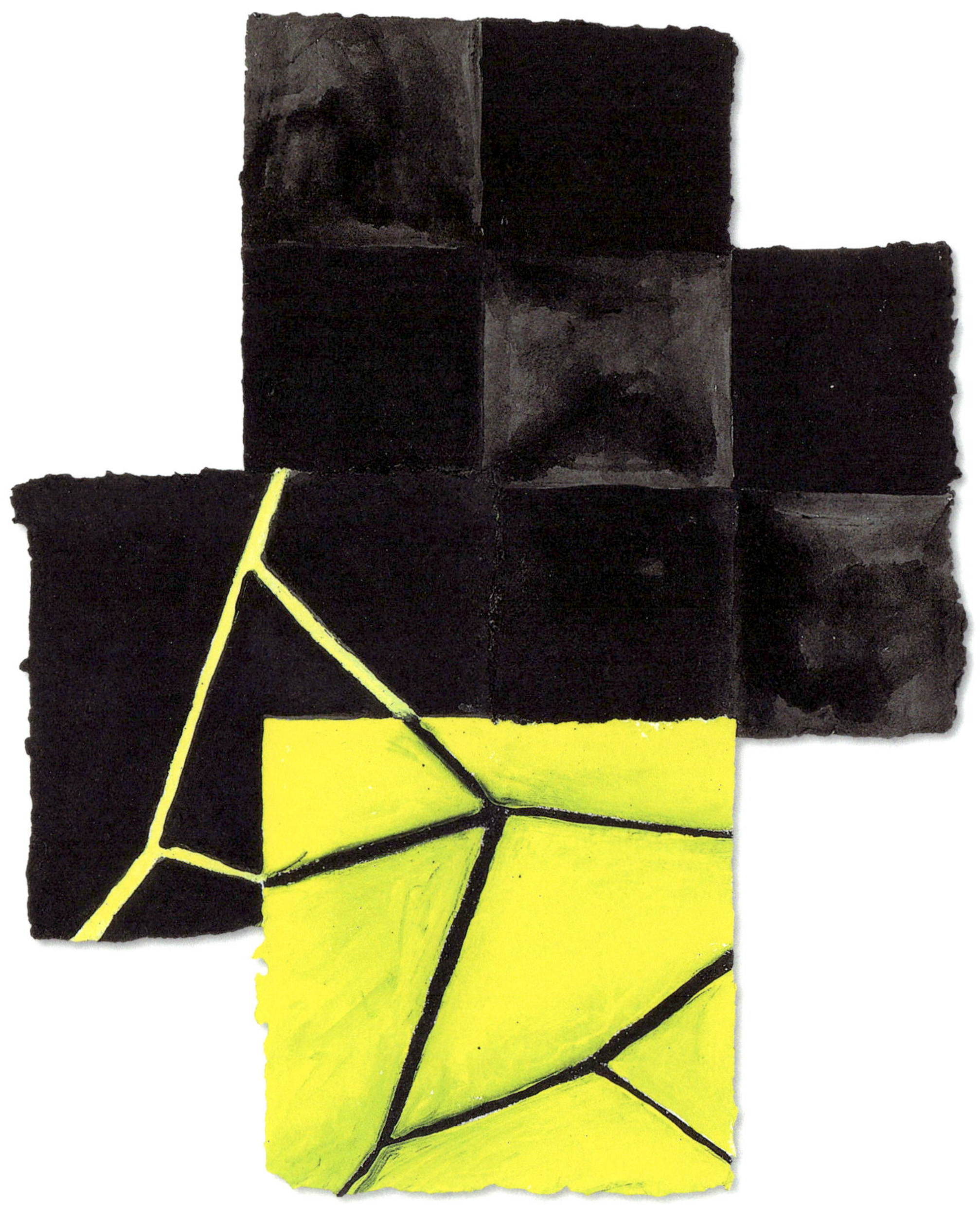

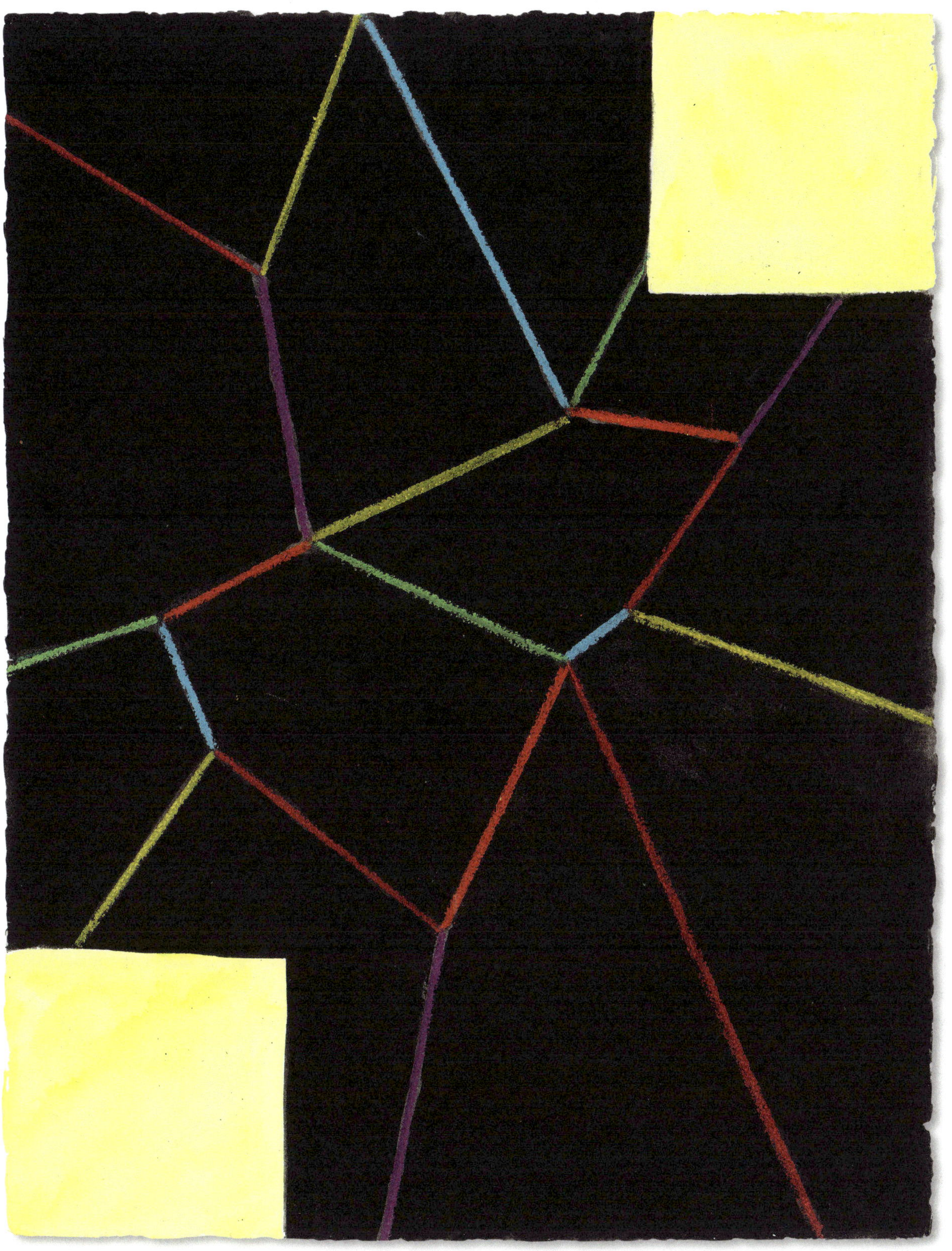

Au Go Go, 1995. Acrylic and pastel on paper, 30 × 22 ½ in. (76.2 × 57.2 cm). Detail, following spread

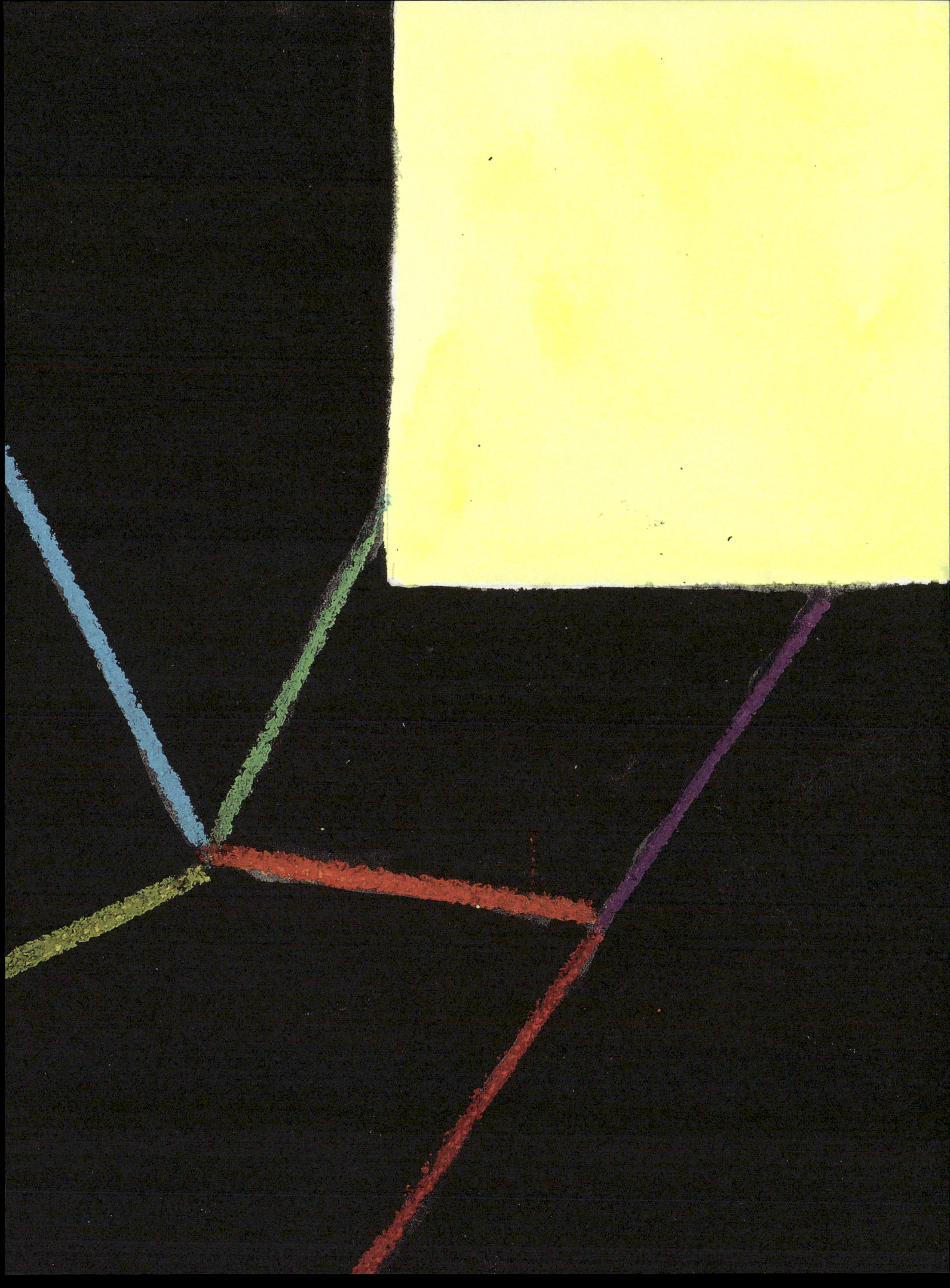

Chartreuse Web, 1991. Oil on handmade paper, 19 × 19 in. (48.3 × 48.3 cm)

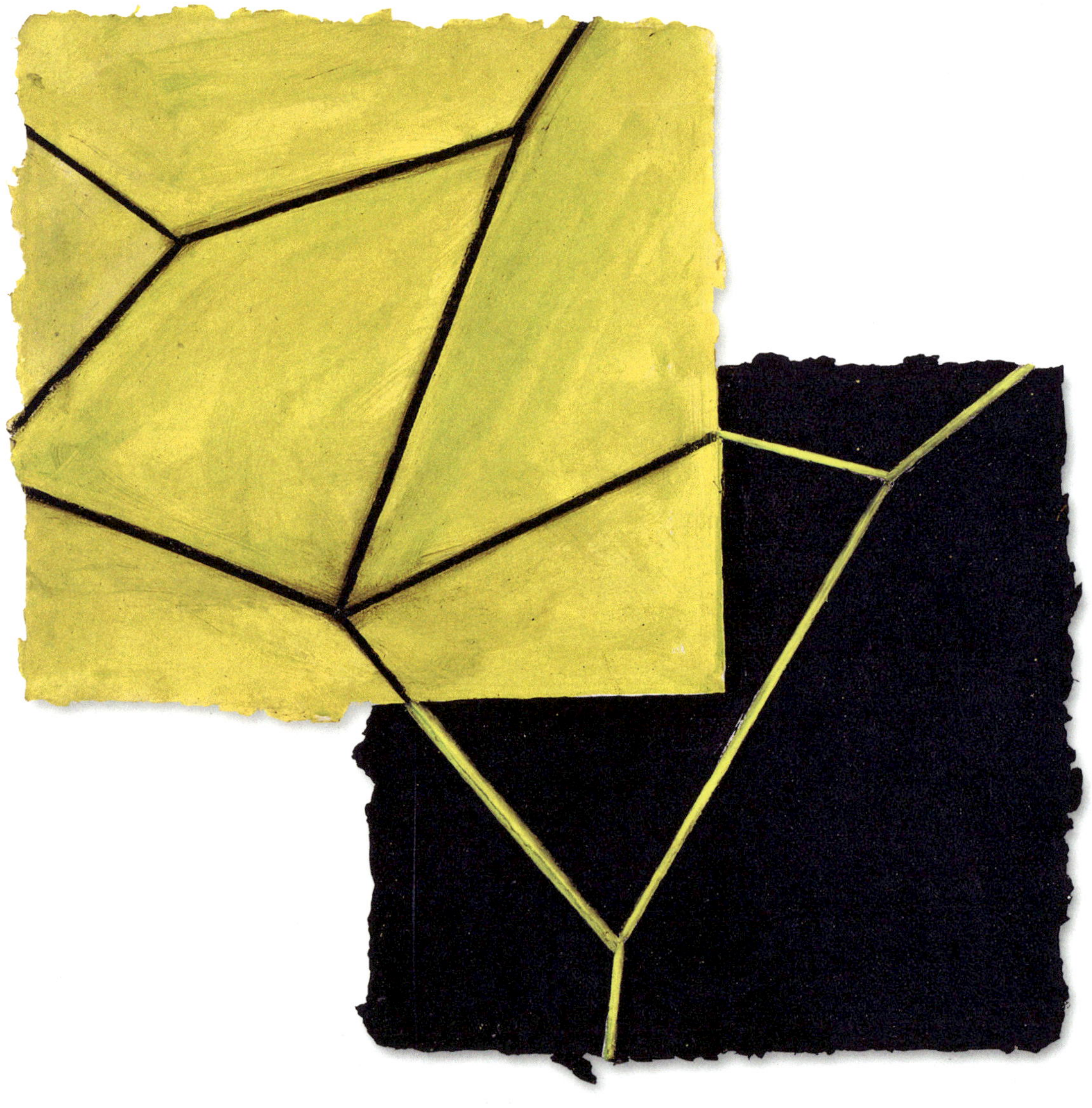

Black Valentine, ca. 1995. Oil and pencil on handmade paper,
12 × 11 ½ in. (30.5 × 29.2 cm)

Untitled, ca. 1990–95. Acrylic on handmade paper, 11 ½ × 11 ½ in.
(29.2 × 29.2 cm). Detail, following spread

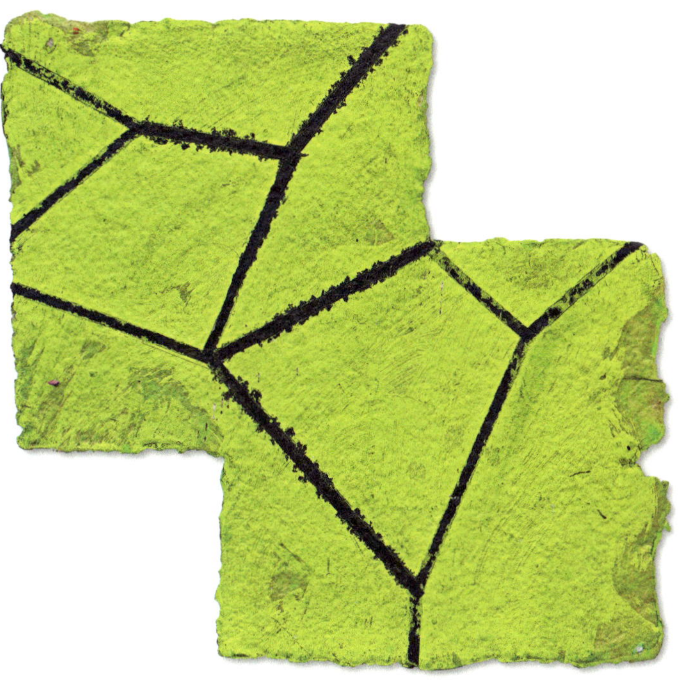

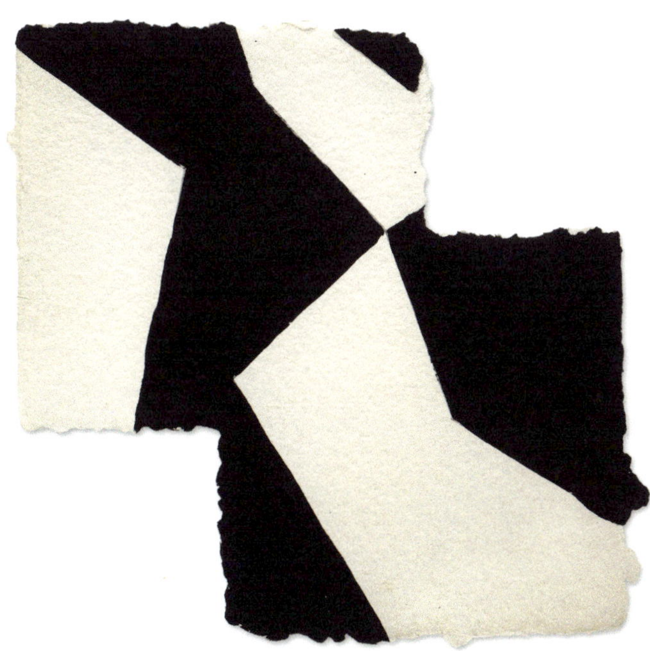

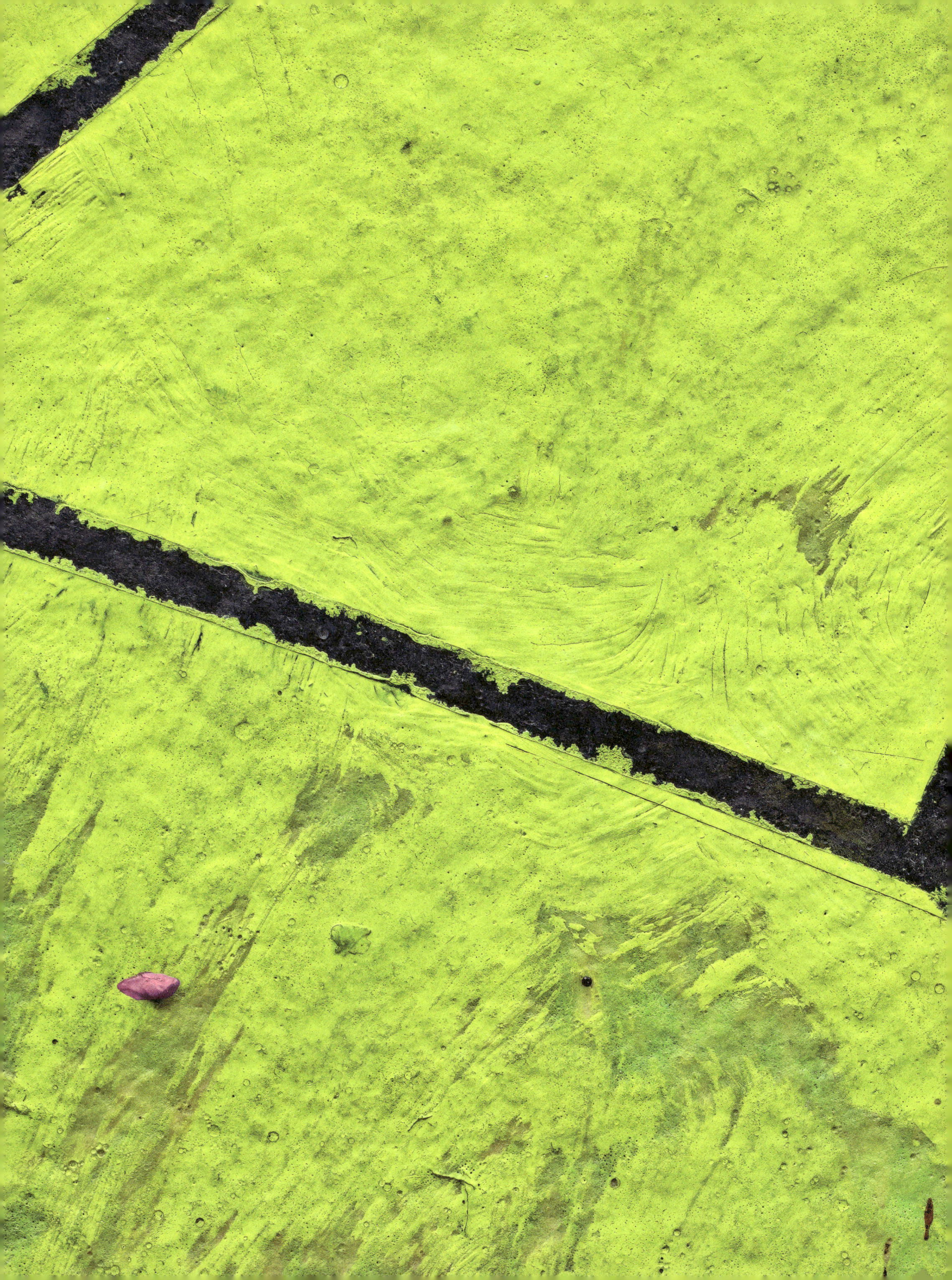

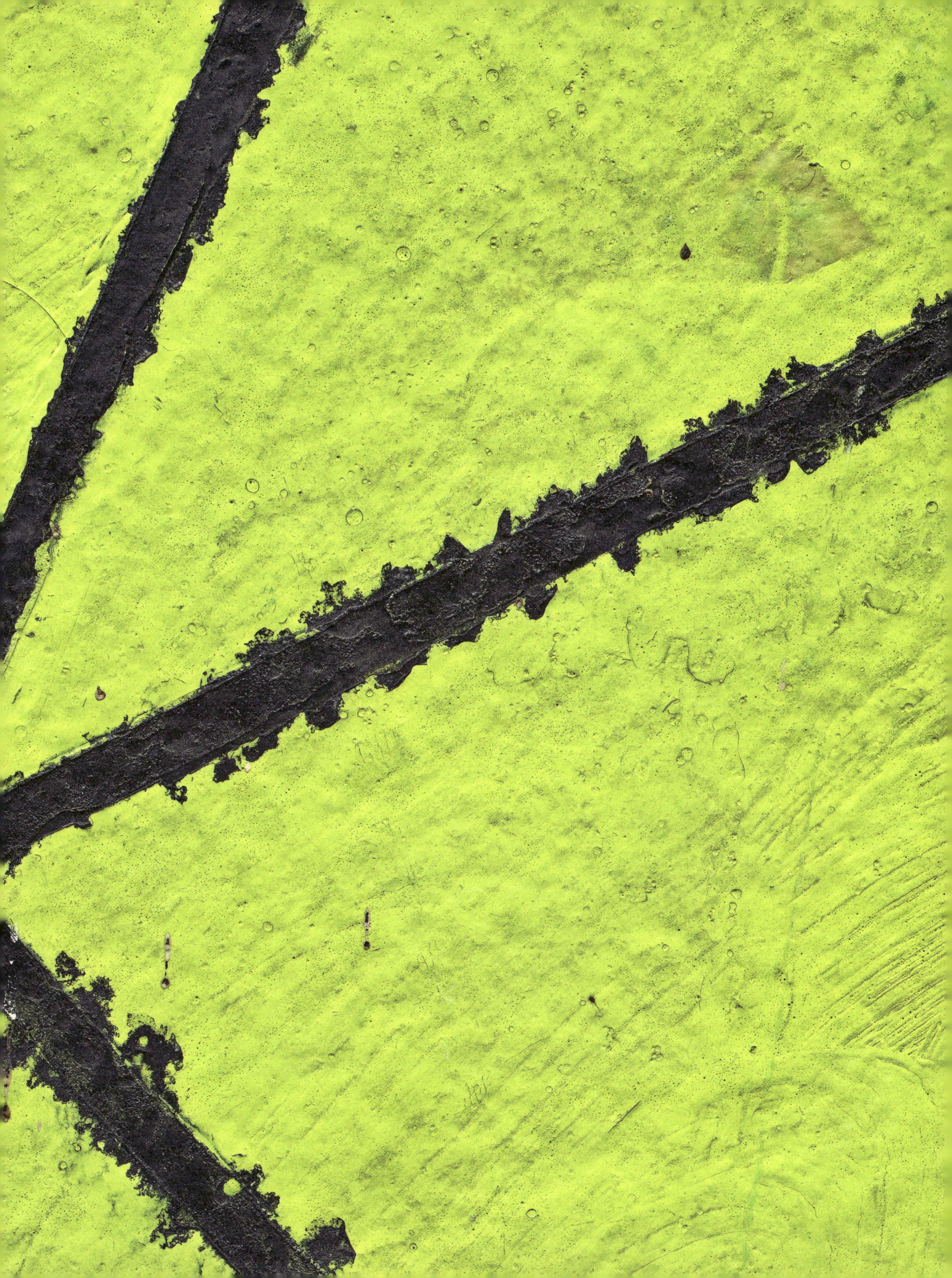

Charming Billy, 2000. Oil on paper, 22 × 15 ⅝ in. (55.9 × 39.7 cm)

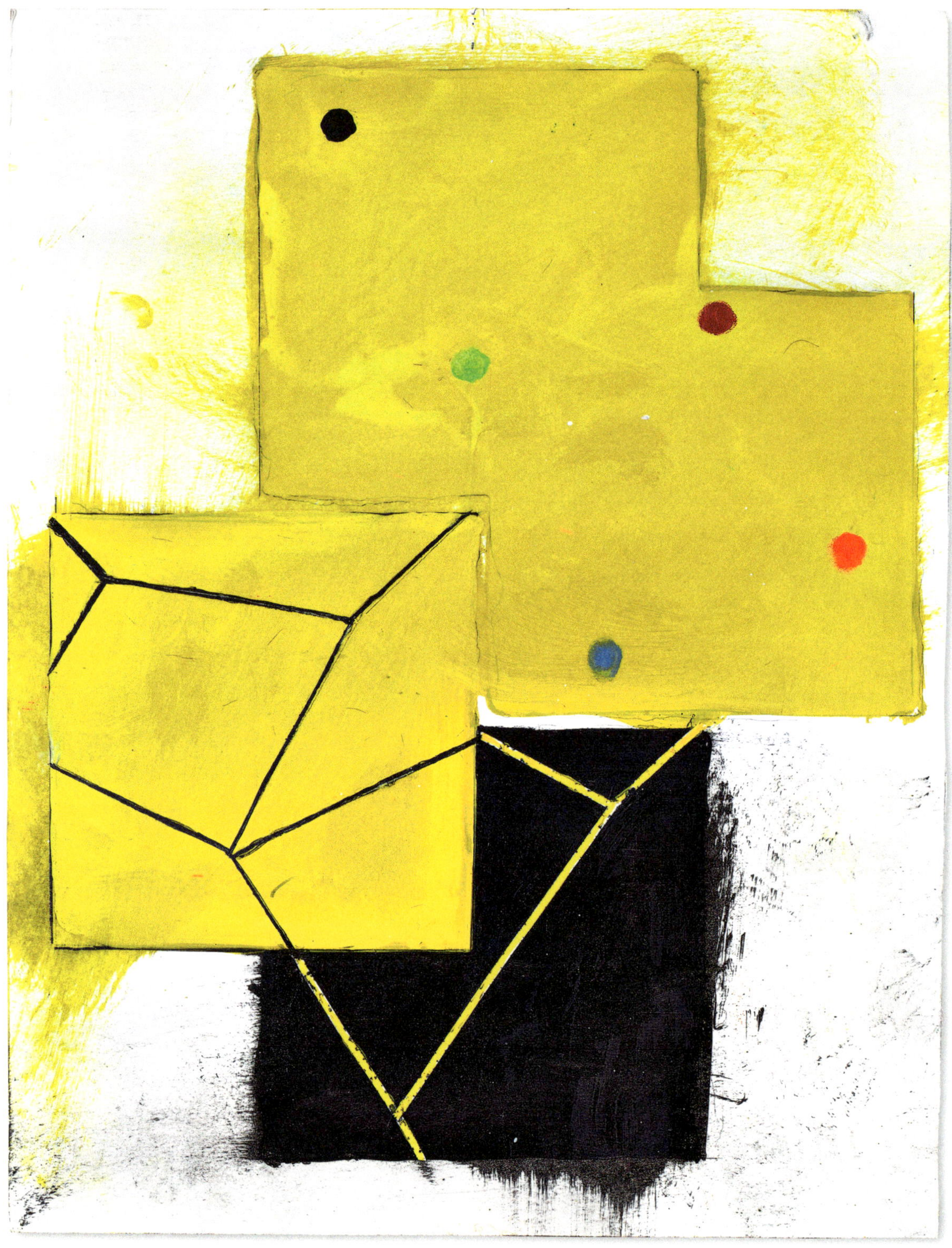

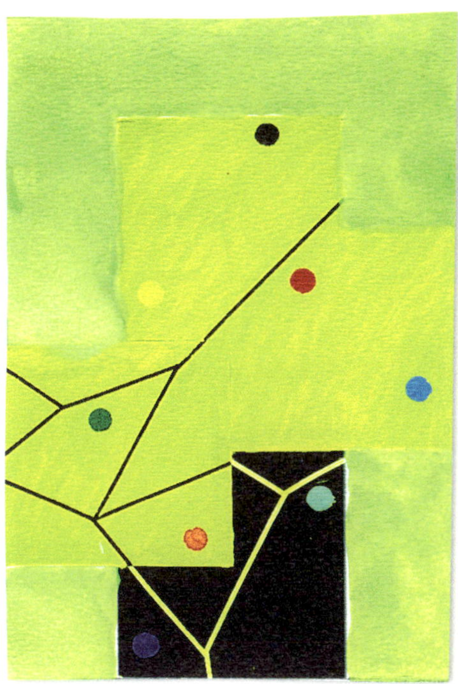

Charming Billy, ca. 2000. Watercolor and digital print on paper, 7 ½ × 4 ⅞ in. (19.1 × 12.4 cm)

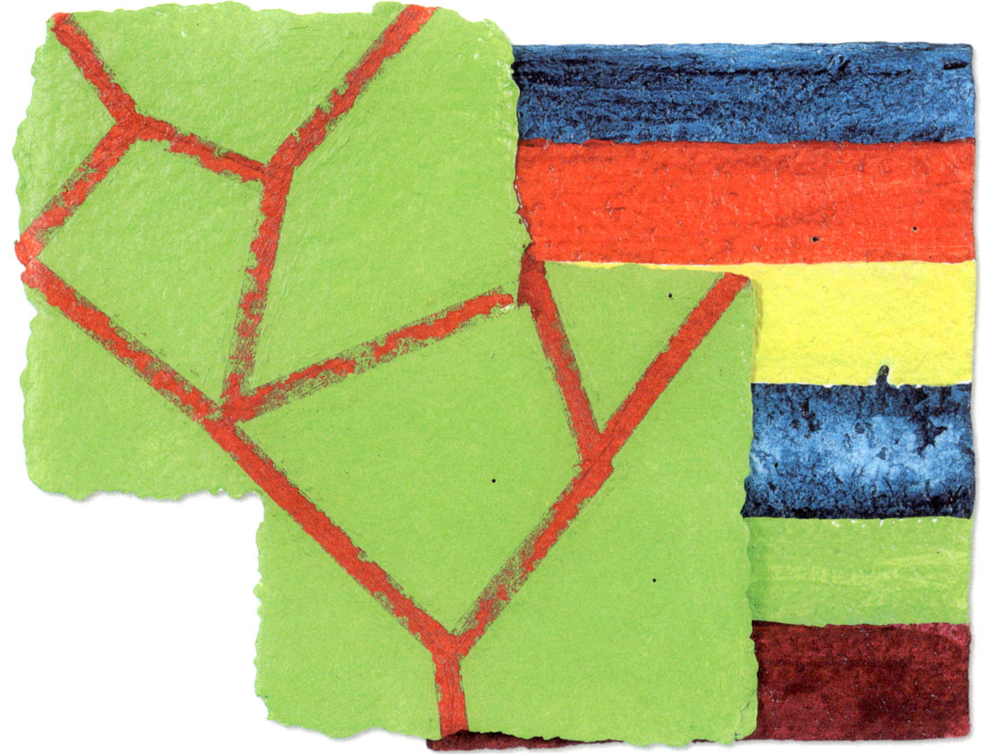

First Date, 2015. Oil on handmade paper, 12 ½ × 15 ⅝ in. (31.8 × 39.7 cm)

Untitled Watercolor Study, ca. 1988–90. Watercolor, crayon, and pencil on paper, 7 × 10 ¼ in. (17.8 × 26 cm)

Untitled Watercolor Study, ca. 1988–90. Watercolor, crayon, and pencil on paper, 10 ¼ × 7 in. (26 × 17.8 cm)

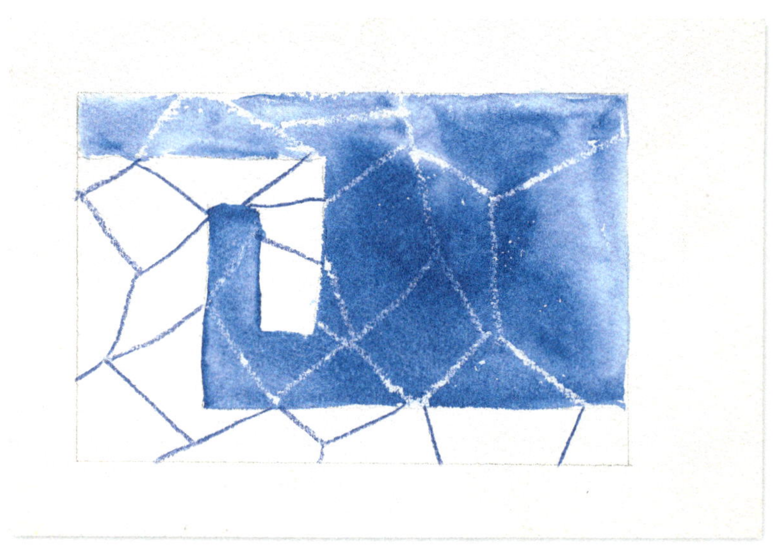

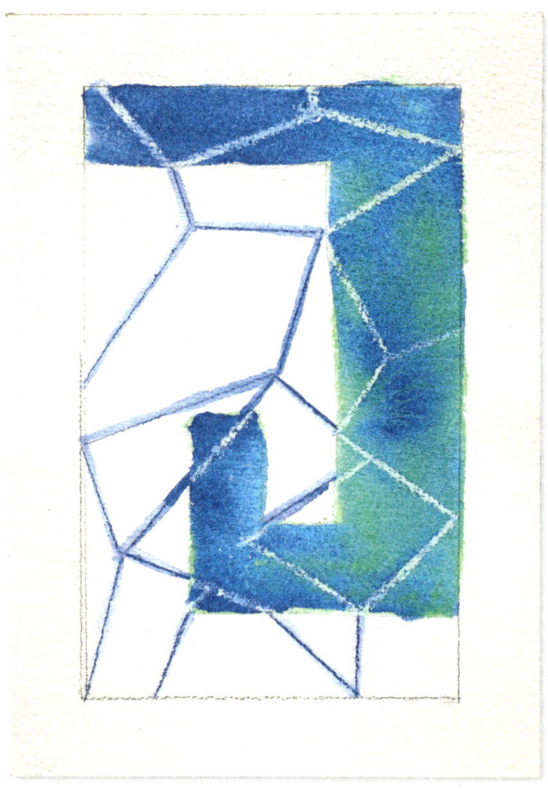

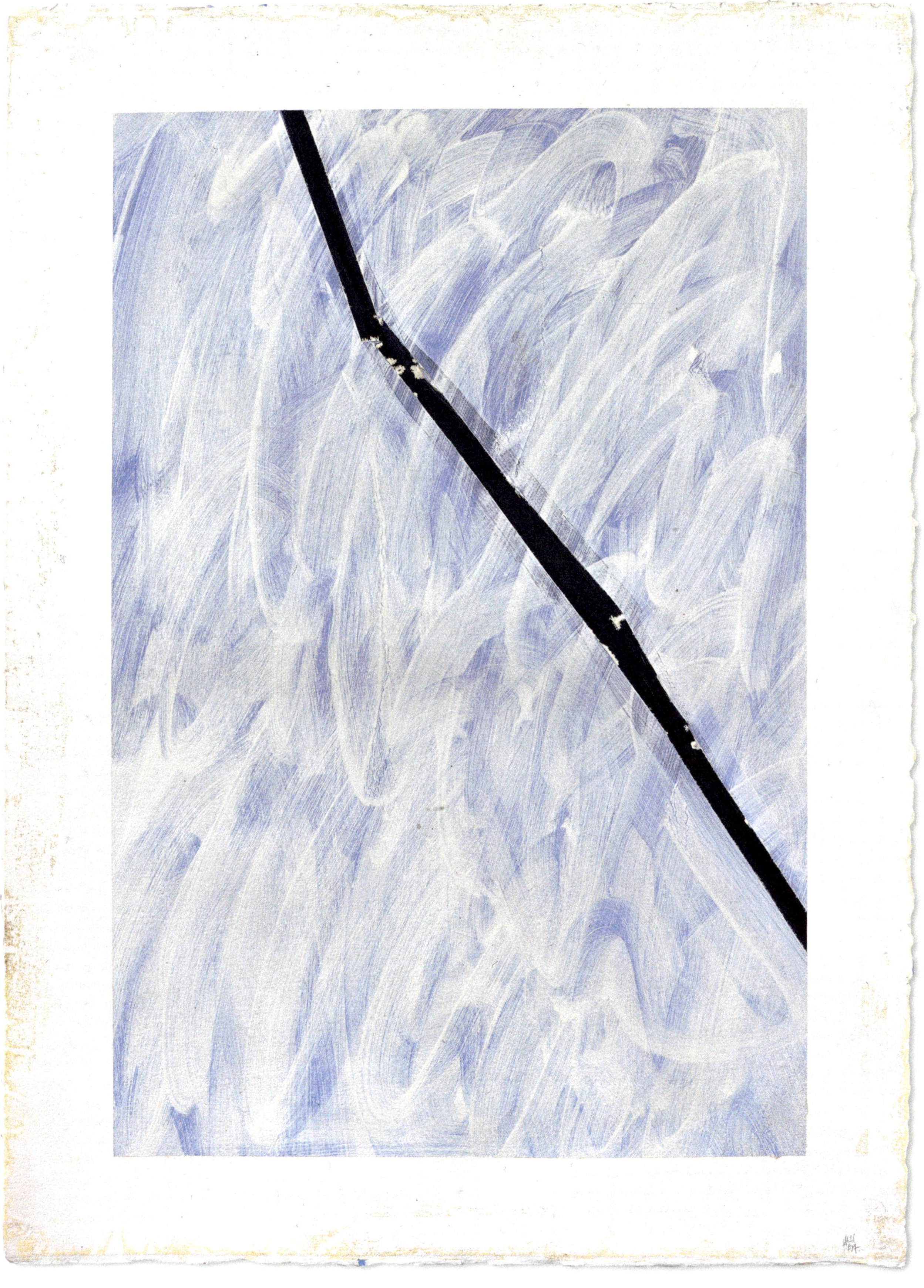

Blue Line, 1997. Oil on gessoed paper, 41 ½ × 29 ¼ in. (105.4 × 74.3 cm)

Untitled Watercolor Study, ca. 1980s. Watercolor on paper, 6 ⅝ × 5 in. (16.8 × 12.7 cm)

Untitled Watercolor Study, ca. 1990s. Watercolor on paper, 10 ⅞ × 14 ⅞ in. (27.6 × 37.8 cm)

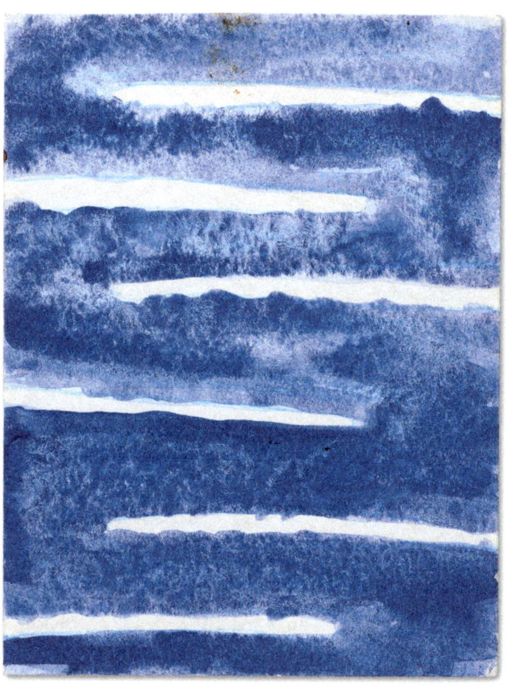

White Water, 1995. Oil on gessoed paper, 41 × 29 ½ in. (104.1 × 74.9 cm)

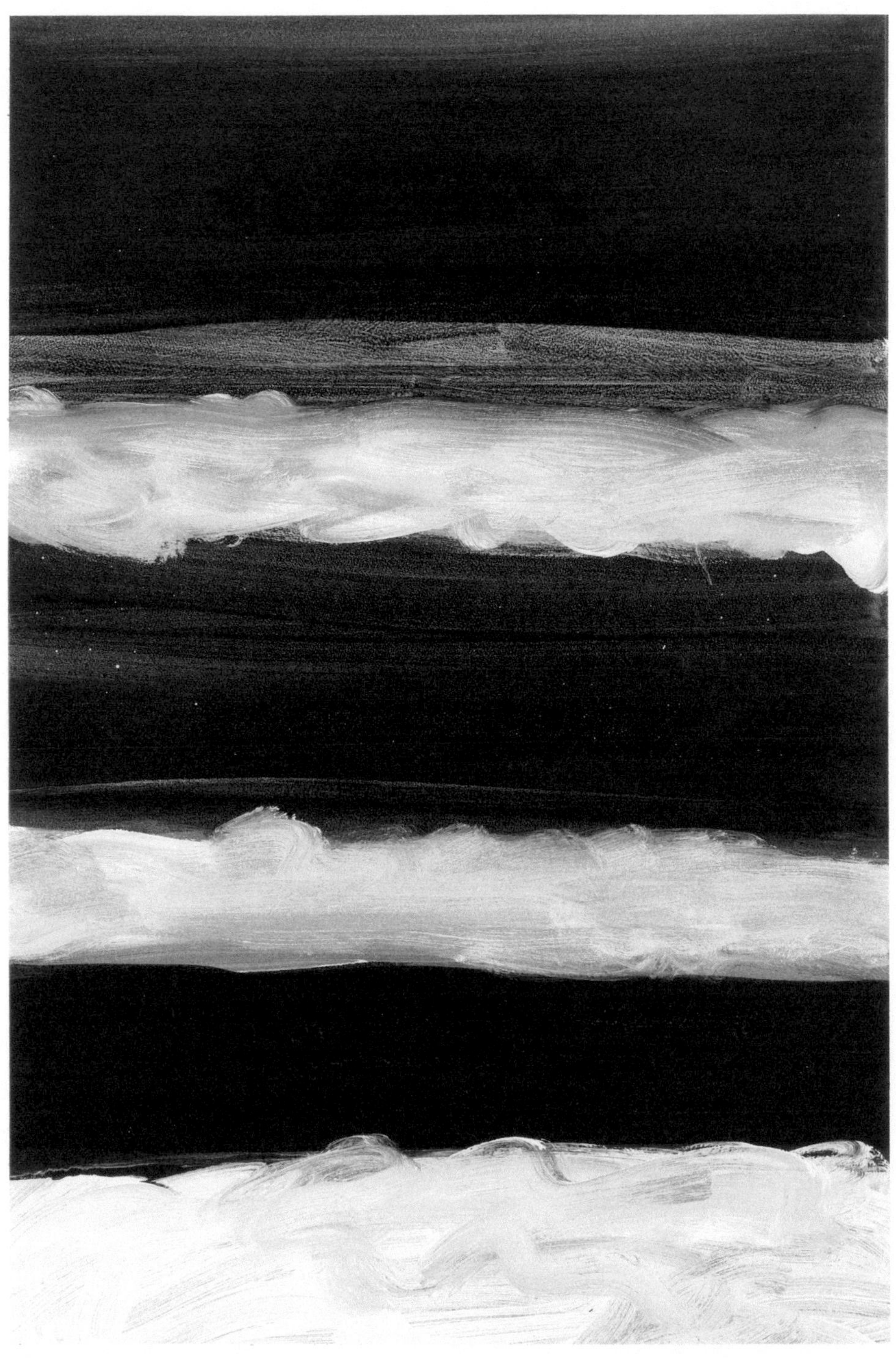

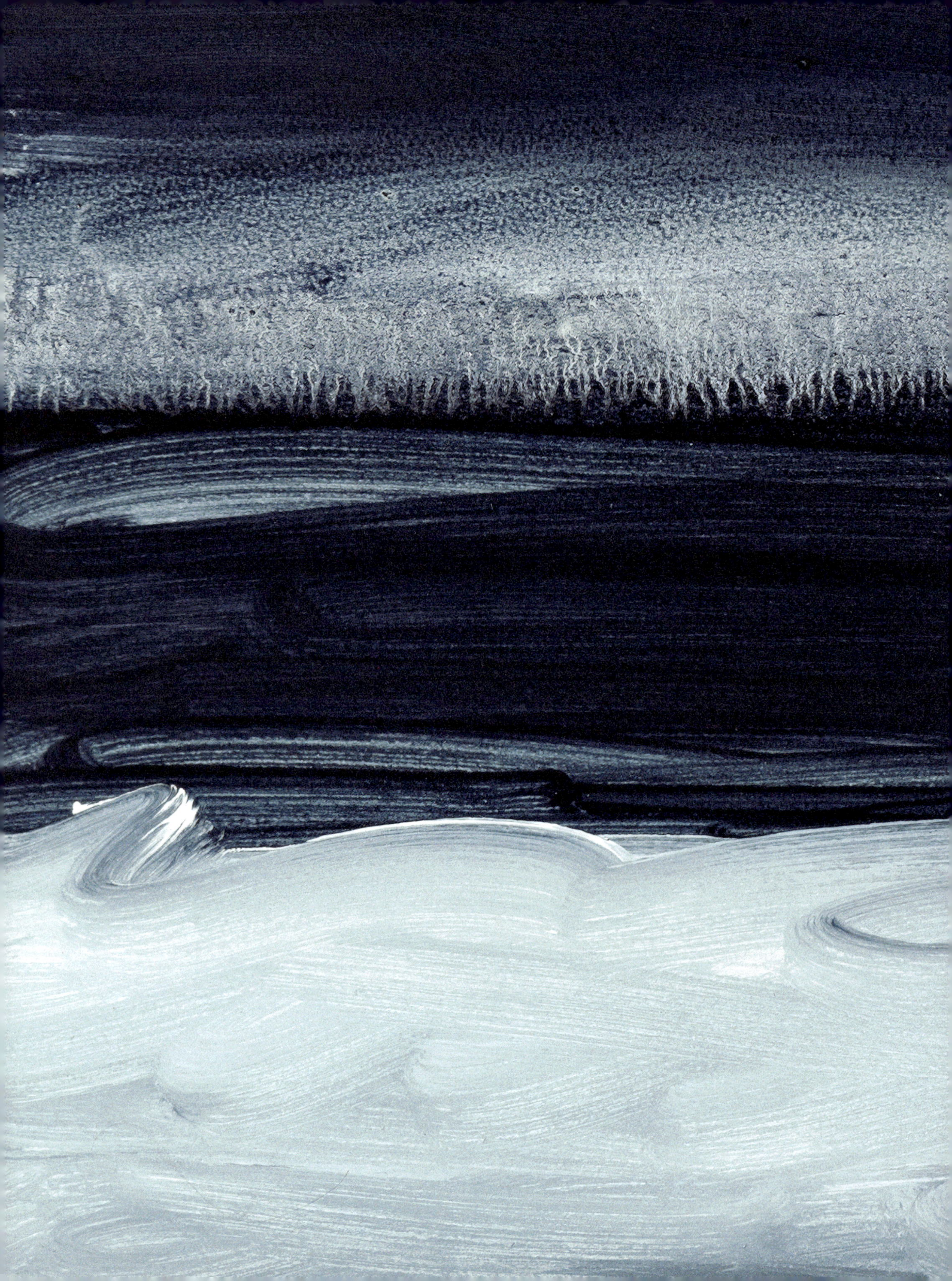

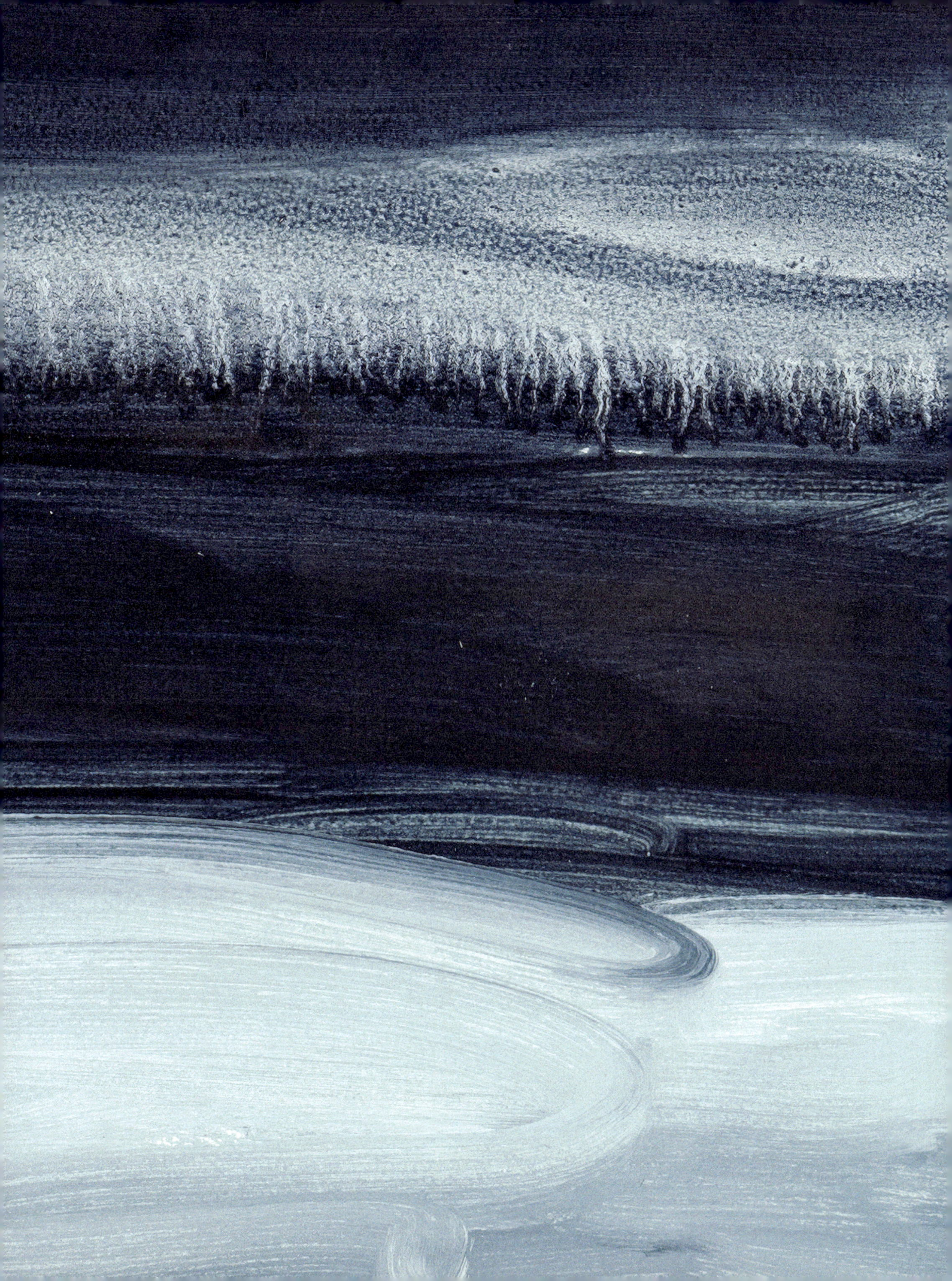

Close Out, 1995. Oil on gessoed paper, 41 × 29 ½ in. (104.1 × 74.9 cm). Detail, previous spread

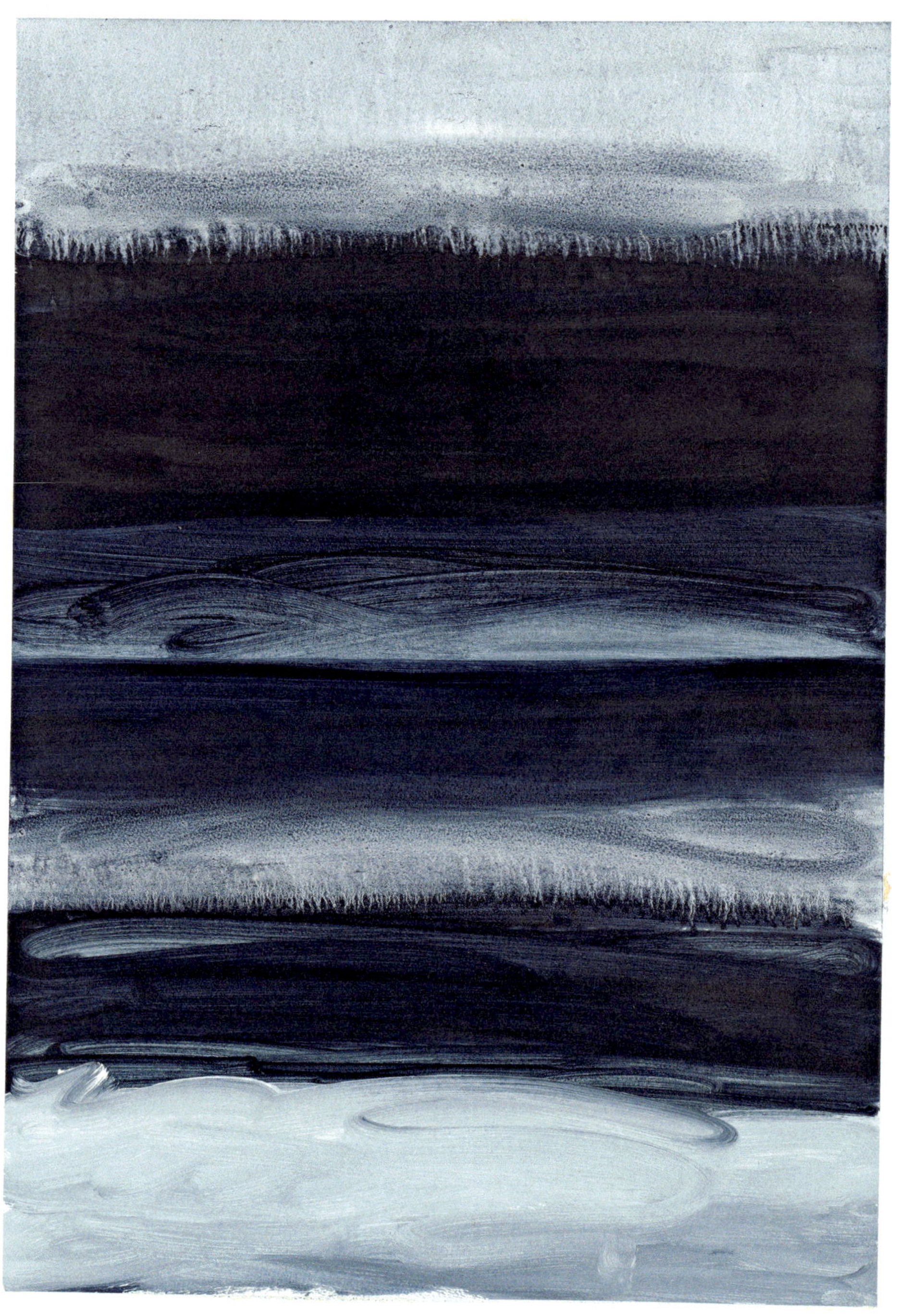

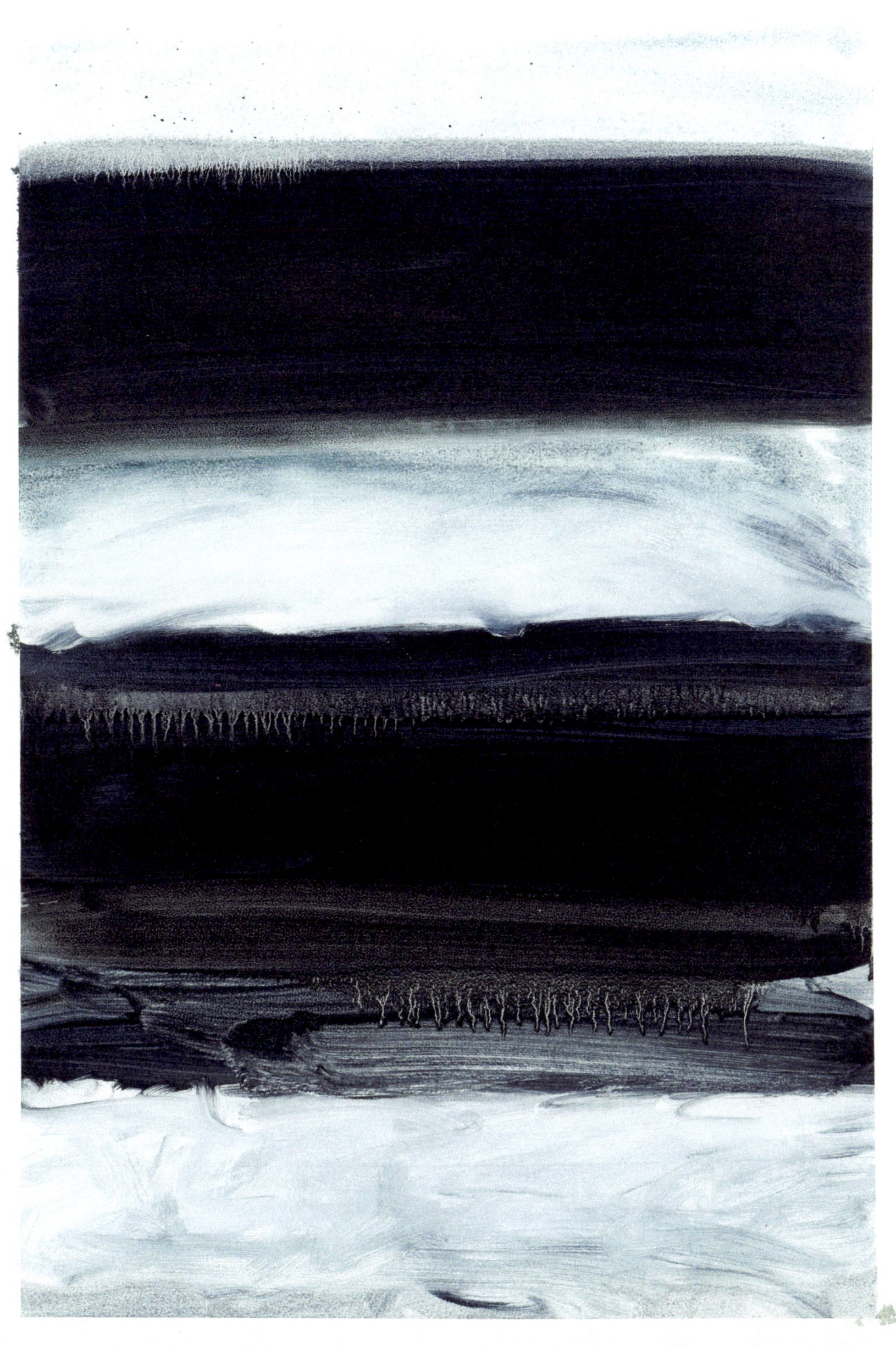

Line Up, 1995. Oil on gessoed paper, 41 × 29 ½ in. (104.1 × 74.9 cm)

Curl, 1995. Oil on gessoed paper, 41 × 29 ½ in. (104.1 × 74.9 cm)

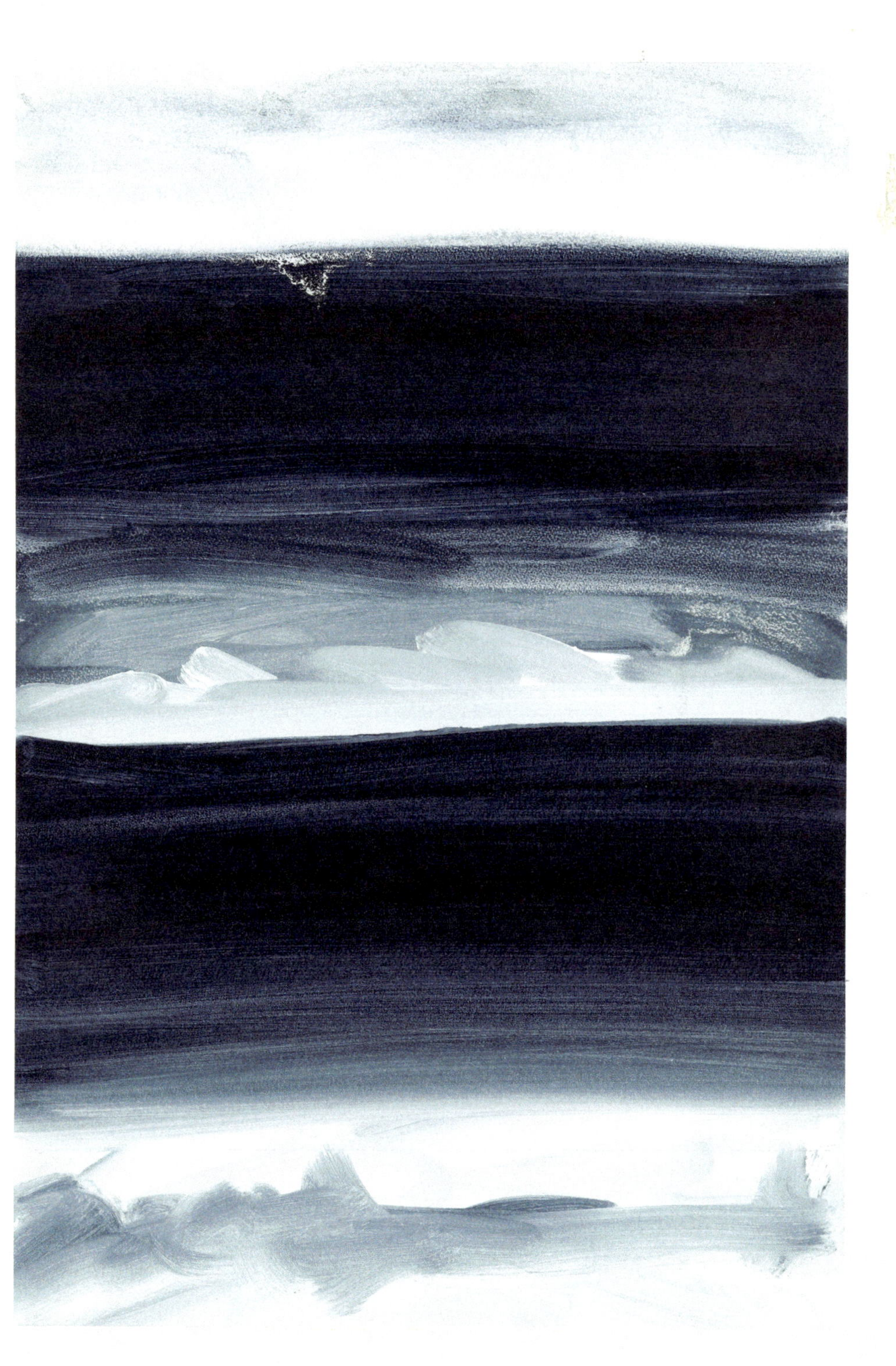

Cloth Study, 2005. Oil on gessoed paper, 41 ¾ × 29 ½ in. (106 × 74.9 cm)

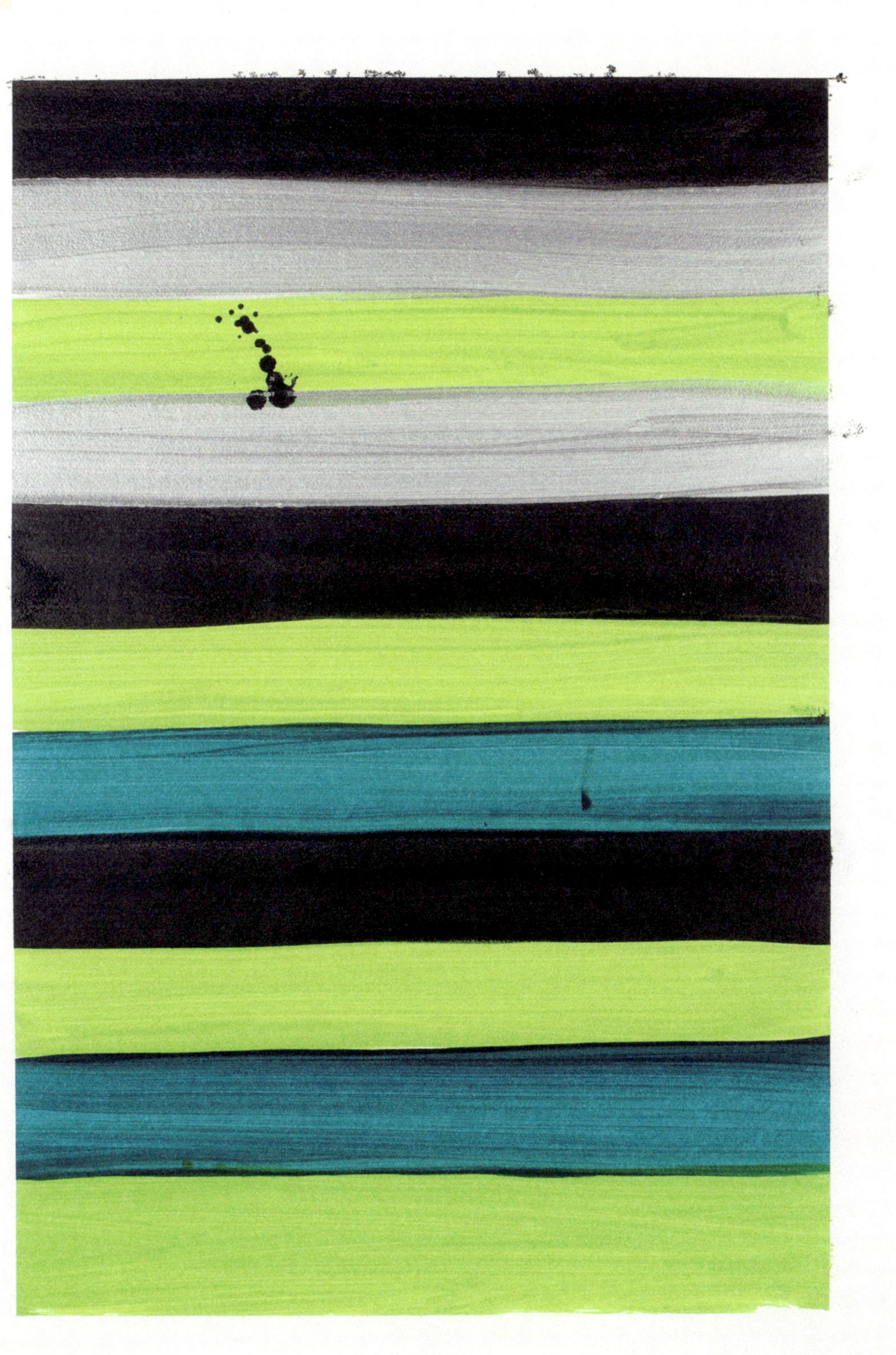

Mirage, ca. 2009. Watercolor on paper, 24 × 18 in. (61 × 45.7 cm)

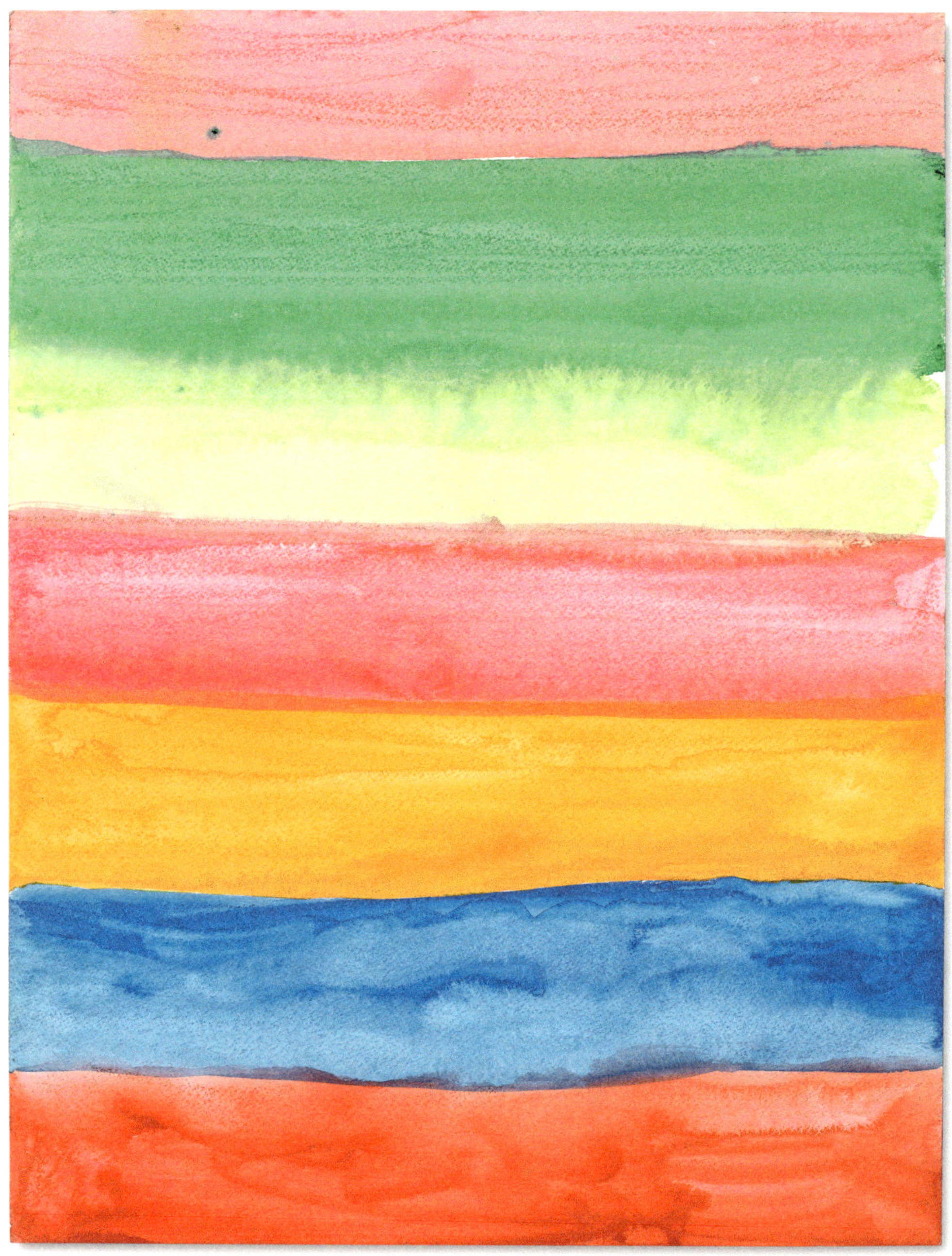

Untitled Study, ca. 1993—97. Acrylic on handmade paper,
15 ¼ × 10 ¼ in. (38.7 × 26 cm)

Untitled Watercolor Study, ca. 1991—92. Watercolor on paper, 7 × 5 in.
(17.8 × 12.7 cm). Detail, following spread

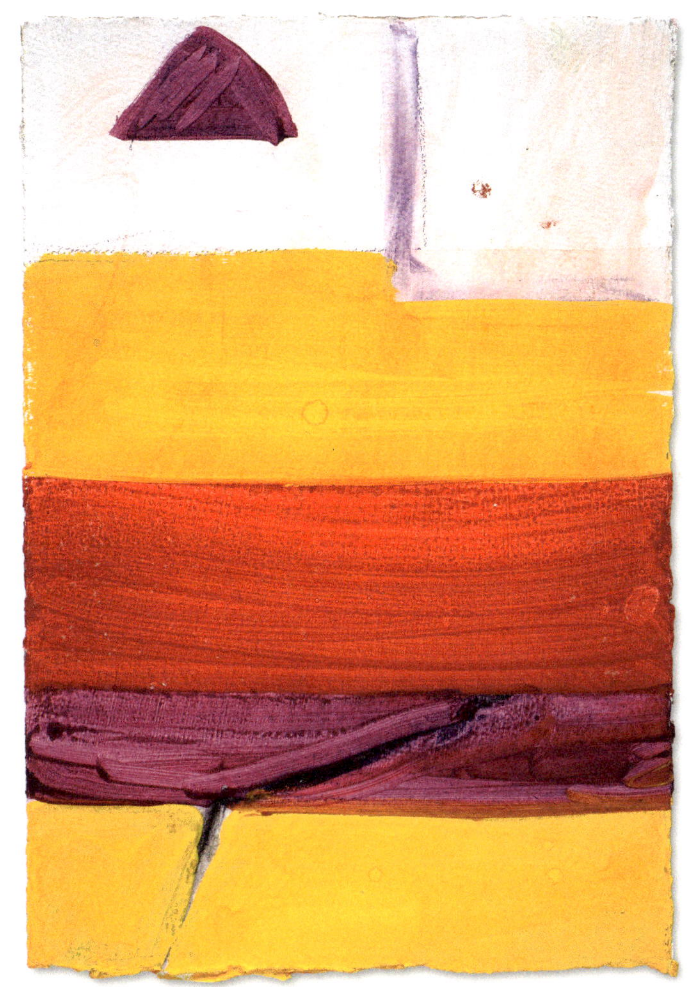

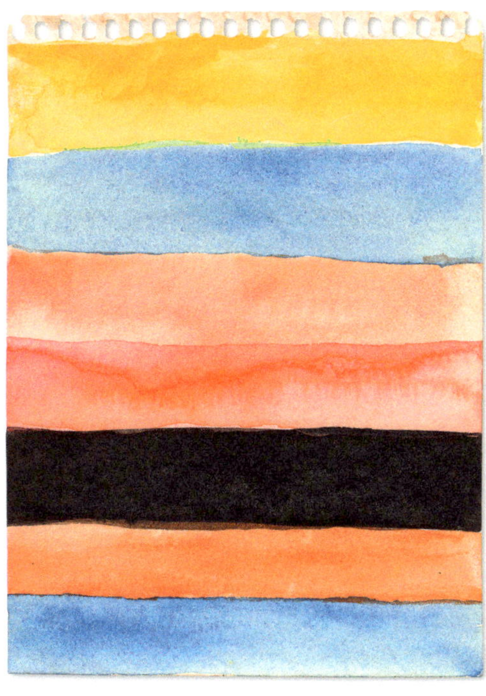

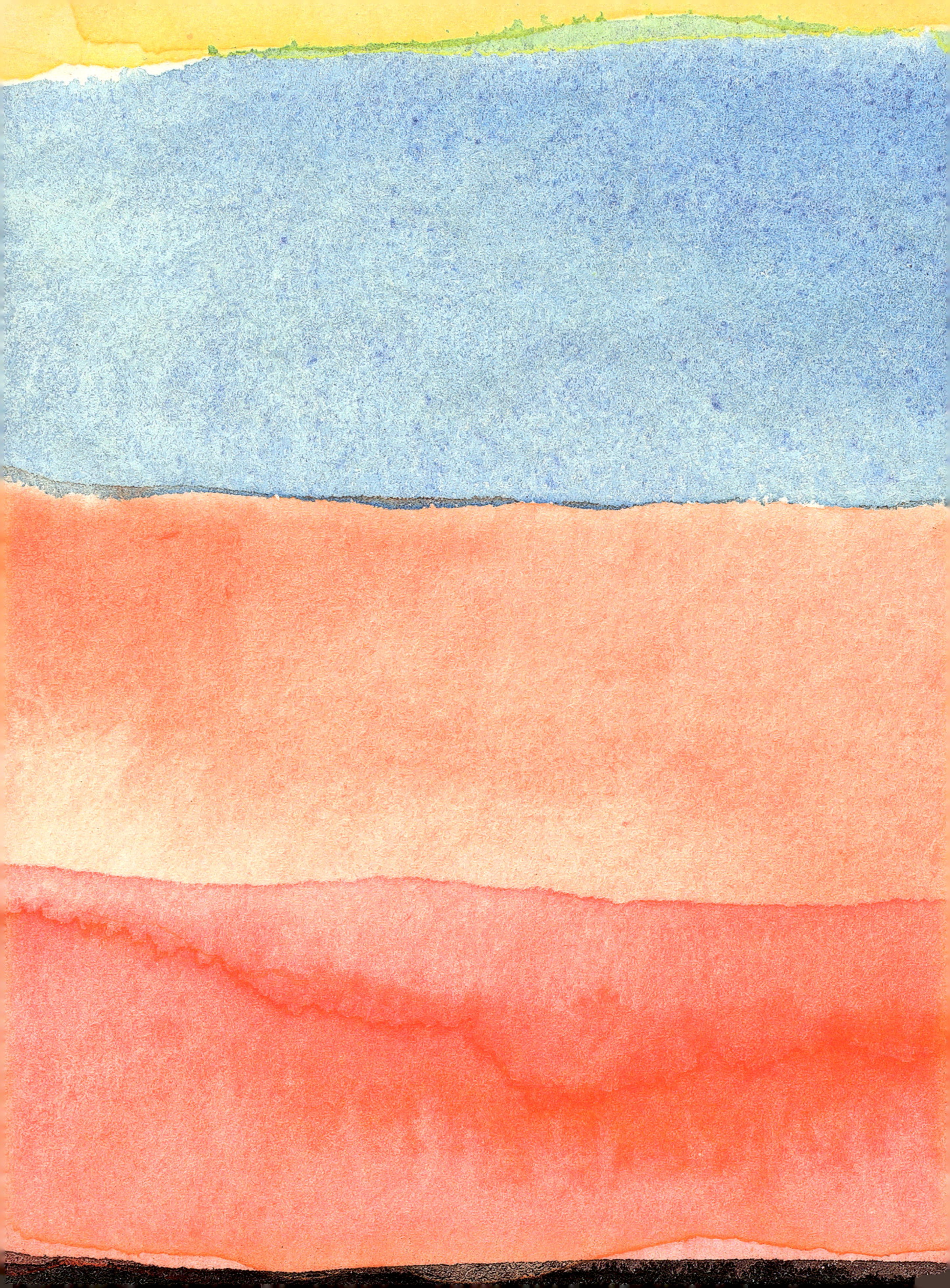

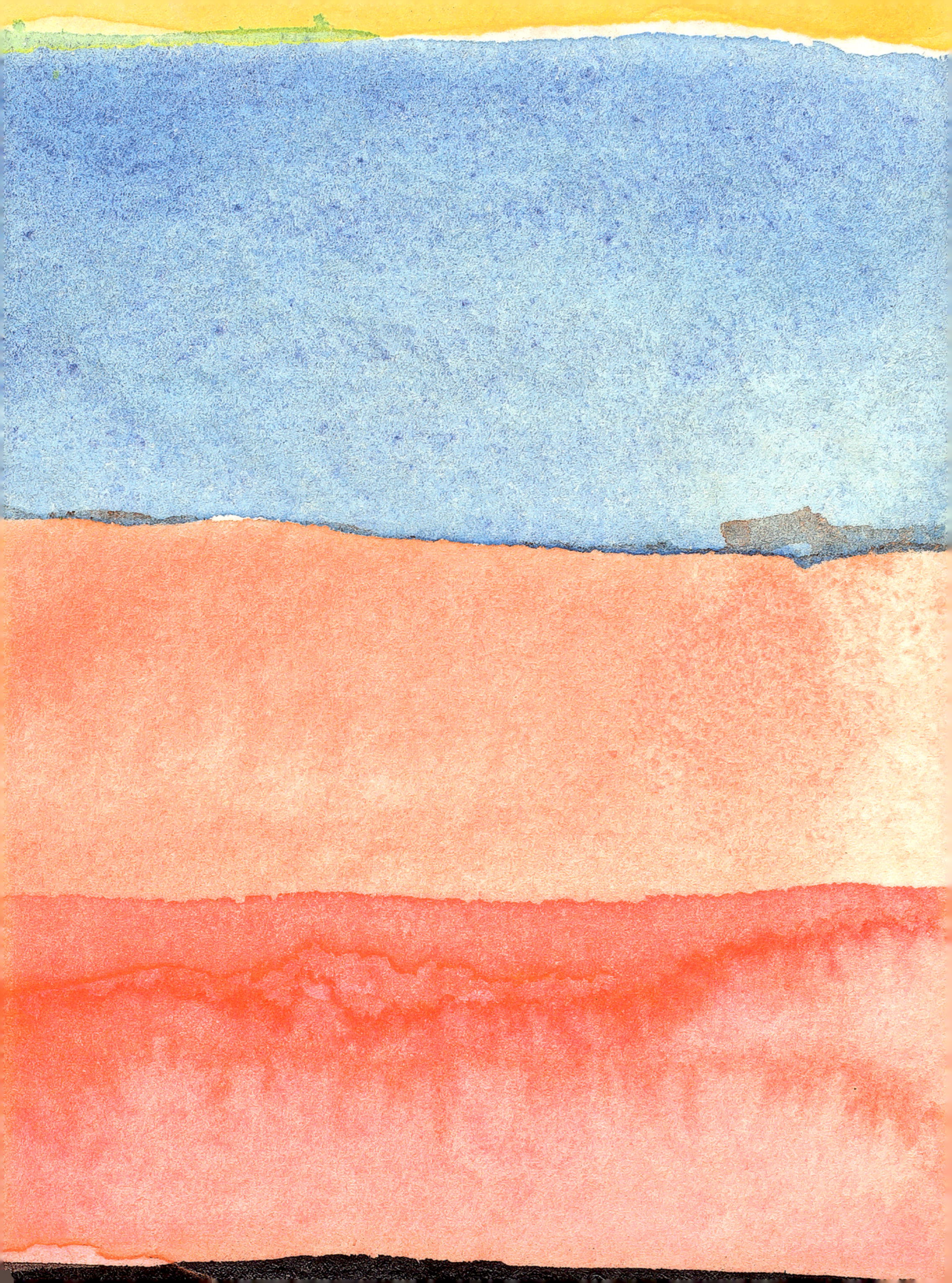

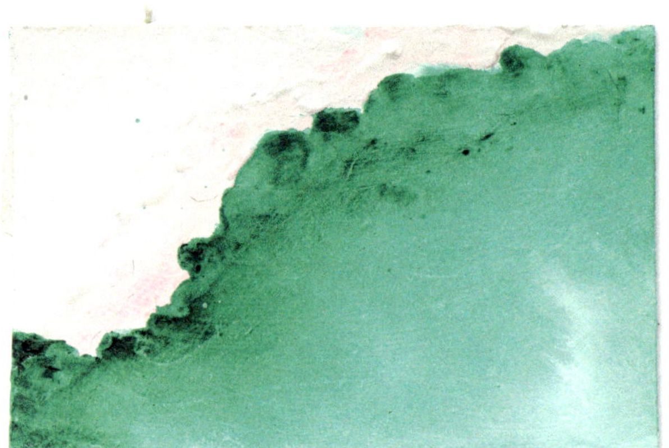

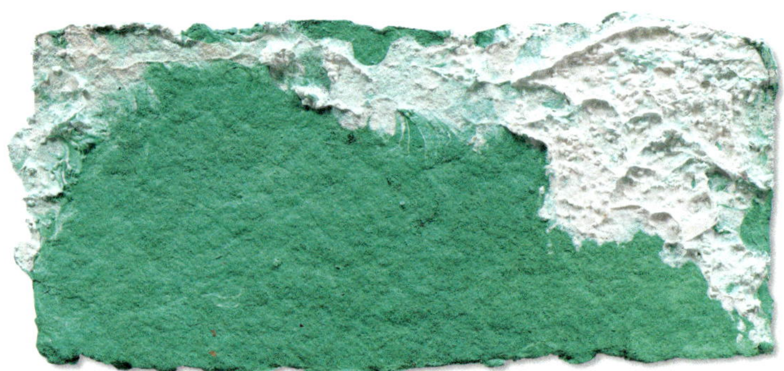

Hawaii, 1975. Ink and acrylic on gessoed paper, 40 × 27 ½ in. (101.6 × 69.9 cm)

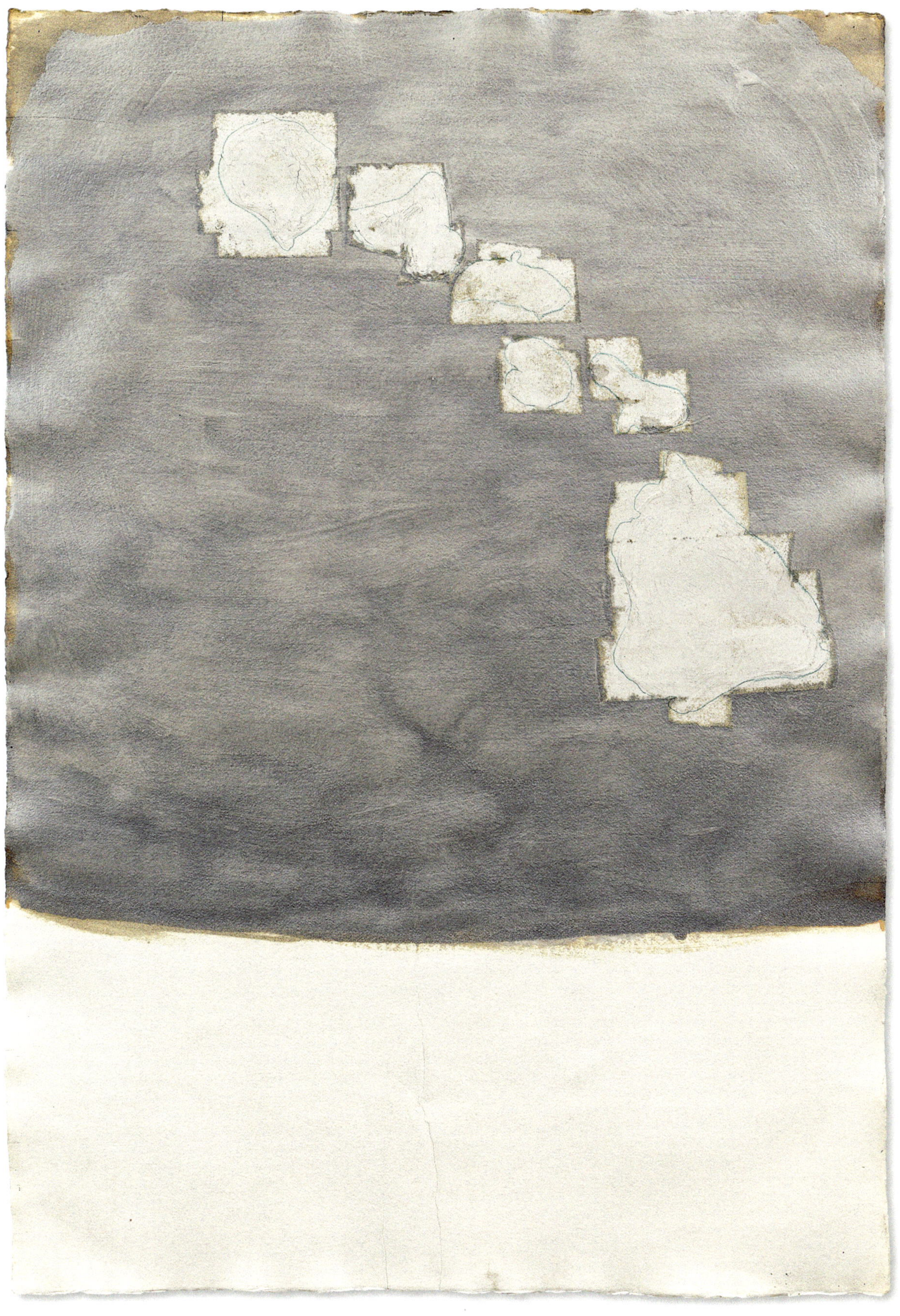

Palm Tree, ca. 1996. Oil on gessoed paper, 41 ½ × 29 ¼ in. (105.4 × 74.3 cm)

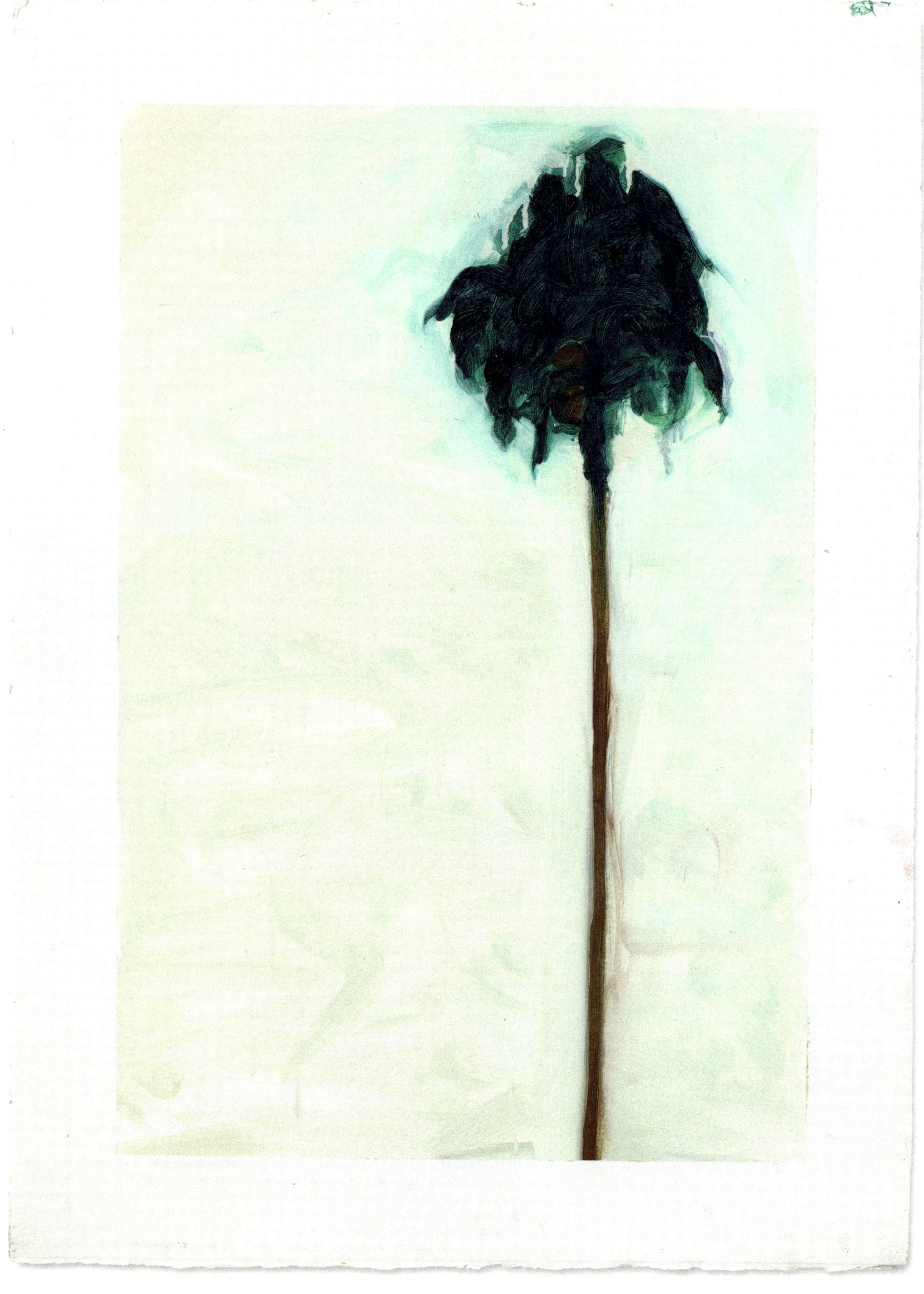

Untitled Watercolor Study, 1995. Watercolor on paper, 5 × 7 in.
(12.7 × 17.8 cm). Detail, following spread

Untitled Watercolor Study, 1995. Watercolor on paper, 5 × 7 in.
(12.7 × 17.8 cm)

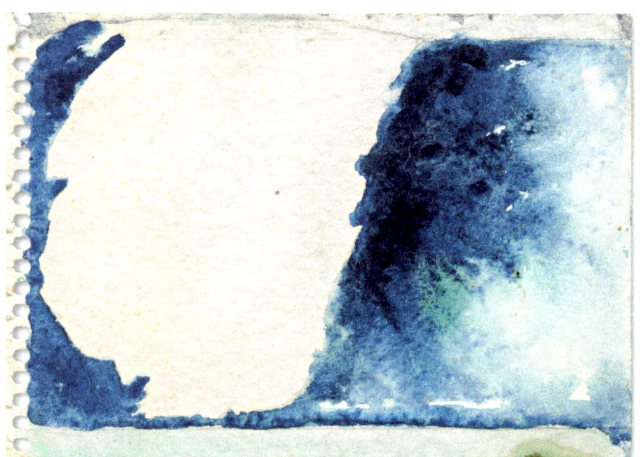

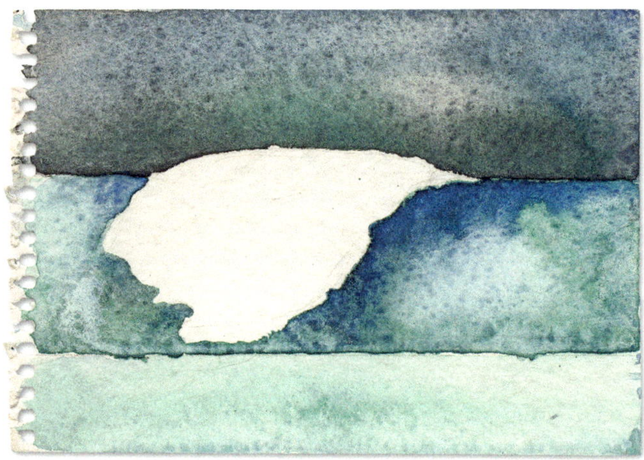

Untitled Watercolor Study, 1995. Watercolor on paper, 5 ⅝ × 4 in. (14.3 × 10.2 cm)

Untitled Watercolor Study, 1995. Watercolor on paper, 4 × 5 ⅝ in. (10.2 × 14.3 cm)

Untitled Watercolor Study, 1995. Watercolor on paper, 4 × 5 ⅝ in. (10.2 × 14.3 cm)

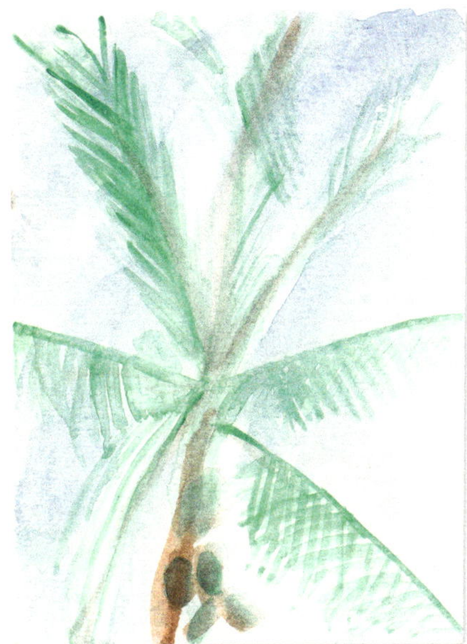

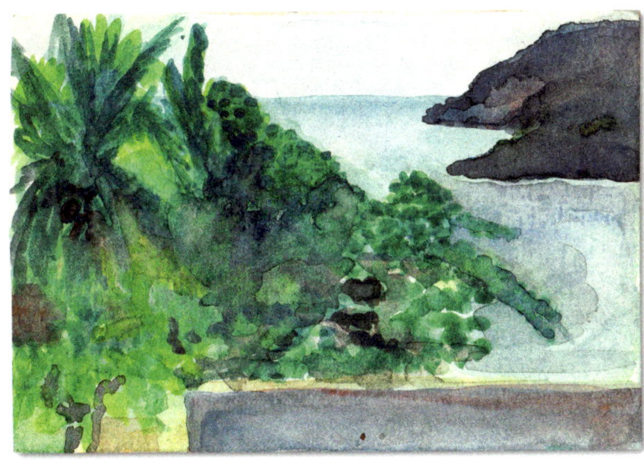

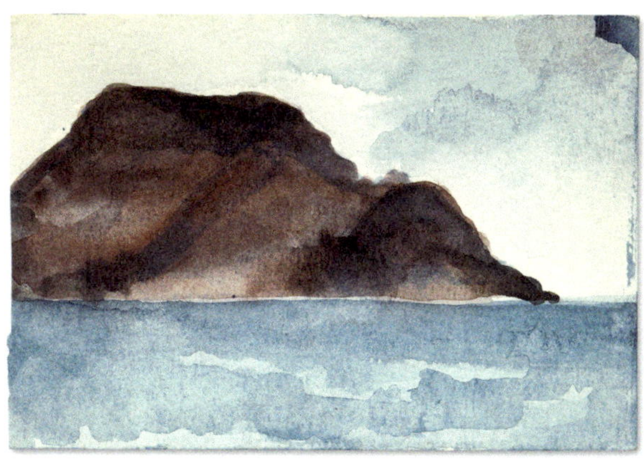

Untitled Study, ca. 1978. Gouache, colored pencil, and pencil on paper,
8 × 6 in. (20.3 × 15.2 cm)

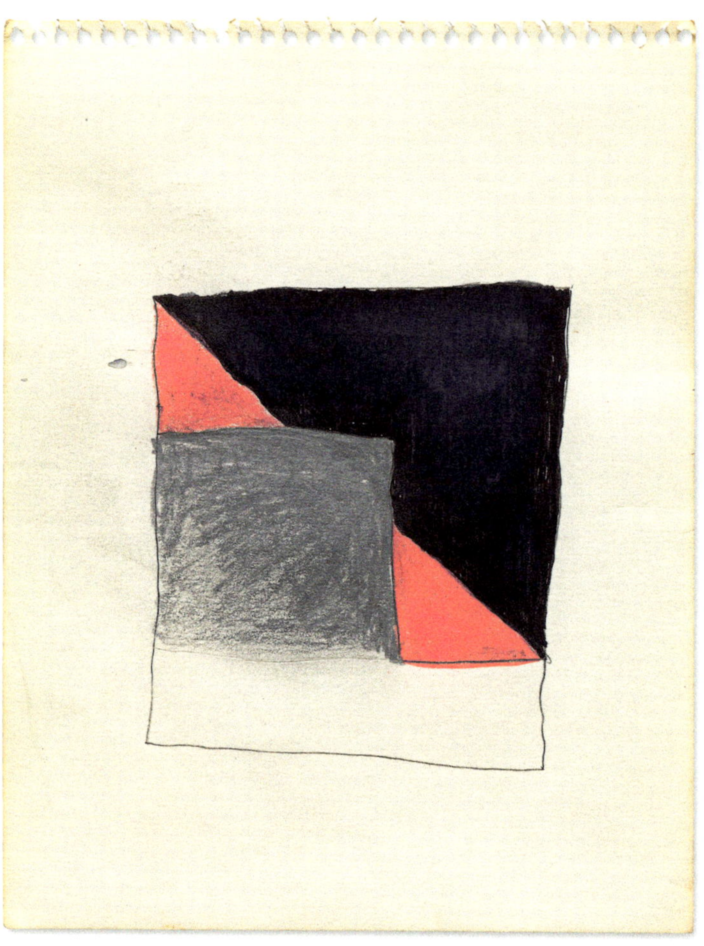

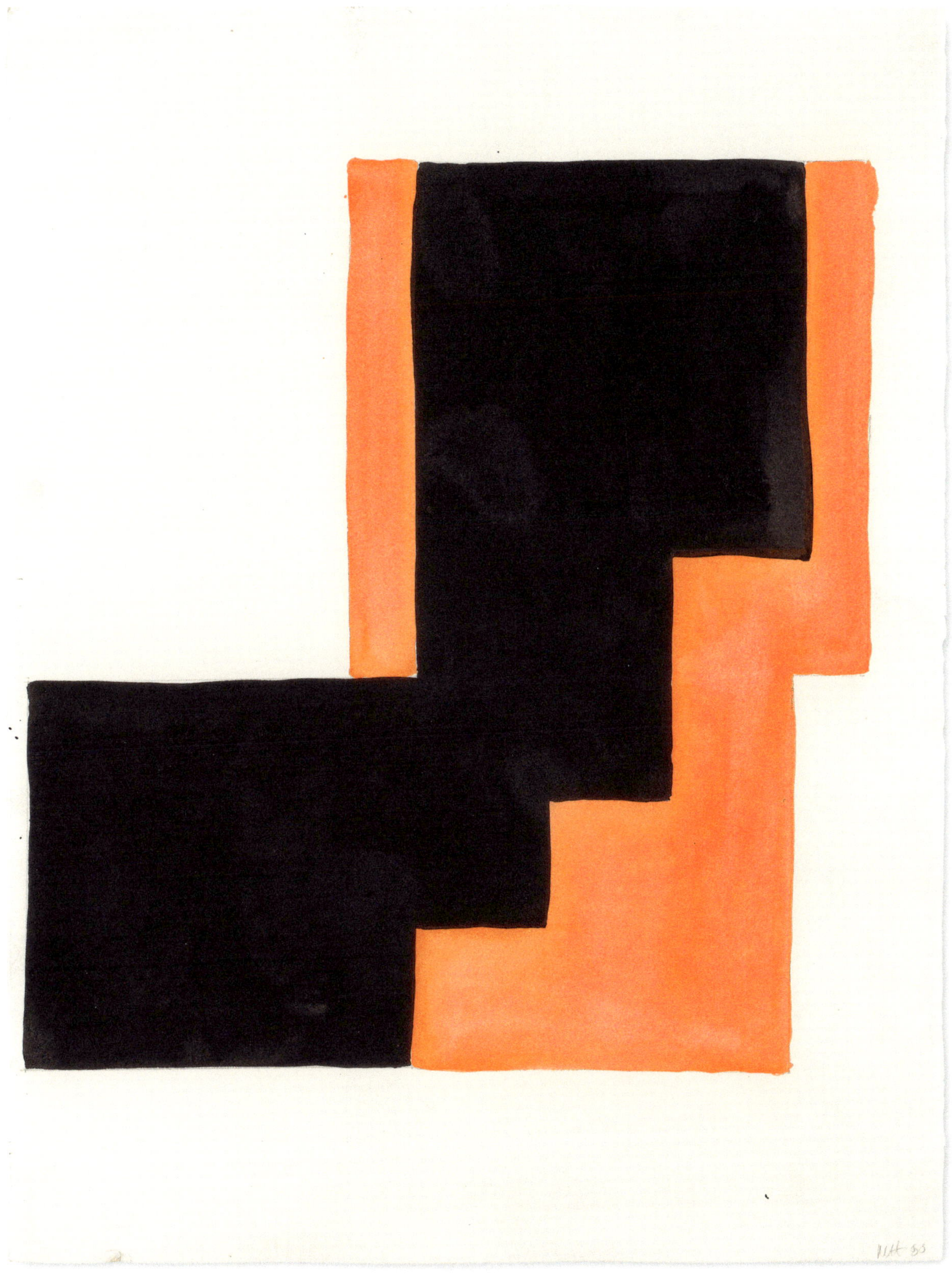

Descent, 1980. Acrylic and watercolor on paper, 29 ⅞ × 22 ¼ in.
(75.9 × 56.5 cm)

Pink Embrace, 1980. Acrylic and watercolor on paper, 29 ⅞ × 22 ⅛ in. (75.9 × 56.2 cm)

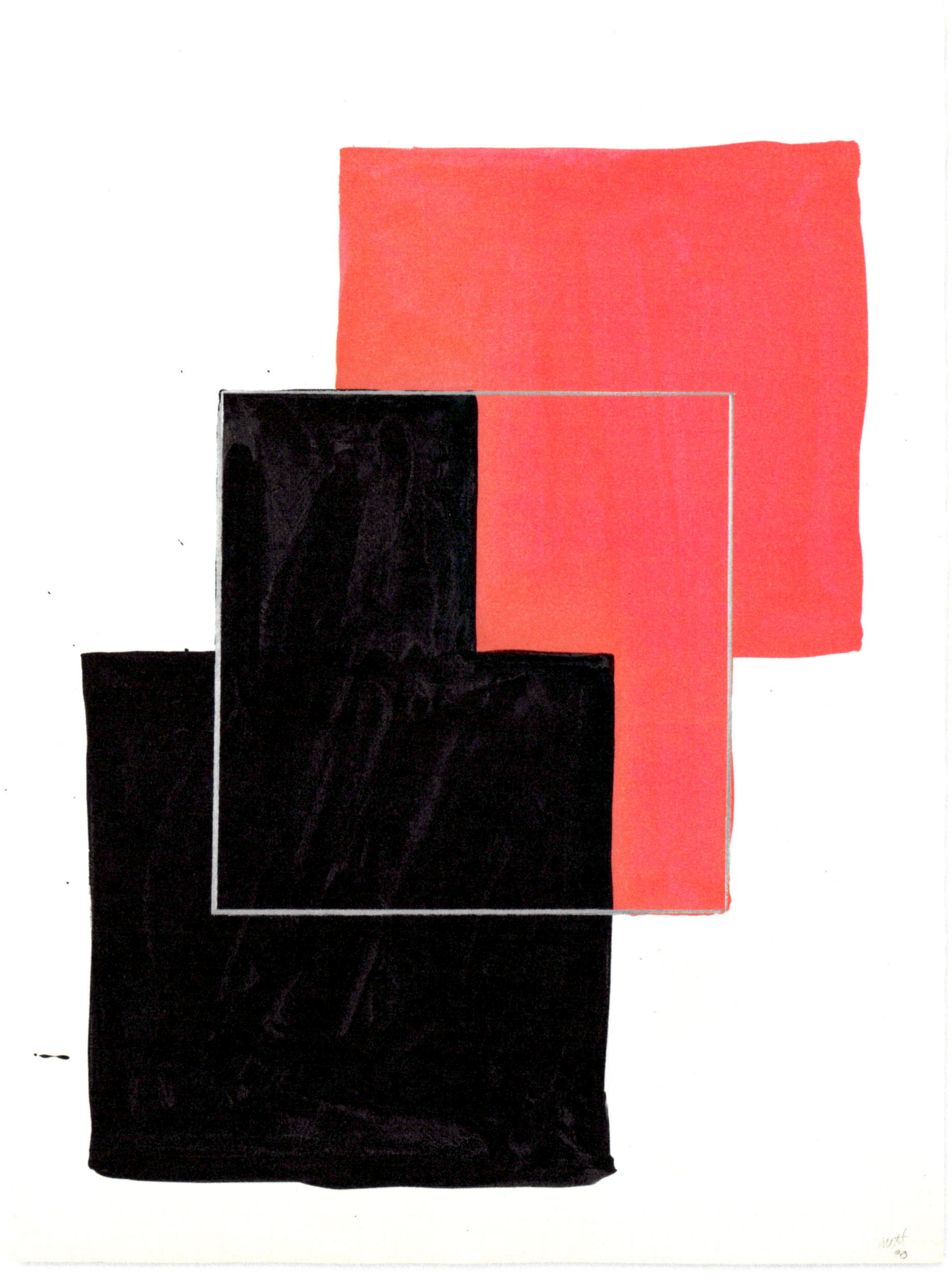

Untitled Watercolor Study, ca. 1980s. Watercolor and pencil on paper,
14 ⅛ × 10 ¾ in. (35.9 × 27.3 cm)

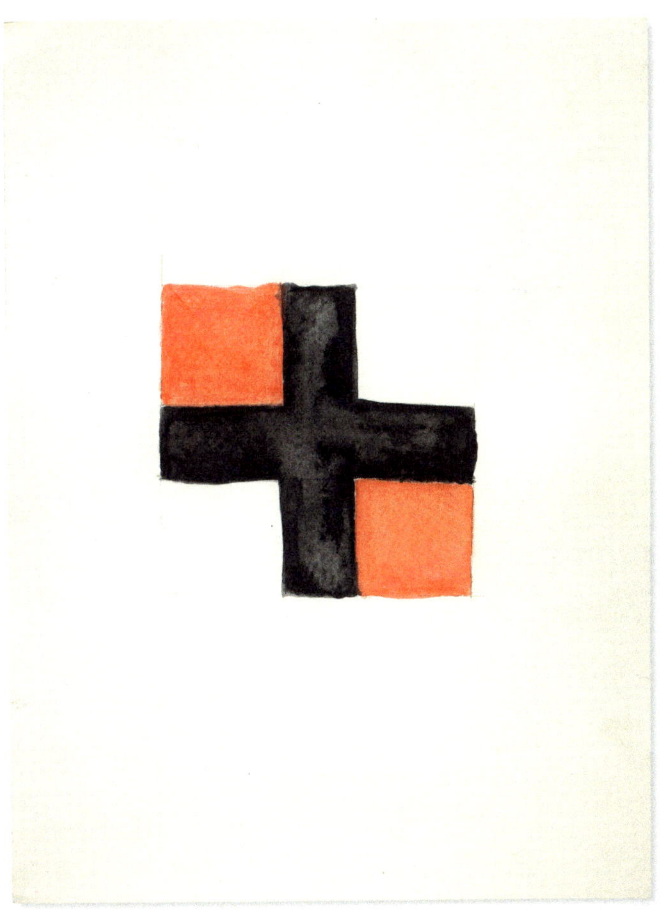

Islands, 1988. Watercolor on paper, 30 × 22 in. (76.2 × 55.9 cm)

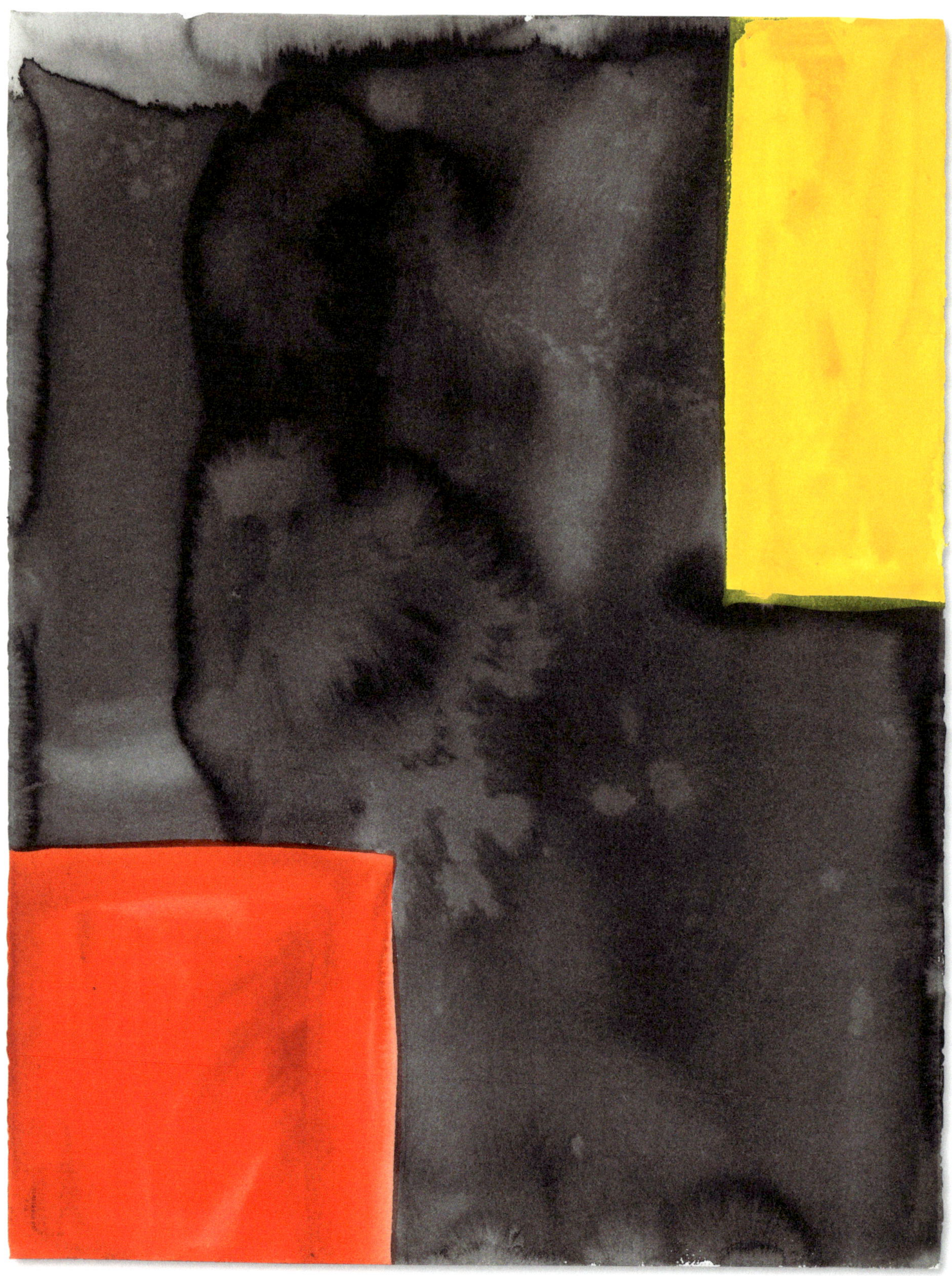

Untitled Watercolor Study, ca. 1982–84. Watercolor and colored pencil on
paper, 3 ⅞ × 5 ⅝ in. (9.8 × 14.3 cm). Detail, following spread

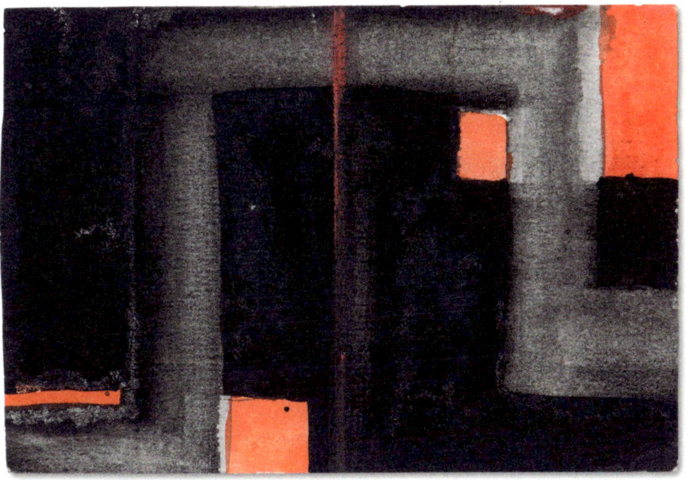

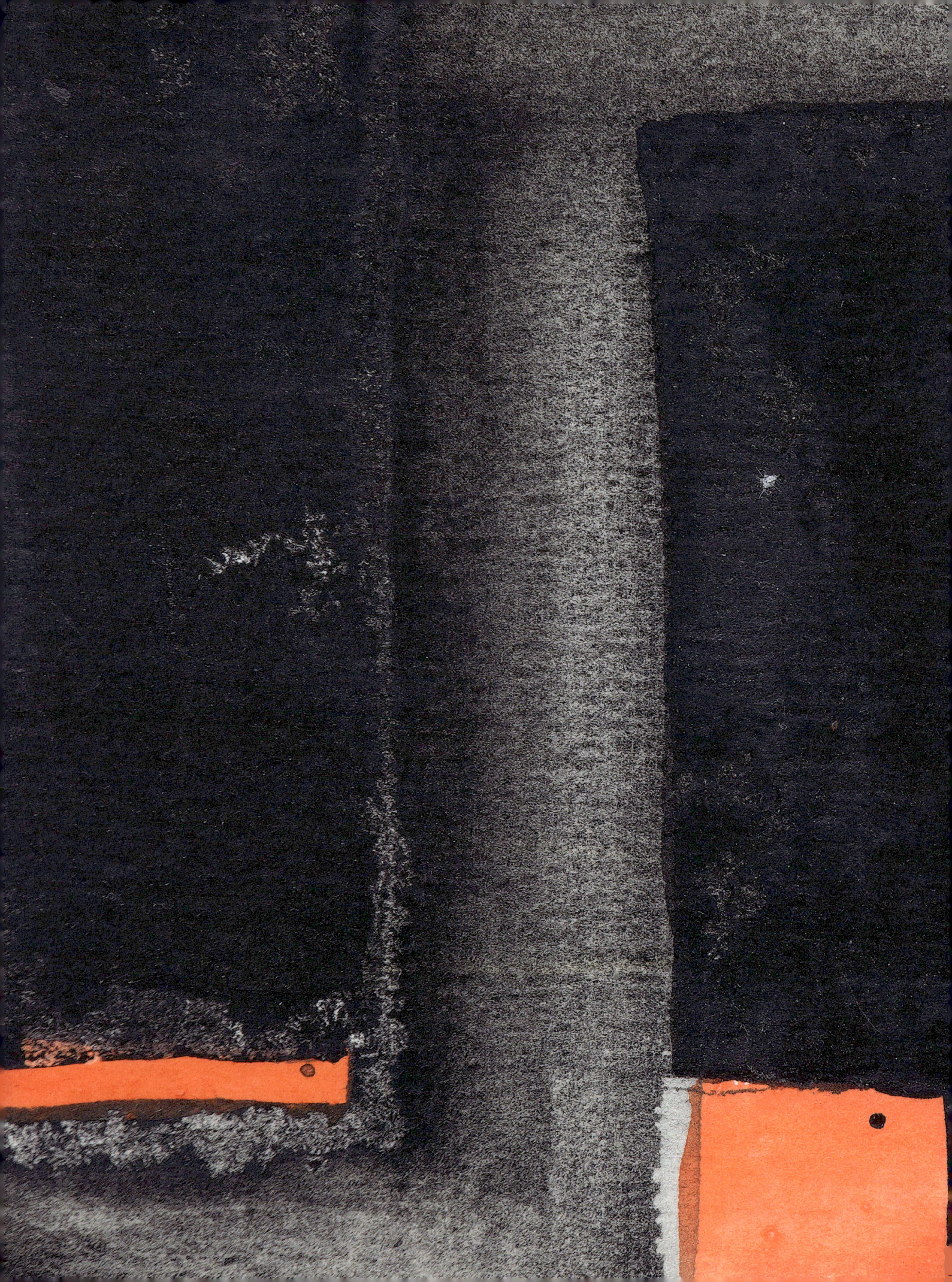

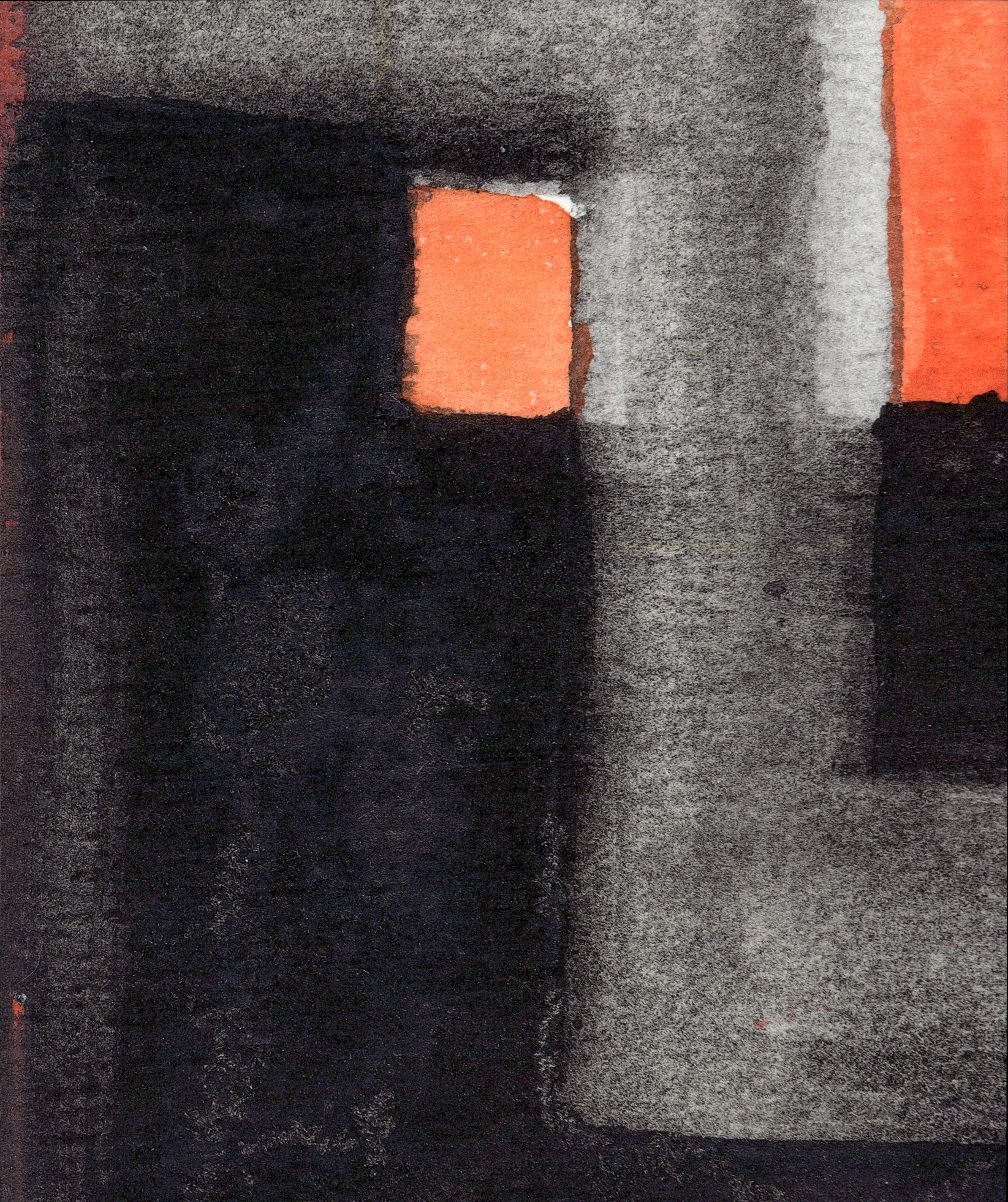

Lavender, 1986. Watercolor on paper, 30 × 42 in. (76.2 × 106.7 cm)

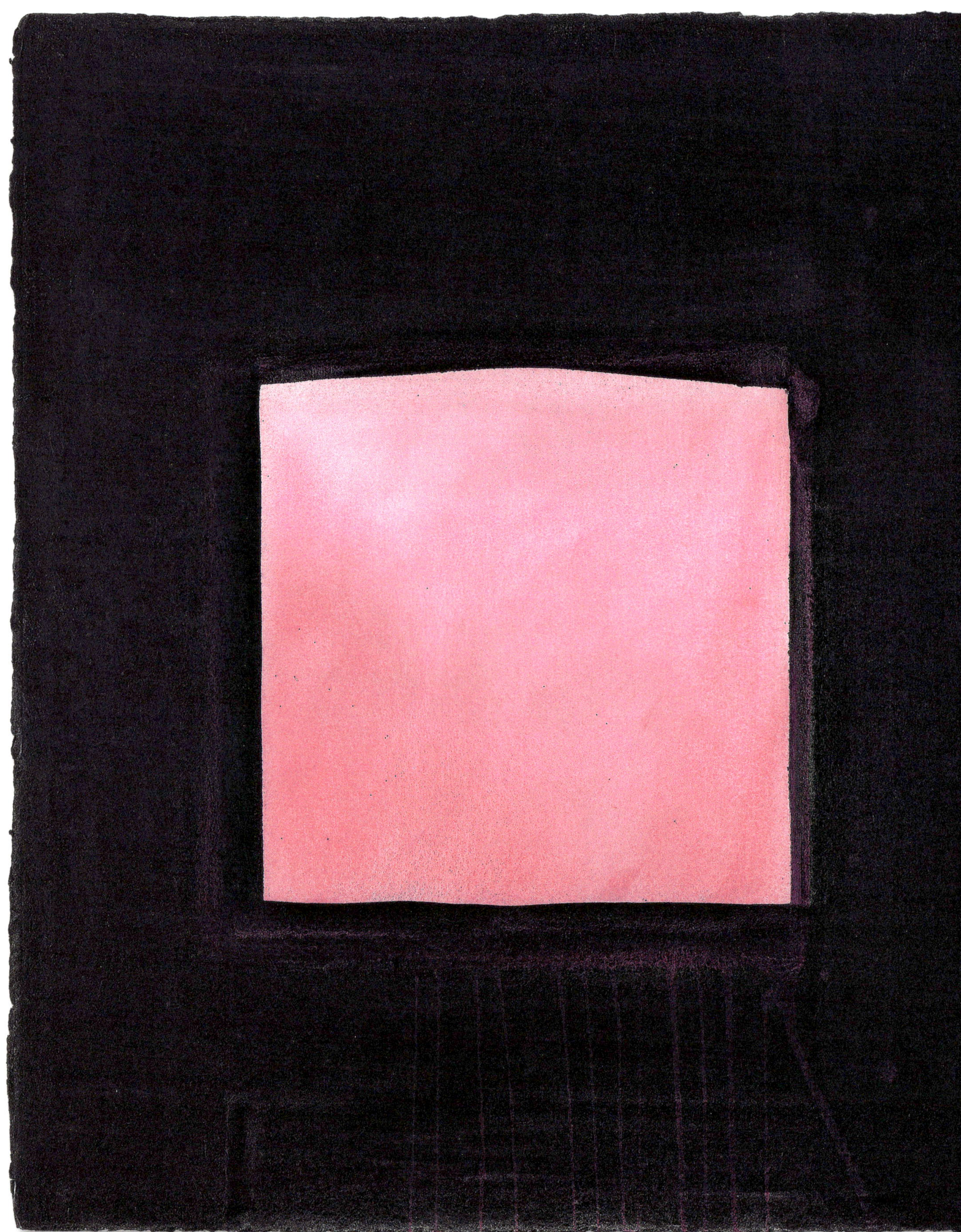

Garden of Allah #2, 1994. Watercolor on paper, 41 × 29 ½ in. (104.1 × 74.9 cm)

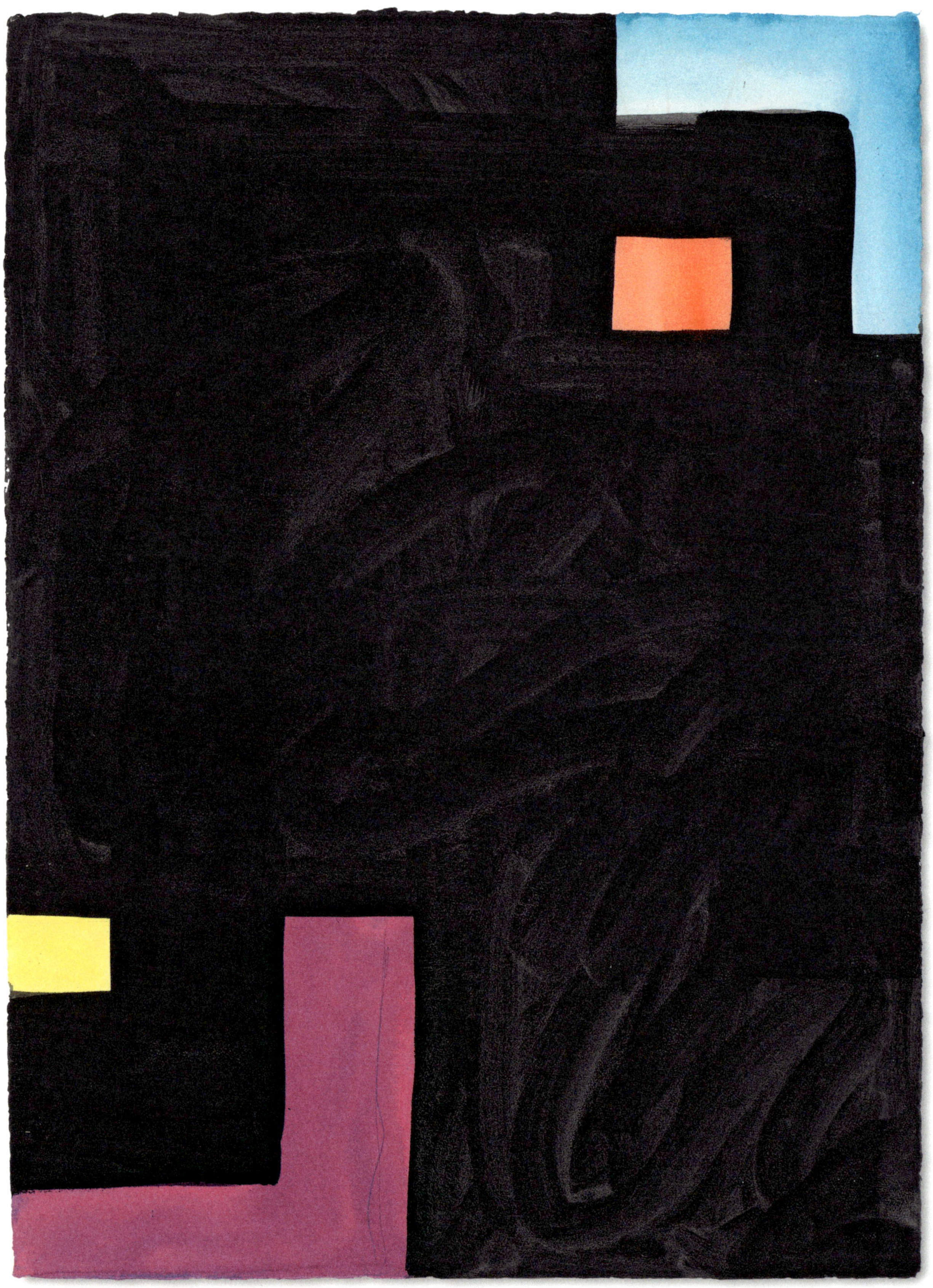

The Kiss (Saturday Nite), 1986. Watercolor on paper, 30 × 22 in. (76.2 × 55.9 cm)

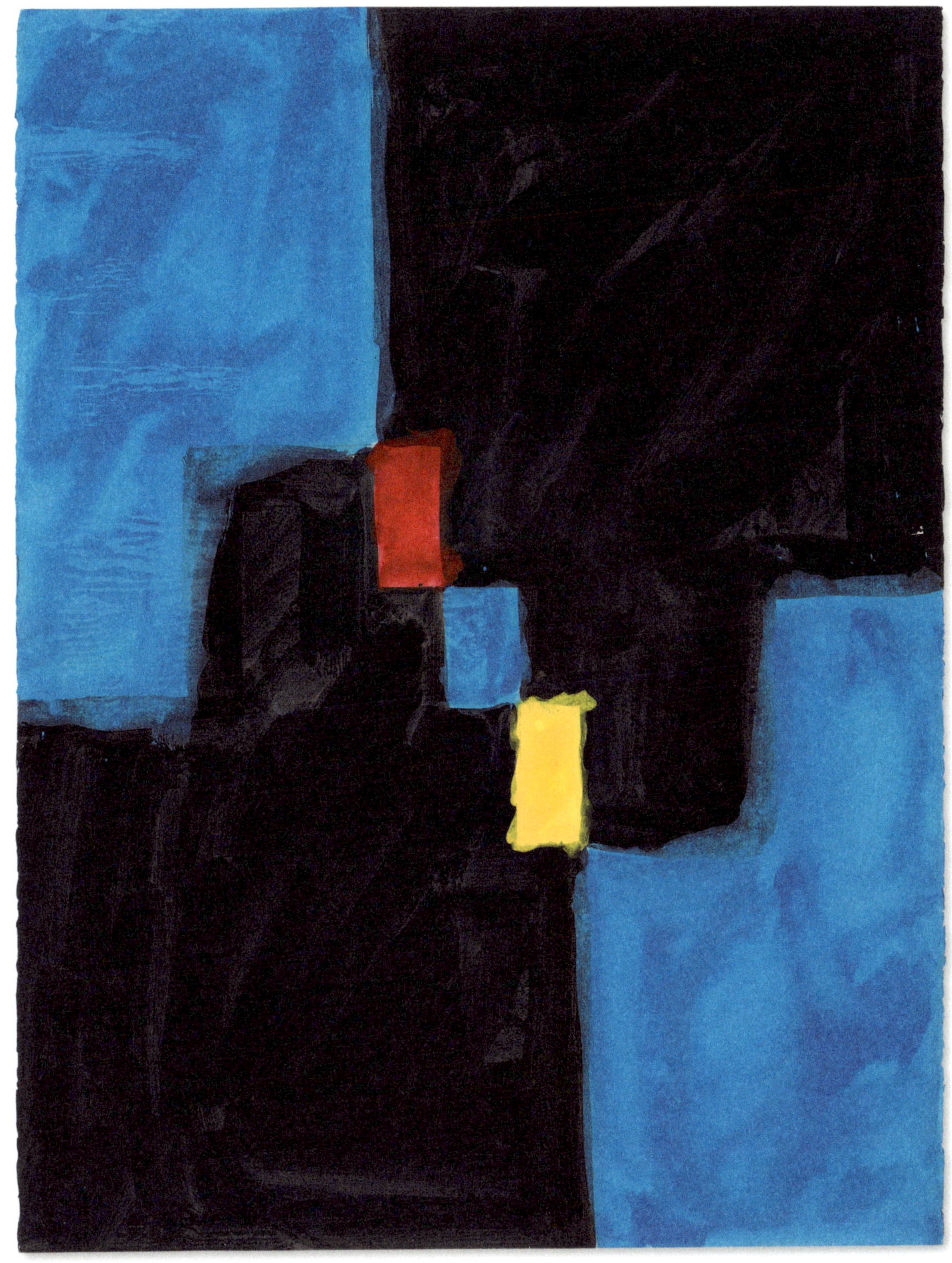

Untitled Watercolor Study, ca. 1986. Watercolor on paper,
5 × 6 ⅝ in. (12.7 × 16.8 cm)

Untitled Watercolor Study, ca. 1986–88. Watercolor and pencil on paper,
5 × 6 ¾ in. (12.7 × 17.1 cm)

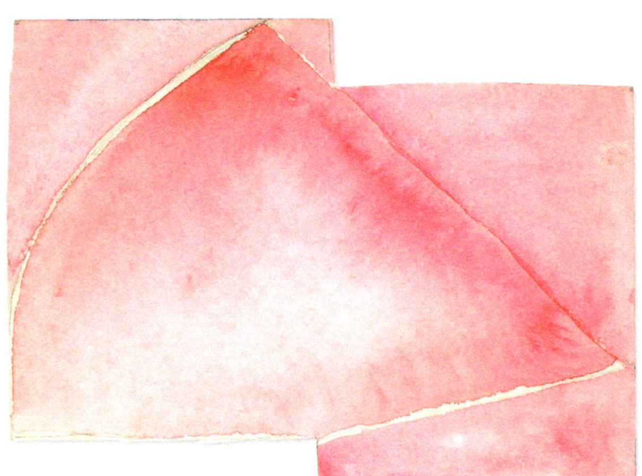

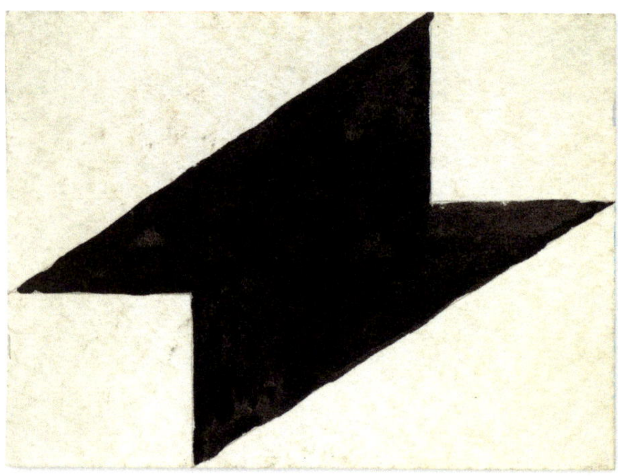

Untitled Watercolor Study, ca. 1986–88. Watercolor on paper,
5 × 6 ½ in. (12.7 × 16.5 cm) (top)

Untitled Watercolor Study, ca. 1986–88. Watercolor and pencil on paper,
5 × 6 ¾ in. (12.7 × 17.1 cm) (center)

Untitled Watercolor Study, ca. 1986–88. Watercolor and pencil on paper,
5 × 6 ⅞ in. (12.7 × 17.5 cm) (bottom). Detail, following spread

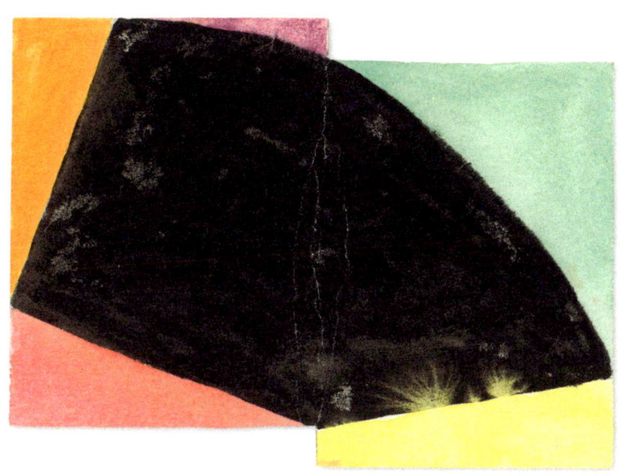

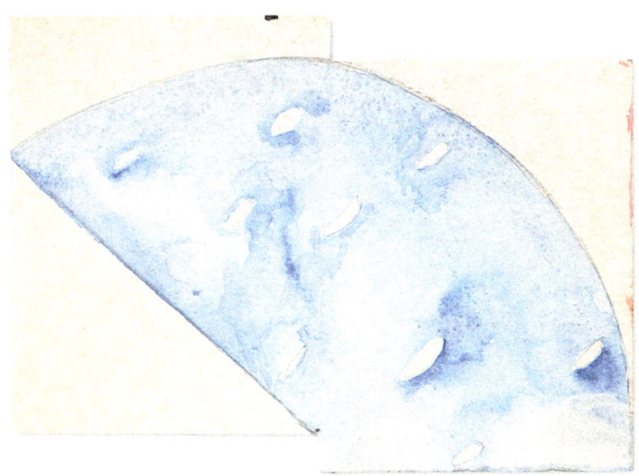

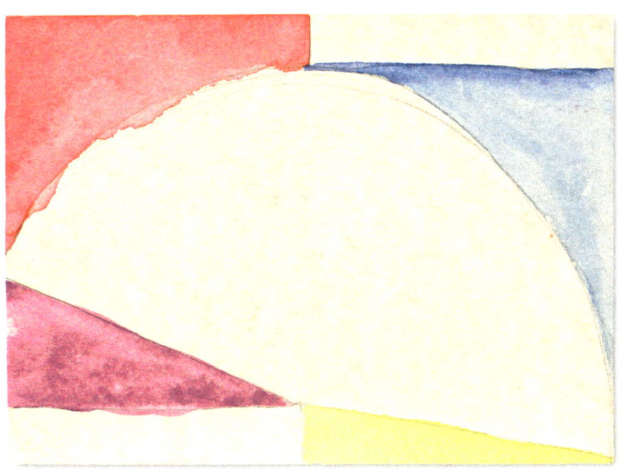

Space Space, 1986. Watercolor on paper, 5 × 7 in. (12.7 × 17.8 cm)

Untitled Watercolor Study, ca. 1986—95. Watercolor and colored pencil on paper, 8 ¾ × 16 ½ in. (22.2 × 41.9 cm)

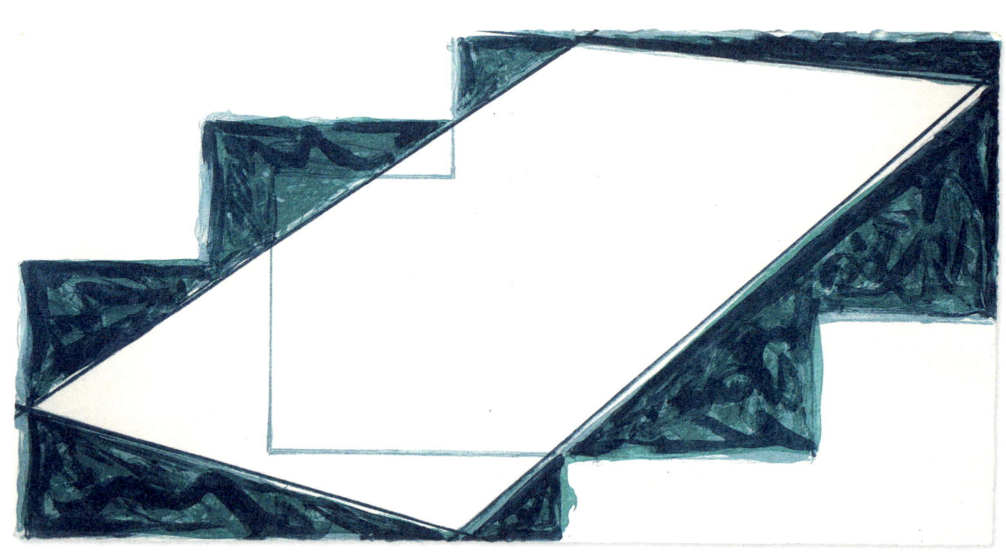

Untitled Watercolor Study, ca. 1988. Watercolor and pencil on paper,
6 × 3 ½ in. (15.2 × 8.9 cm)

Untitled Watercolor Study, ca. 1988. Watercolor and pencil on paper,
6 ¼ × 3 ½ in. (15.9 × 8.9 cm)

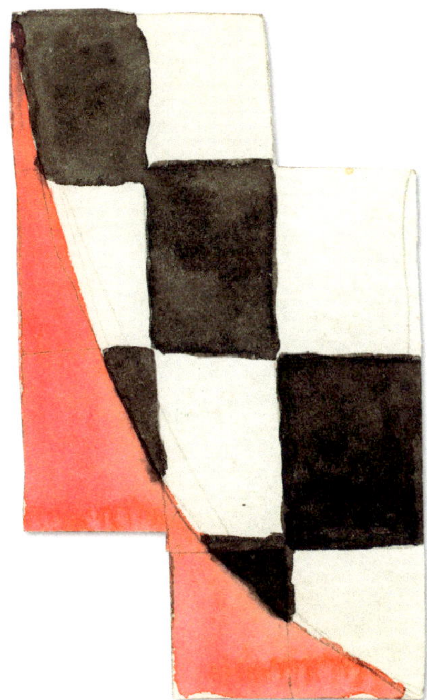

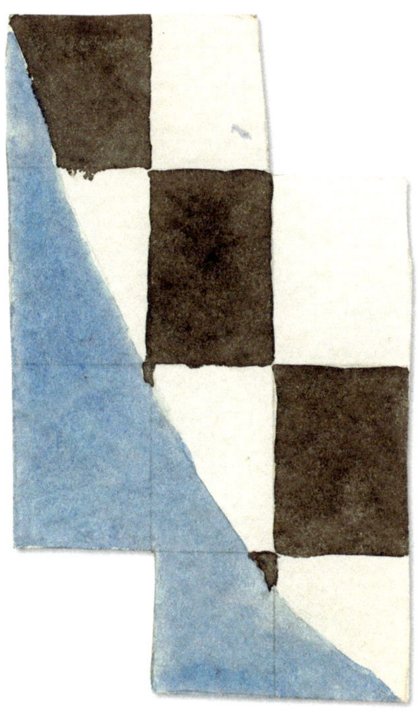

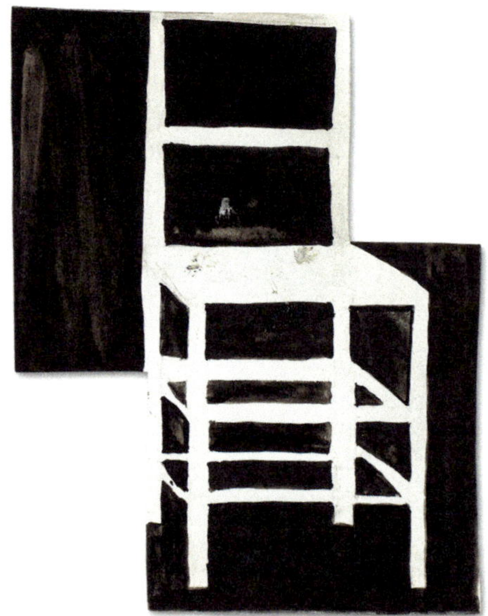

Untitled Watercolor Study, ca. 1987–89. Watercolor and pencil on paper, 11 × 8 ½ in. (27.9 × 21.6 cm)

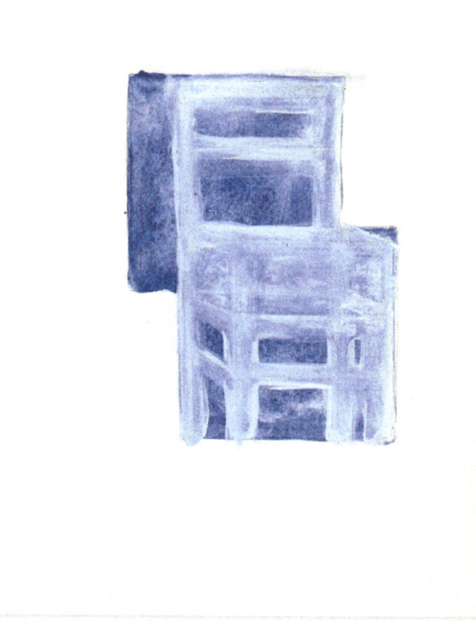

Untitled Watercolor Study, ca. 1987–89. Watercolor on paper, 14 ⅜ × 10 ¼ in. (36.5 × 26 cm)

Untitled Watercolor Study (Self-Portrait), ca. 1989. Colored pencil and watercolor on paper, 16 ⅜ × 12 ⅜ in. (41.6 × 31.4 cm)

Untitled Watercolor Study (Self-Portrait), ca. 1989. Watercolor on paper, 16 ⅜ × 12 ⅜ in. (41.6 × 31.4 cm)

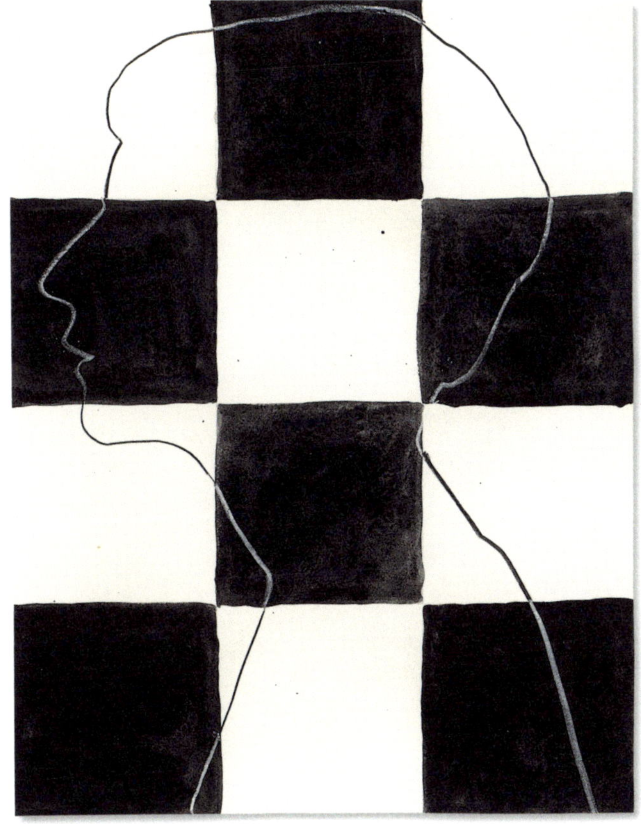

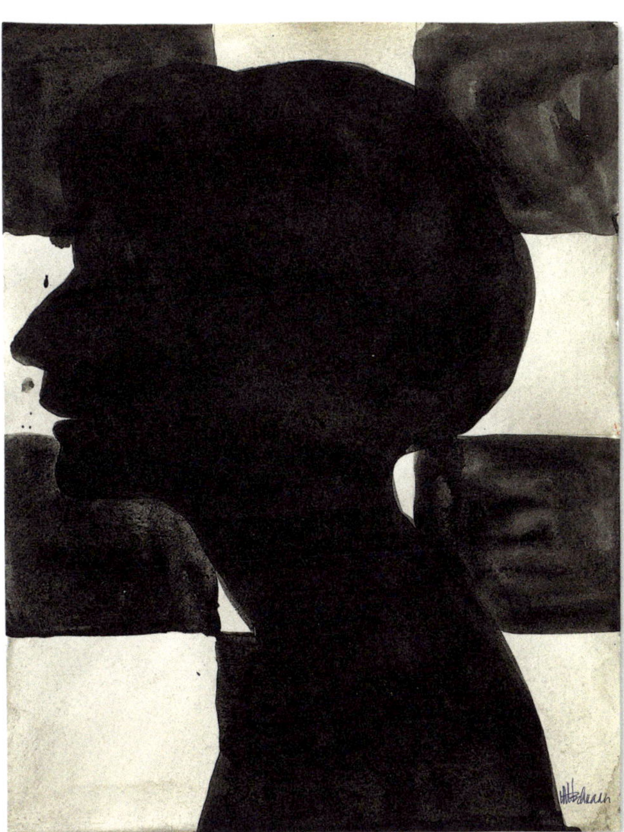

Untitled Study, ca. 1989. Gouache and pencil on paper, 7 × 5 in.
(17.8 × 12.7 cm)

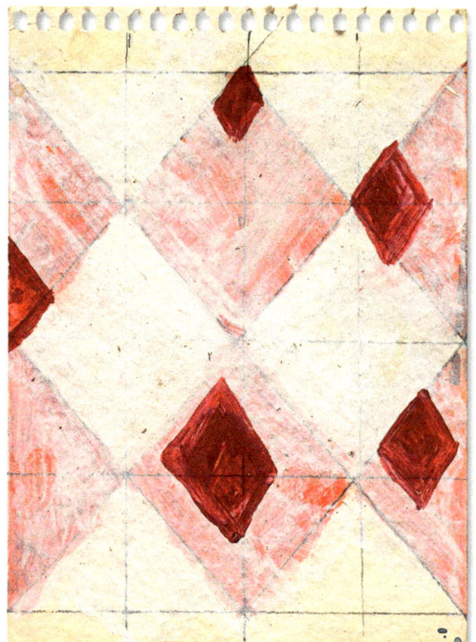

Untitled, ca. 1990—95. Acrylic and watercolor on handmade paper,
11 1/2 × 11 1/2 in. (29.2 × 29.2 cm)

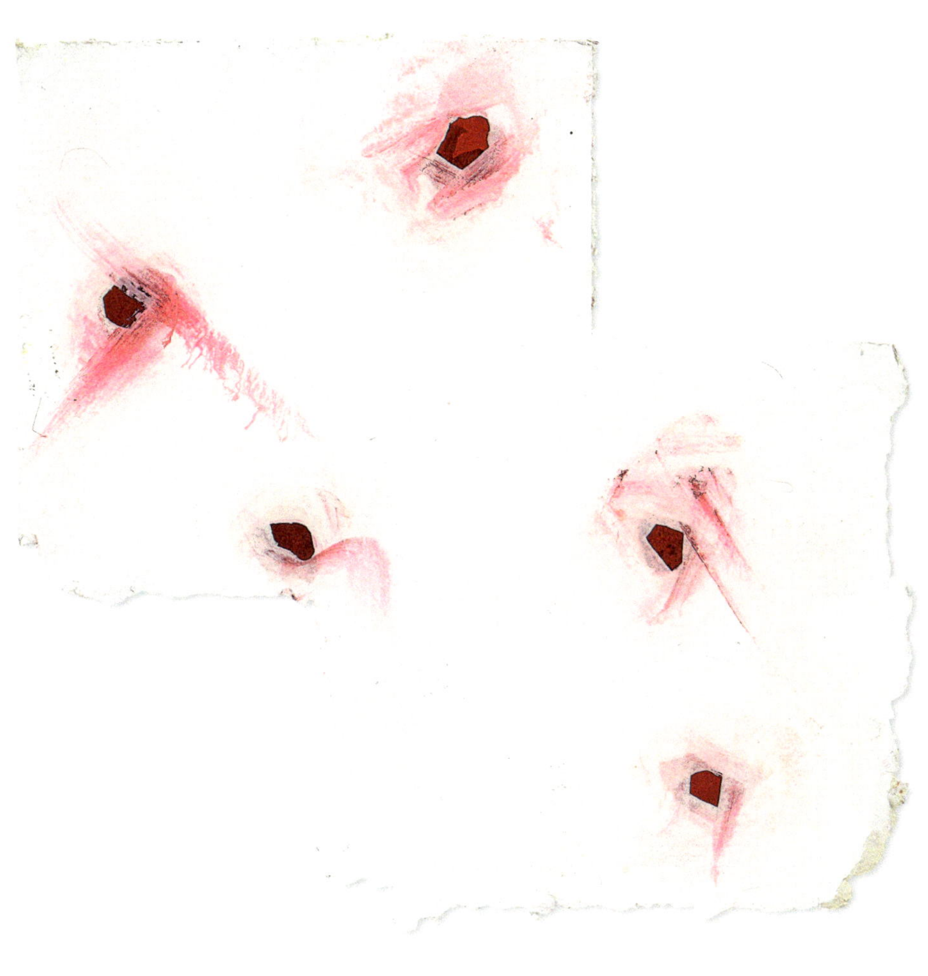

Untitled Watercolor Study, ca. 1989. Watercolor on paper, 6 ¾ × 5 in.
(17.1 × 12.7 cm)

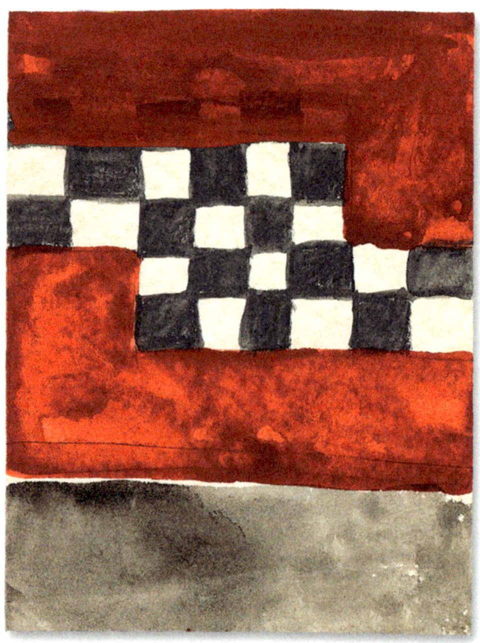

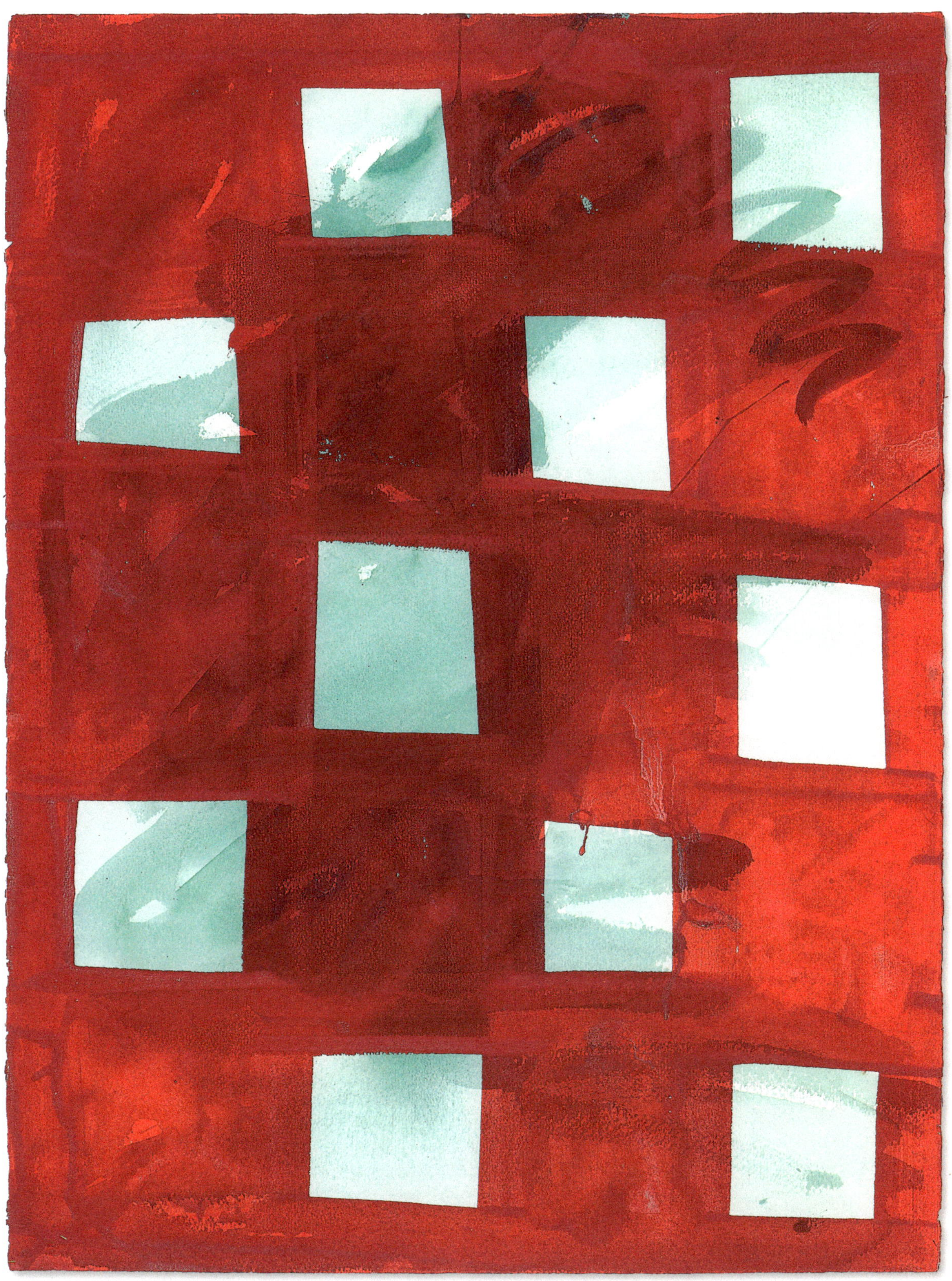

The Red Screen, 1995. Oil on gessoed paper, 42 ⅛ × 29 ⅞ in. (107 × 75.9 cm)

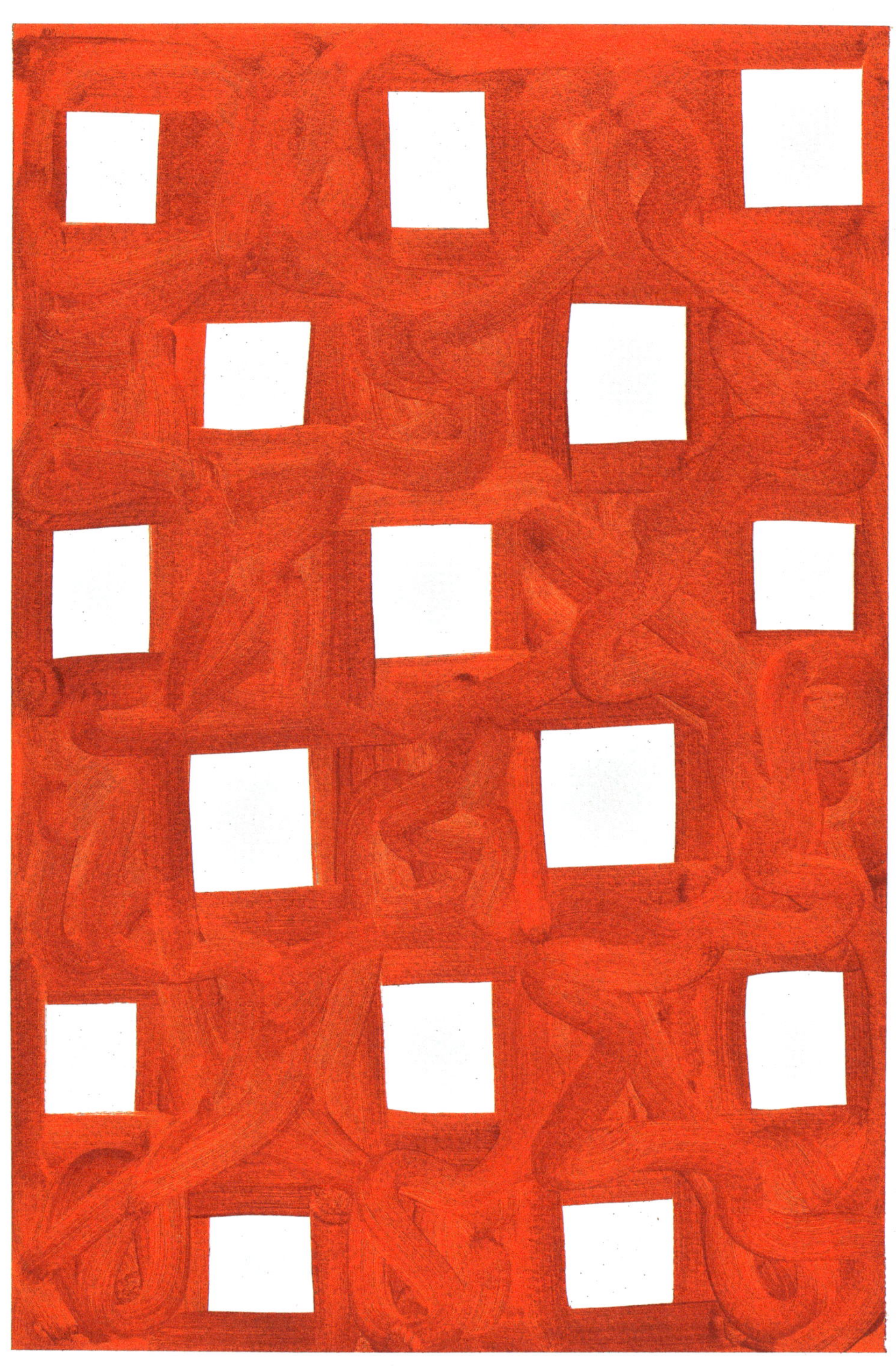

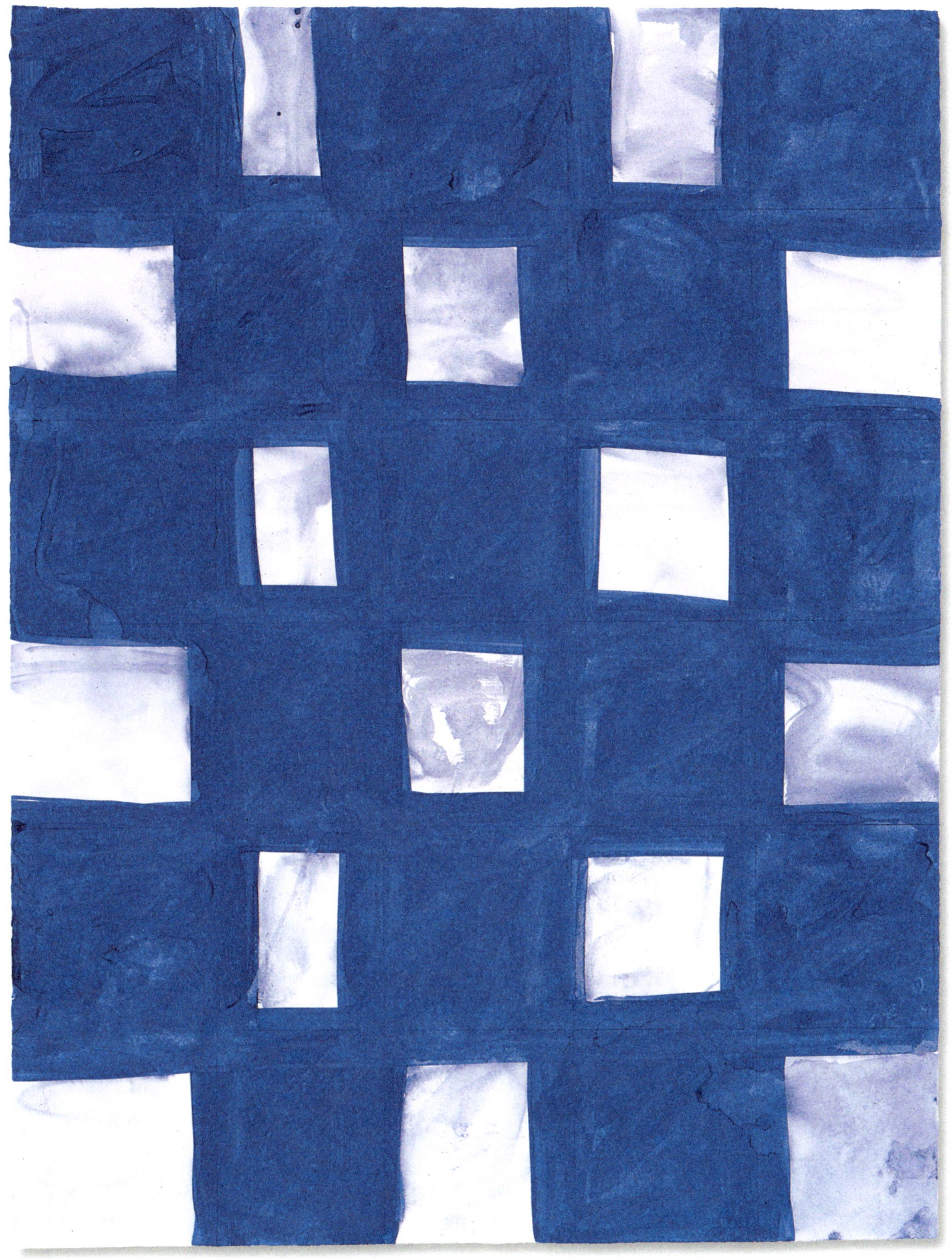

Blumoon, 1990. Watercolor on paper, 30 ⅛ × 22 ¼ in. (76.5 × 56.5 cm)

Untitled Watercolor Study, ca. 1991–97. Watercolor on paper,
14 ⁷⁄₈ × 10 ⁷⁄₈ in. (37.8 × 27.6 cm). Detail, following spread

Untitled Watercolor Study, ca. 1990–92. Watercolor and pencil on paper,
5 ¼ × 4 in. (13.3 × 10.2 cm)

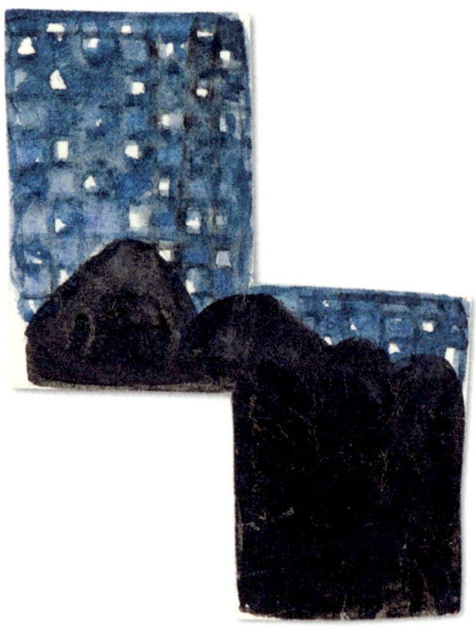

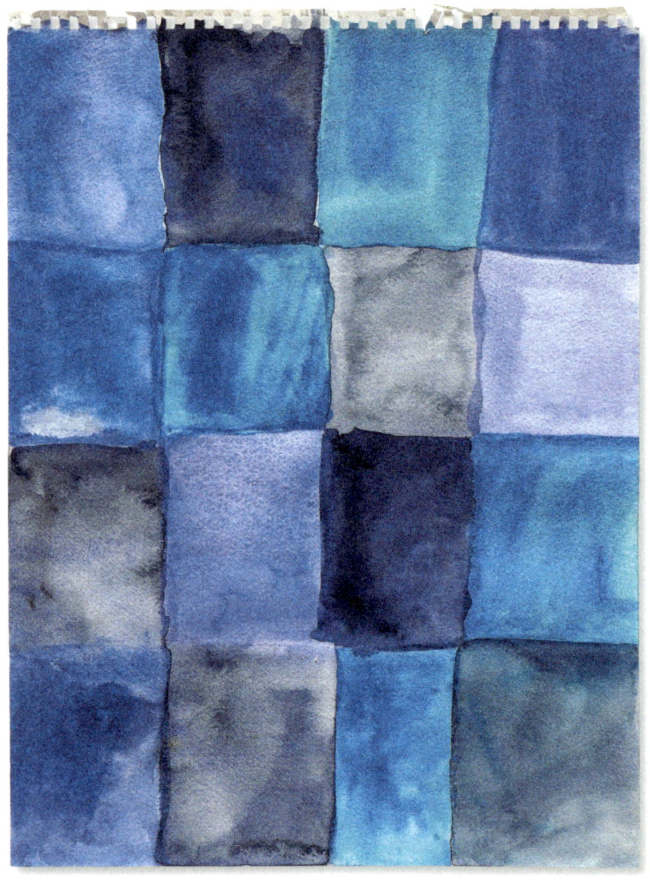

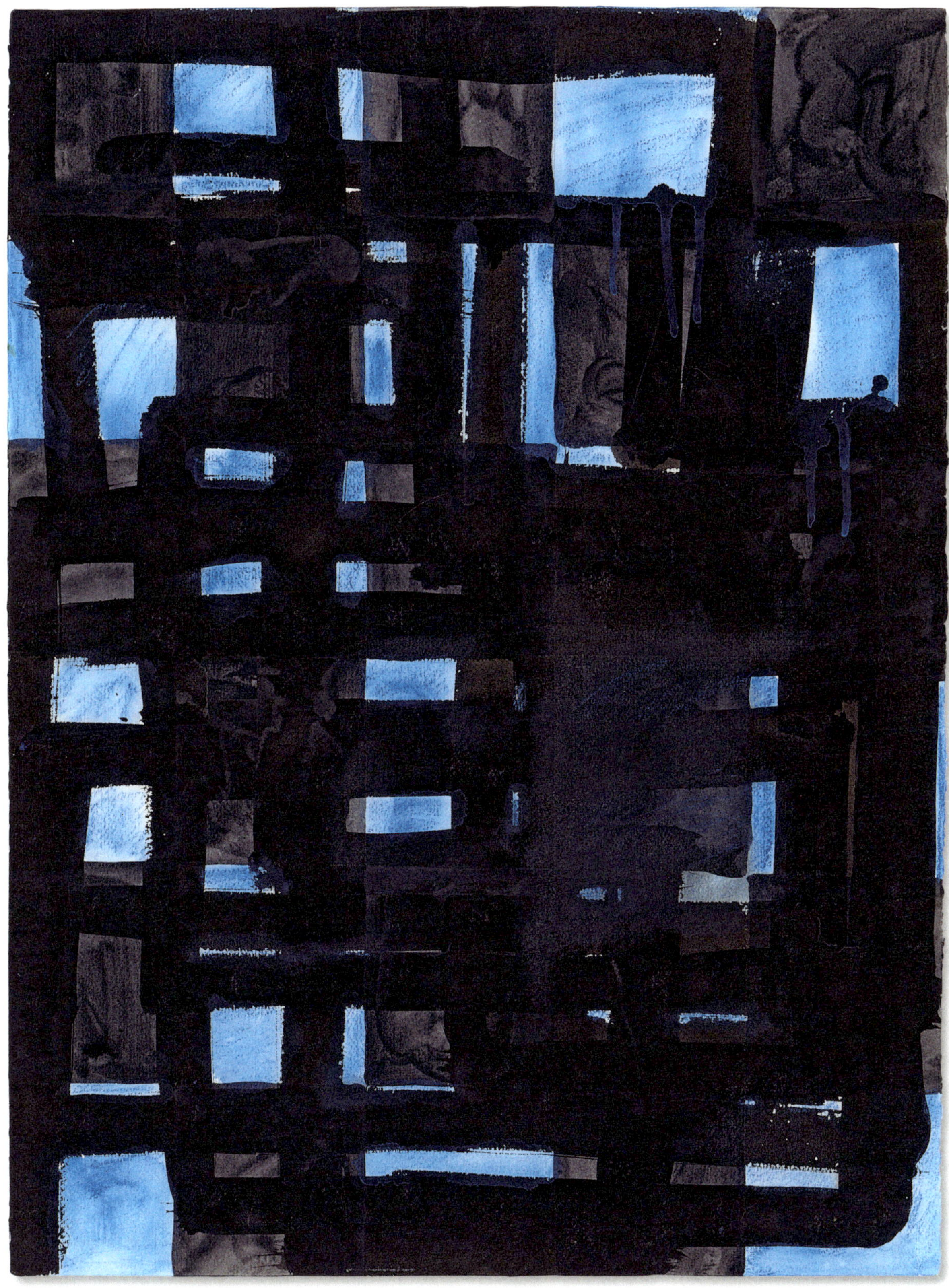

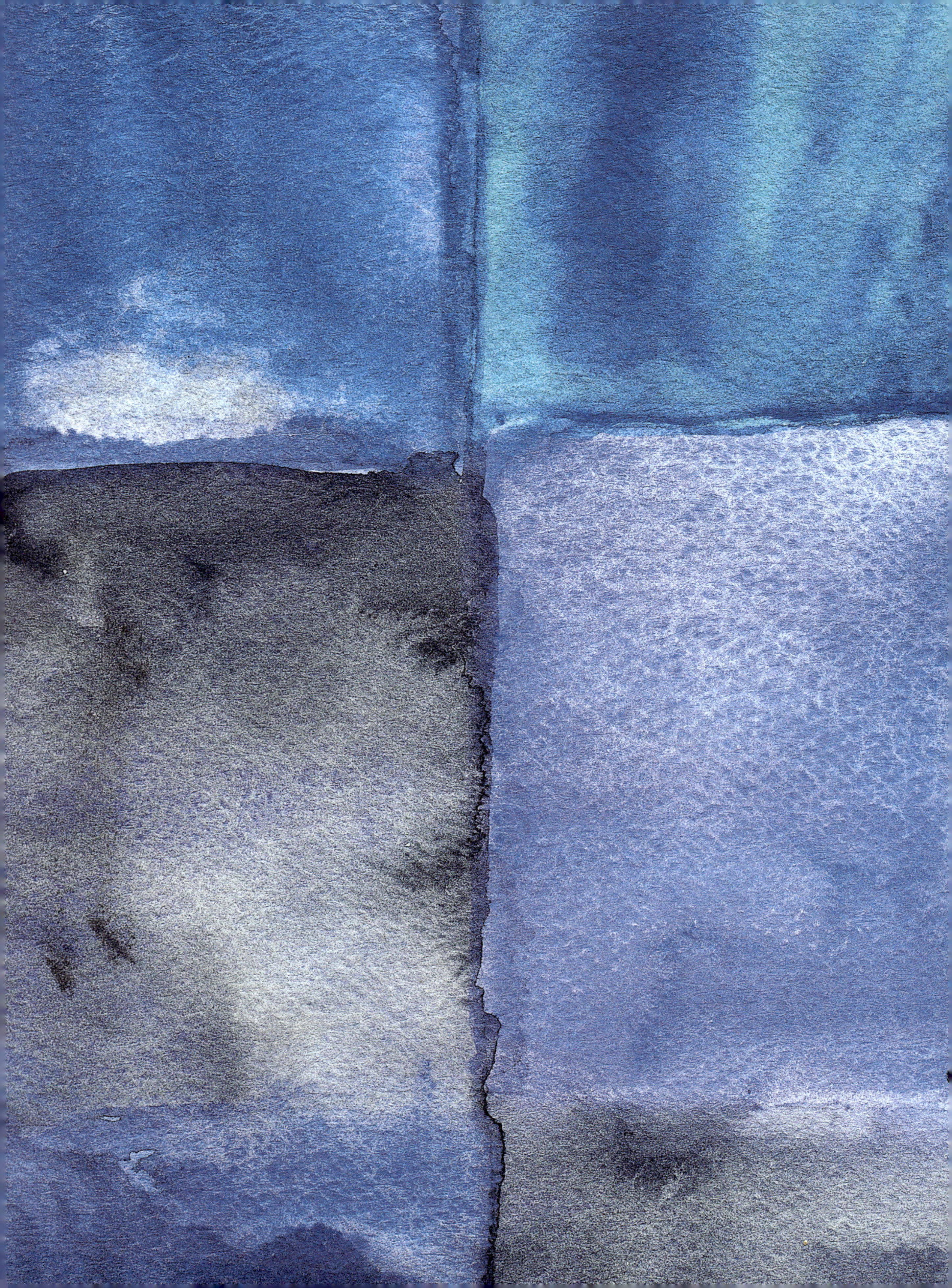

Untitled Watercolor Study, ca. 1980s. Watercolor on paper, 6 ⅞ × 4 ⅞ in. (17.5 × 12.4 cm)

Untitled Watercolor Study, ca. 2019. Watercolor on paper, 5 × 3 ⅜ in. (12.7 × 8.6 cm)

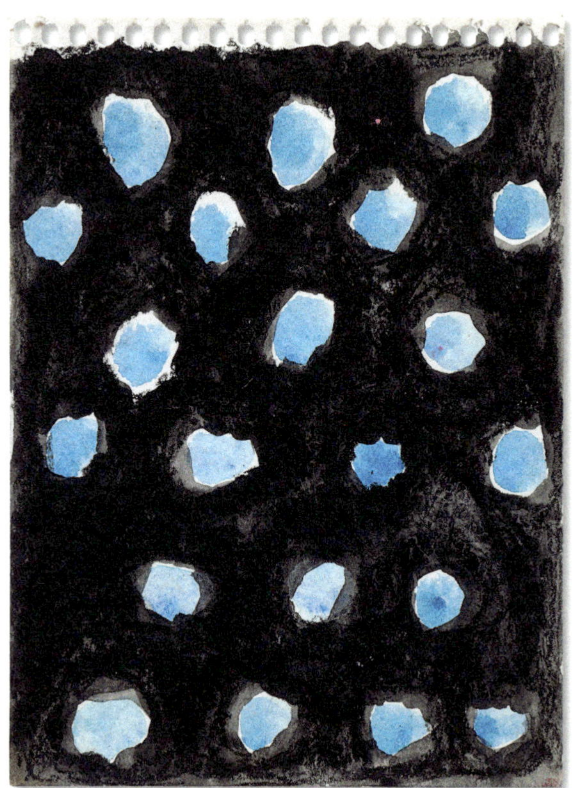

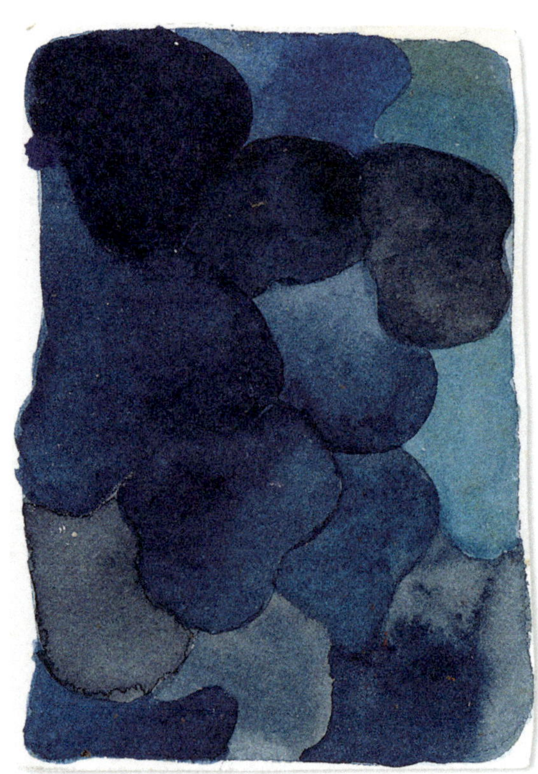

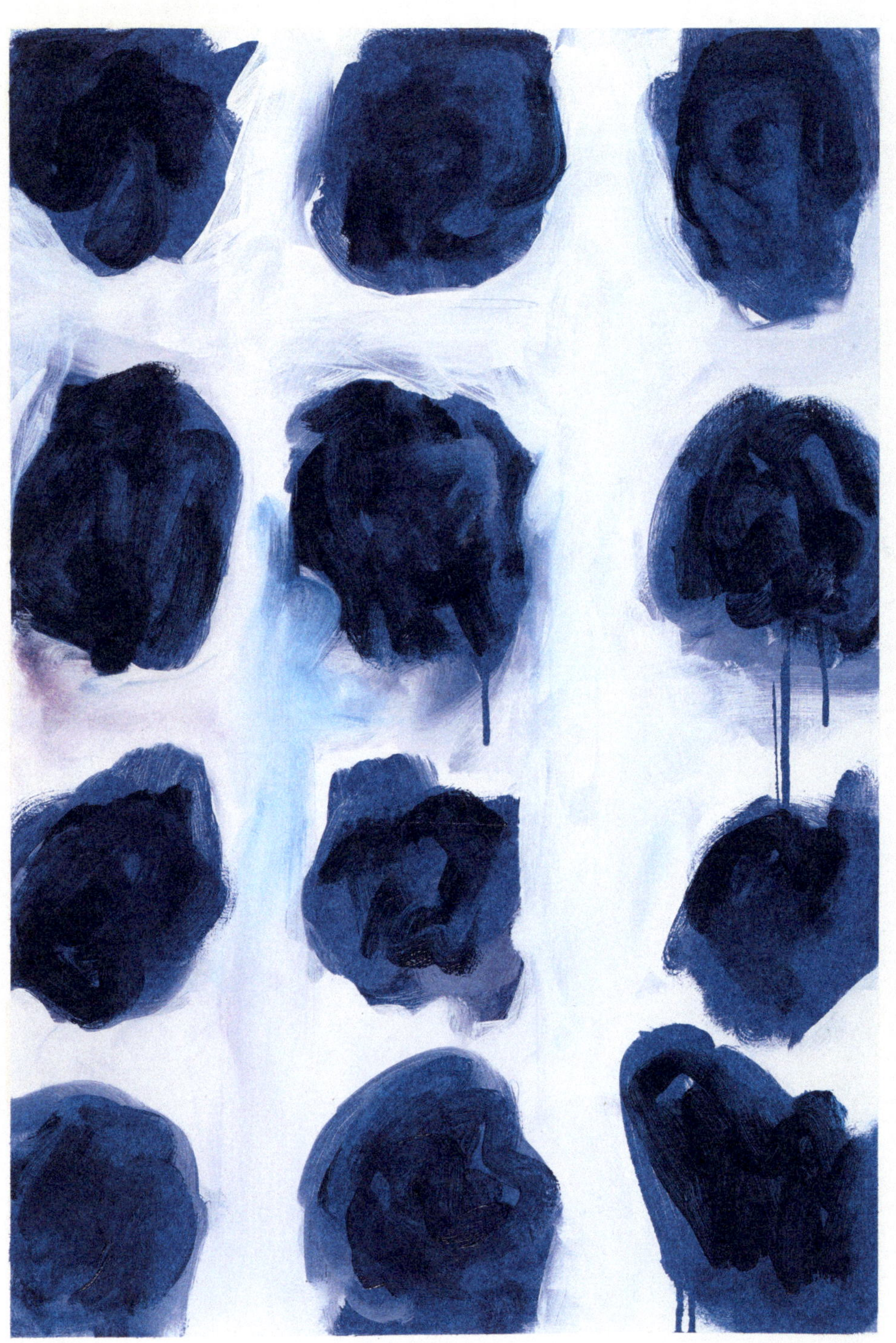

Hydrangia, 1995. Oil on gessoed paper, 41 × 29 ½ in. (104.1 × 74.9 cm)

Untitled Watercolor Study, ca. 1982–84. Watercolor and pencil on paper,
12 ¼ × 10 in. (31.1 × 25.4 cm)

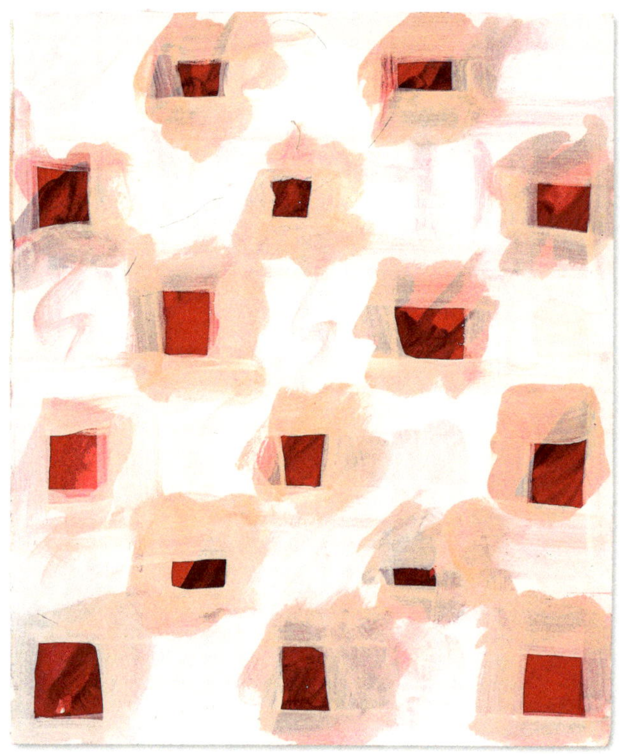

White Screen, 1995. Oil on gessoed paper, 41 × 29 ½ in. (104.1 × 74.9 cm)

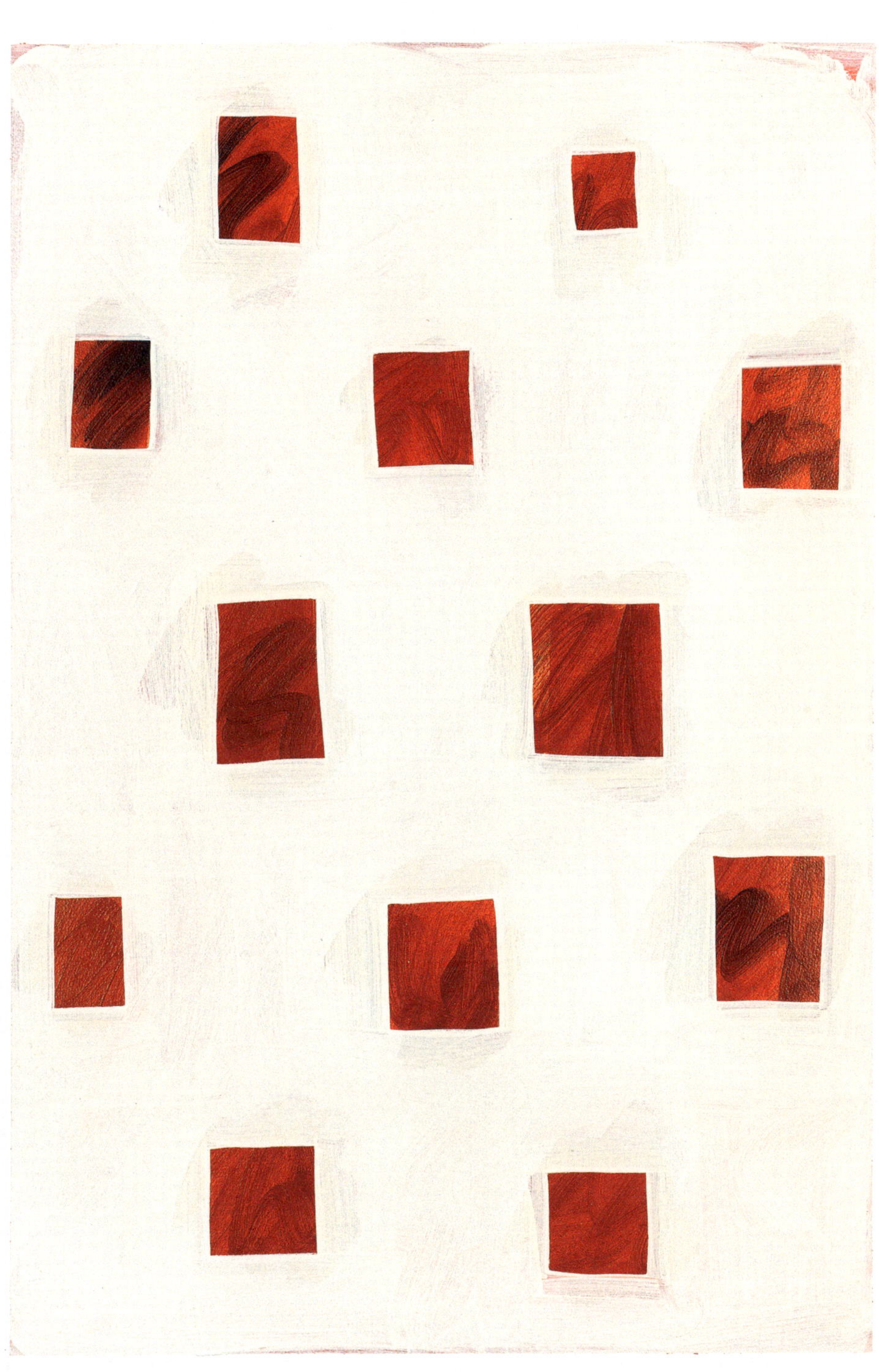

Untitled, 1983. Pencil, crayon, and watercolor on paper, 27 ½ × 39 ¼ in. (69.9 × 99.7 cm)

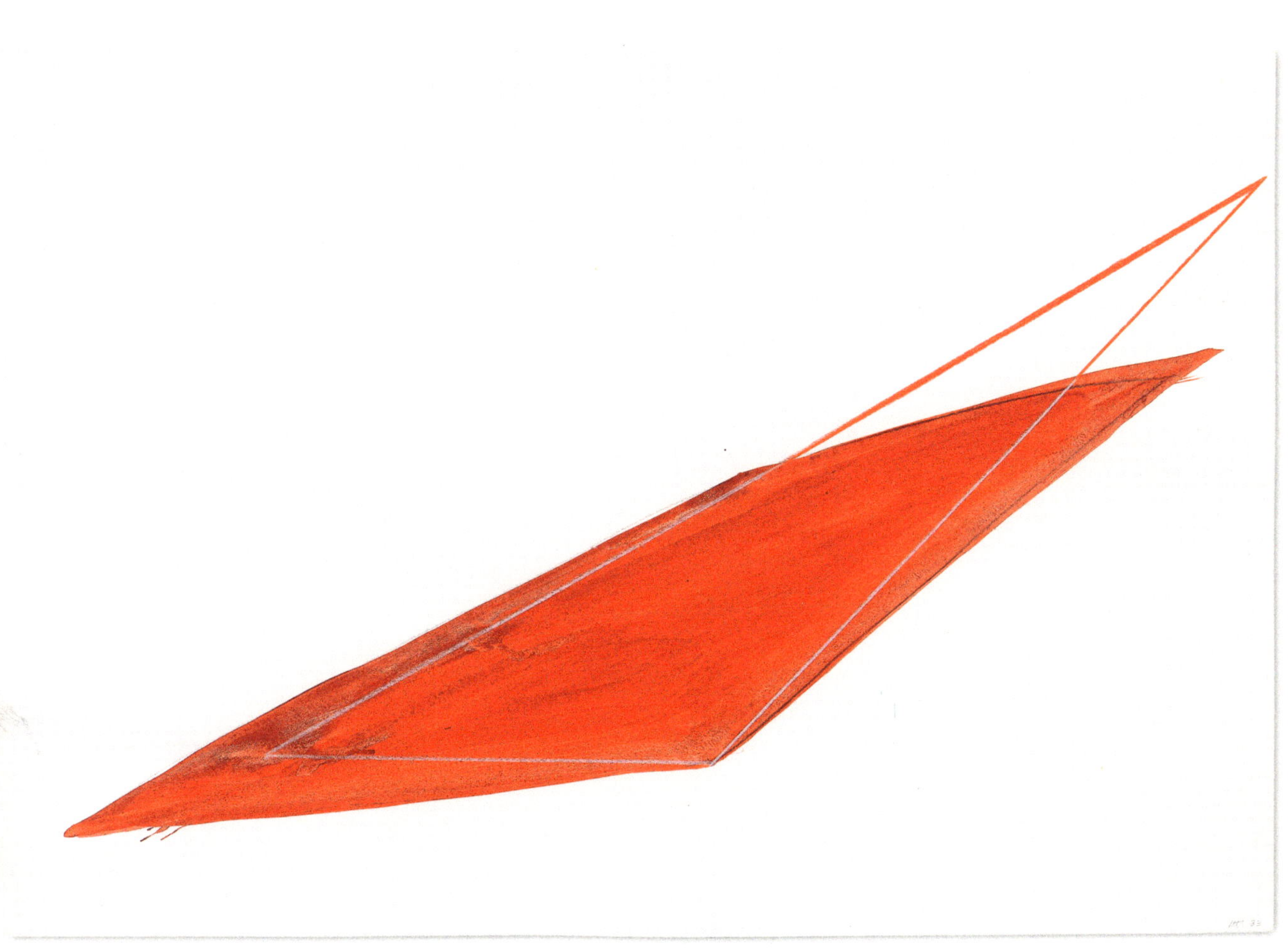

Red Flat Cup, ca. 1983. Watercolor on paper, dimensions unknown

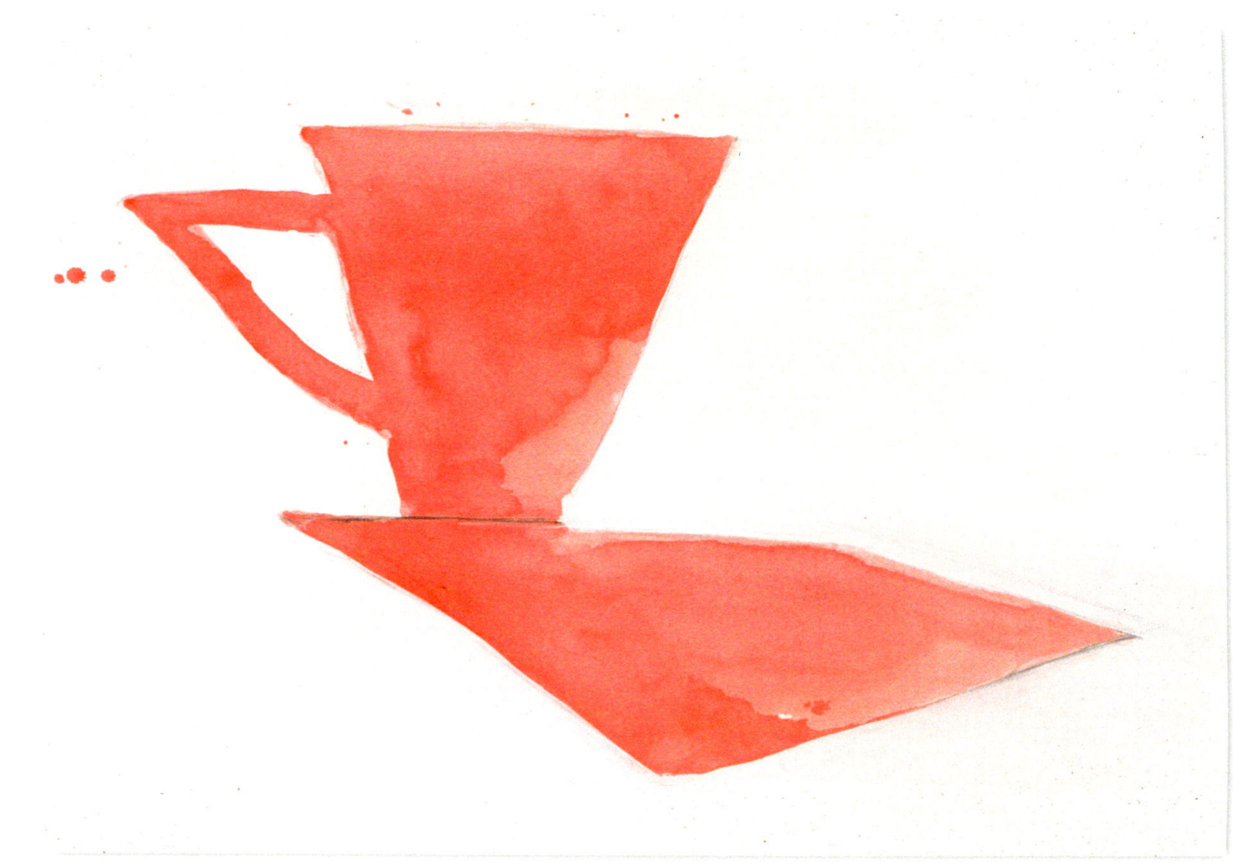

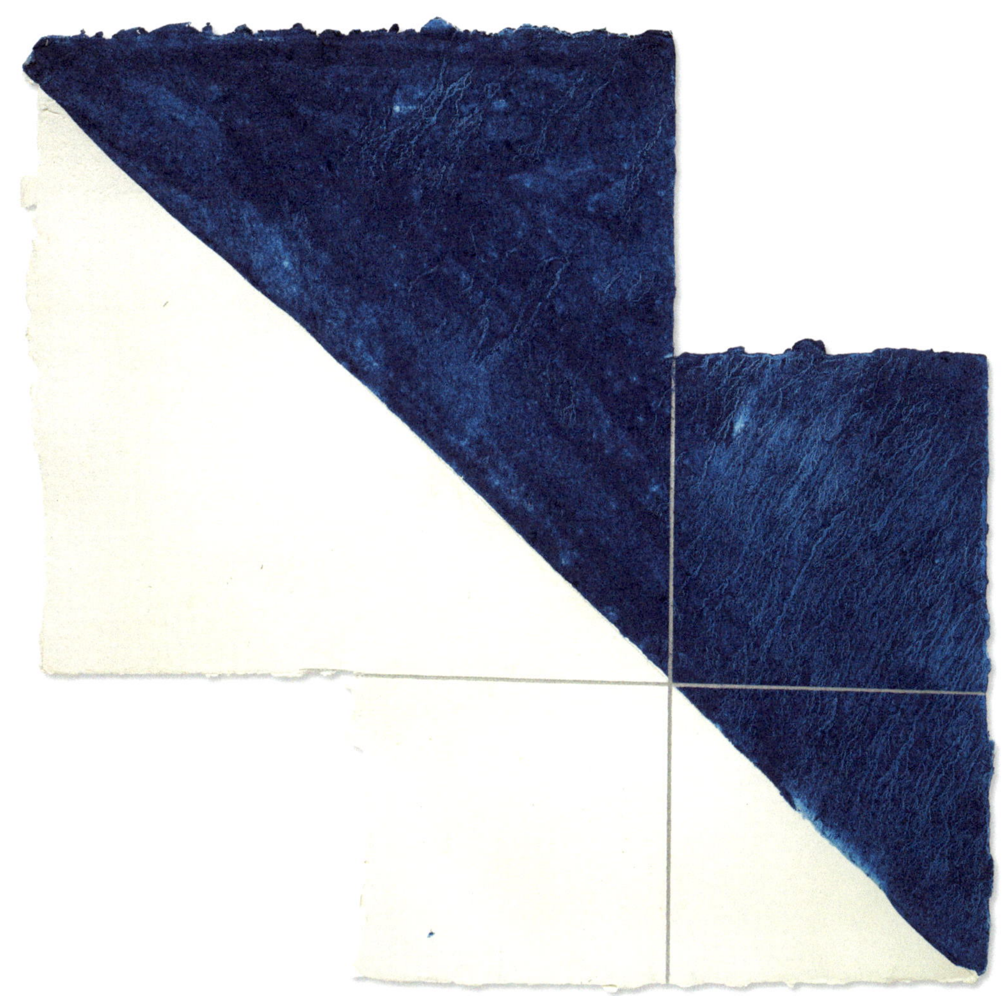

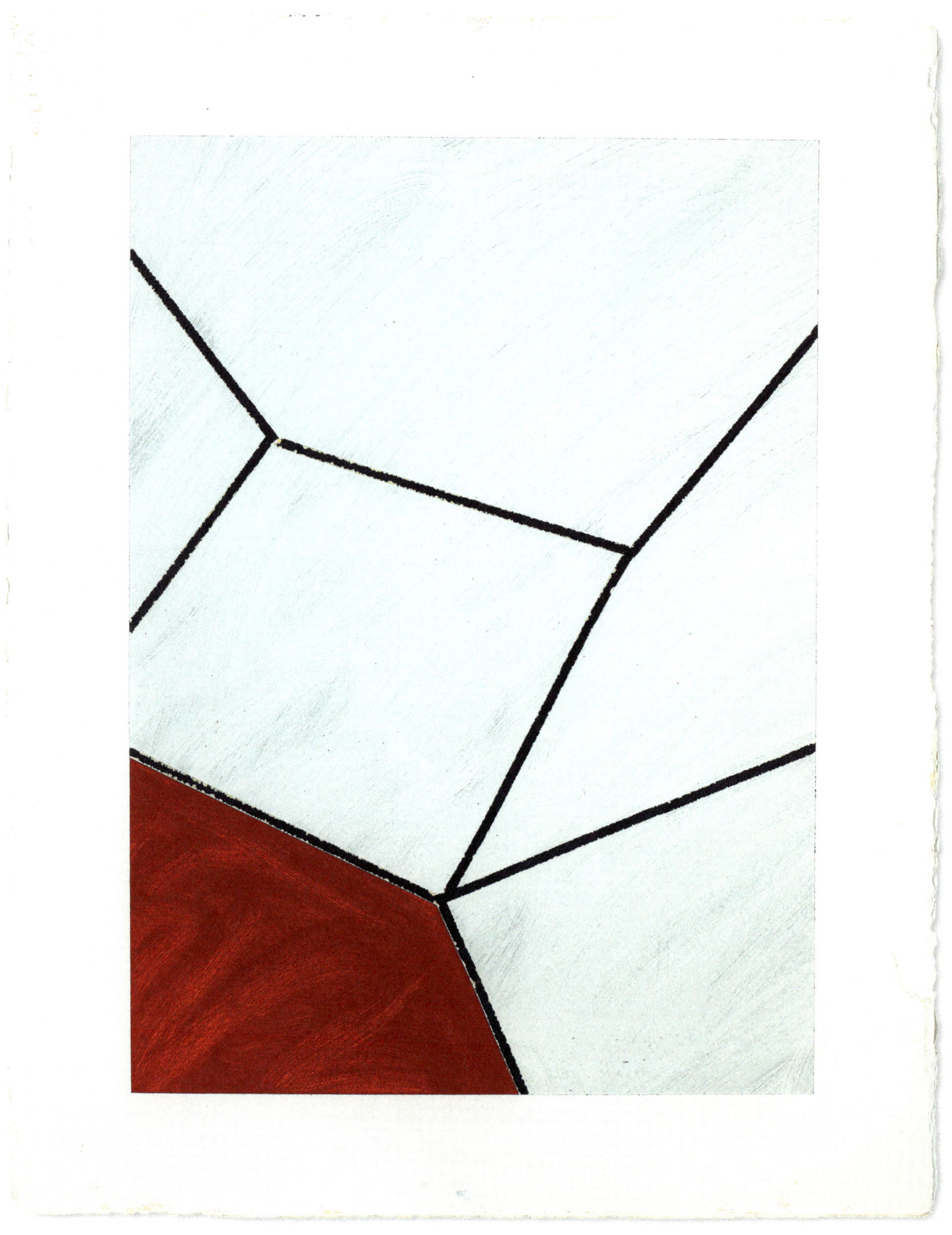

Red Corner, 1995. Oil on gessoed paper, 30 × 22 in. (76.2 × 55.9 cm)

Tricky, 1995. Oil on gessoed paper, 41 ½ × 29 ½ in. (105.4 × 74.9 cm). Detail, following spread.

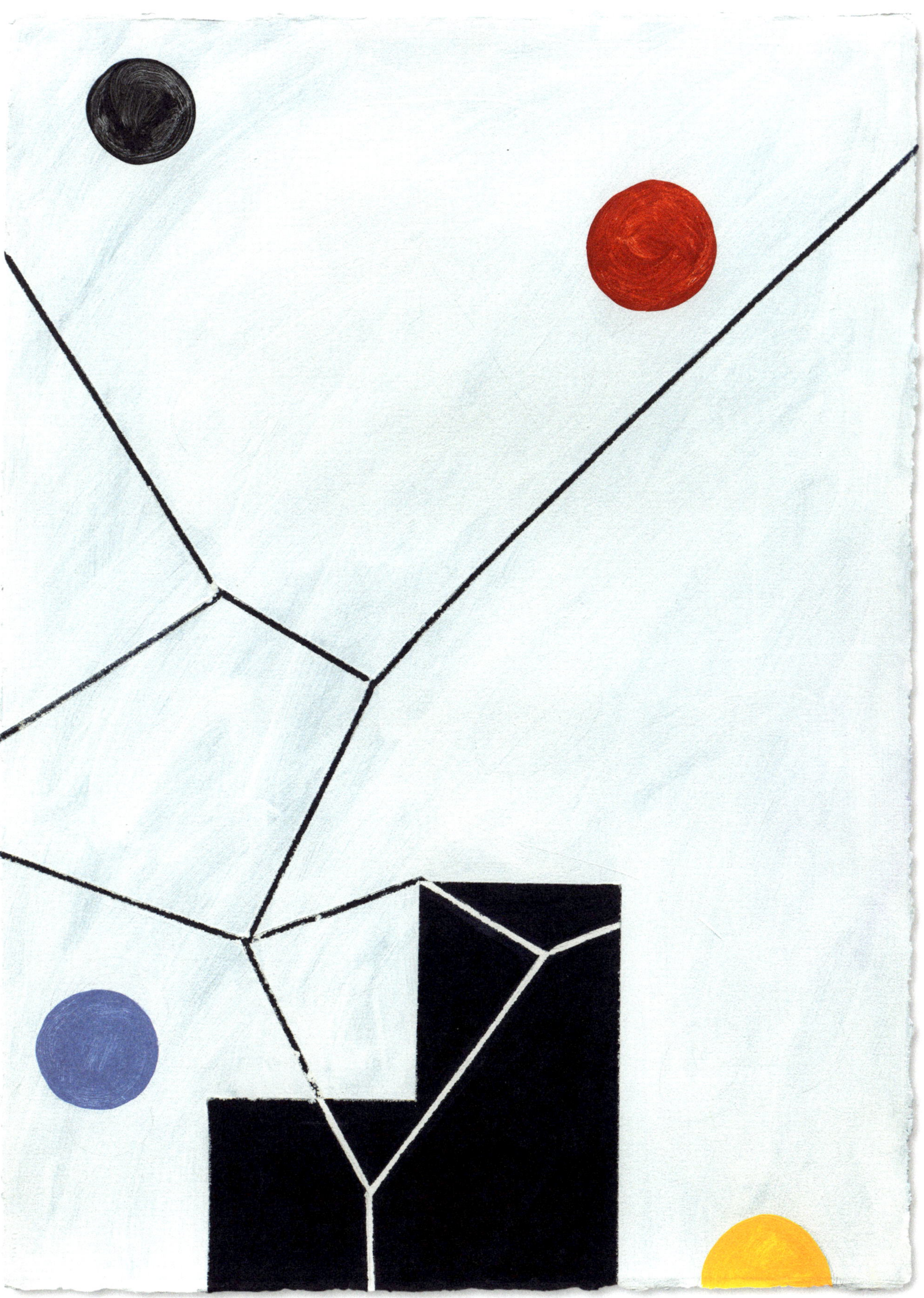

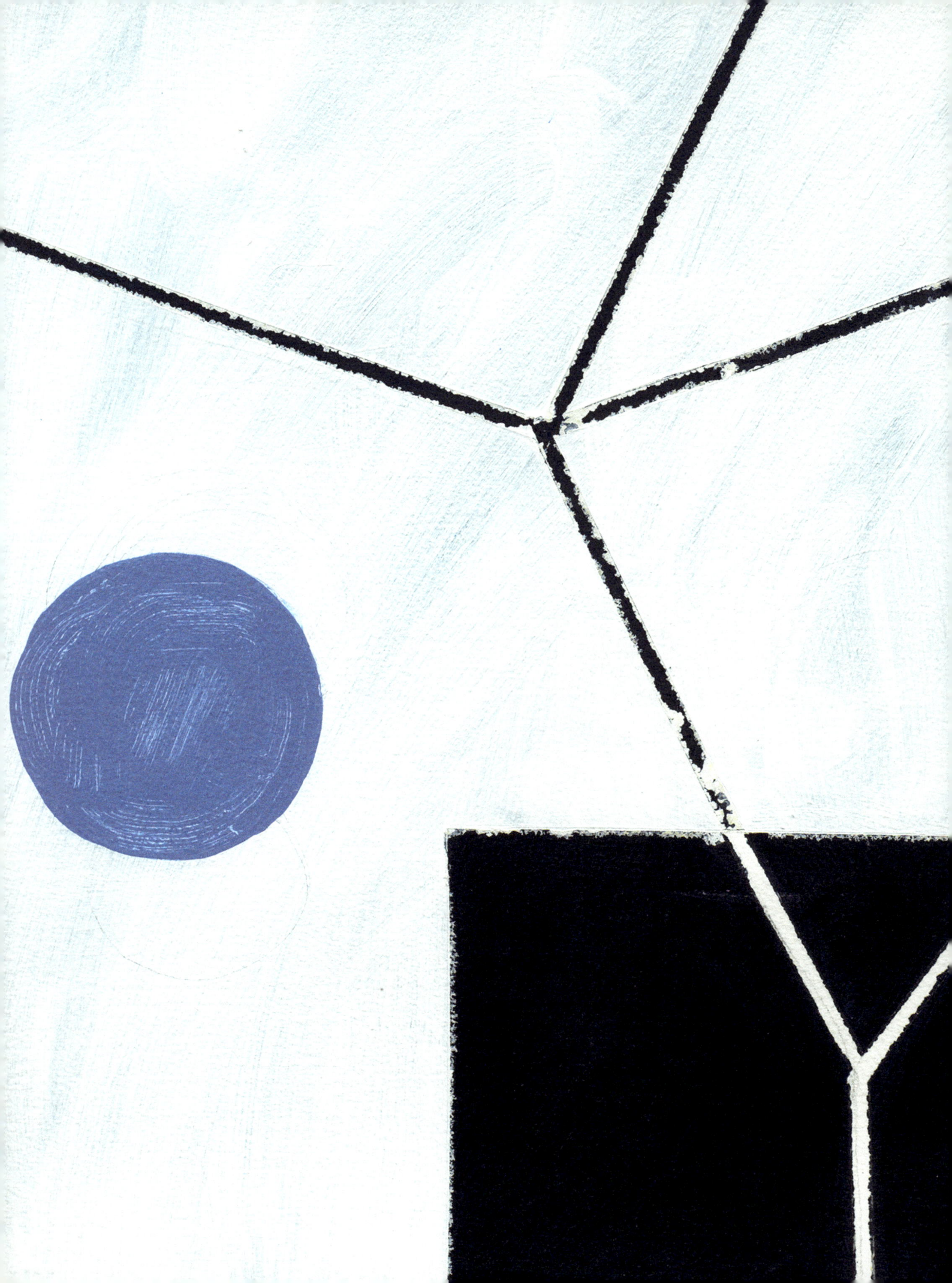

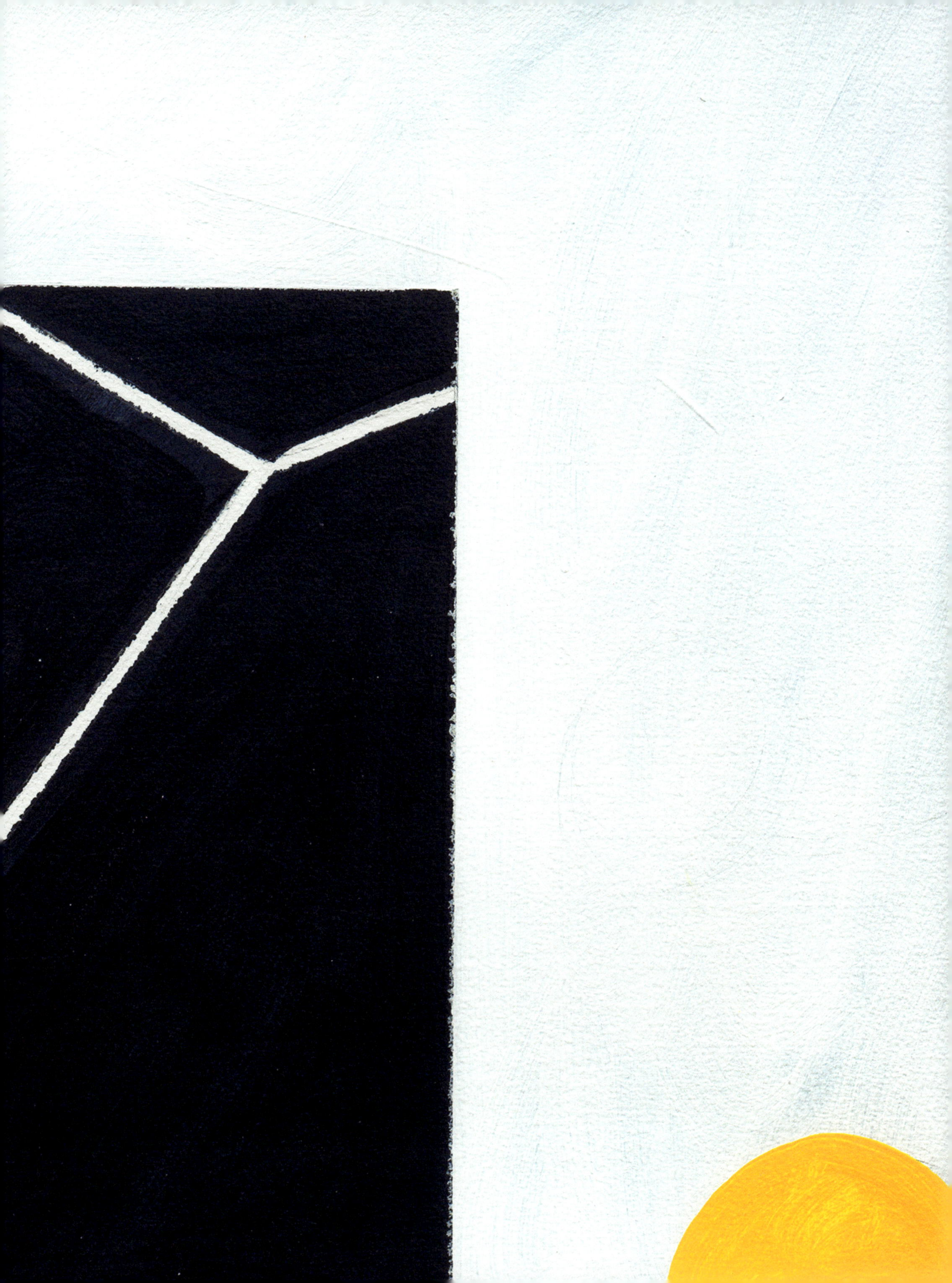

Half Jack, 2005. Oil on gessoed paper, 41 ½ × 29 ¼ in. (105.4 × 74.3 cm)

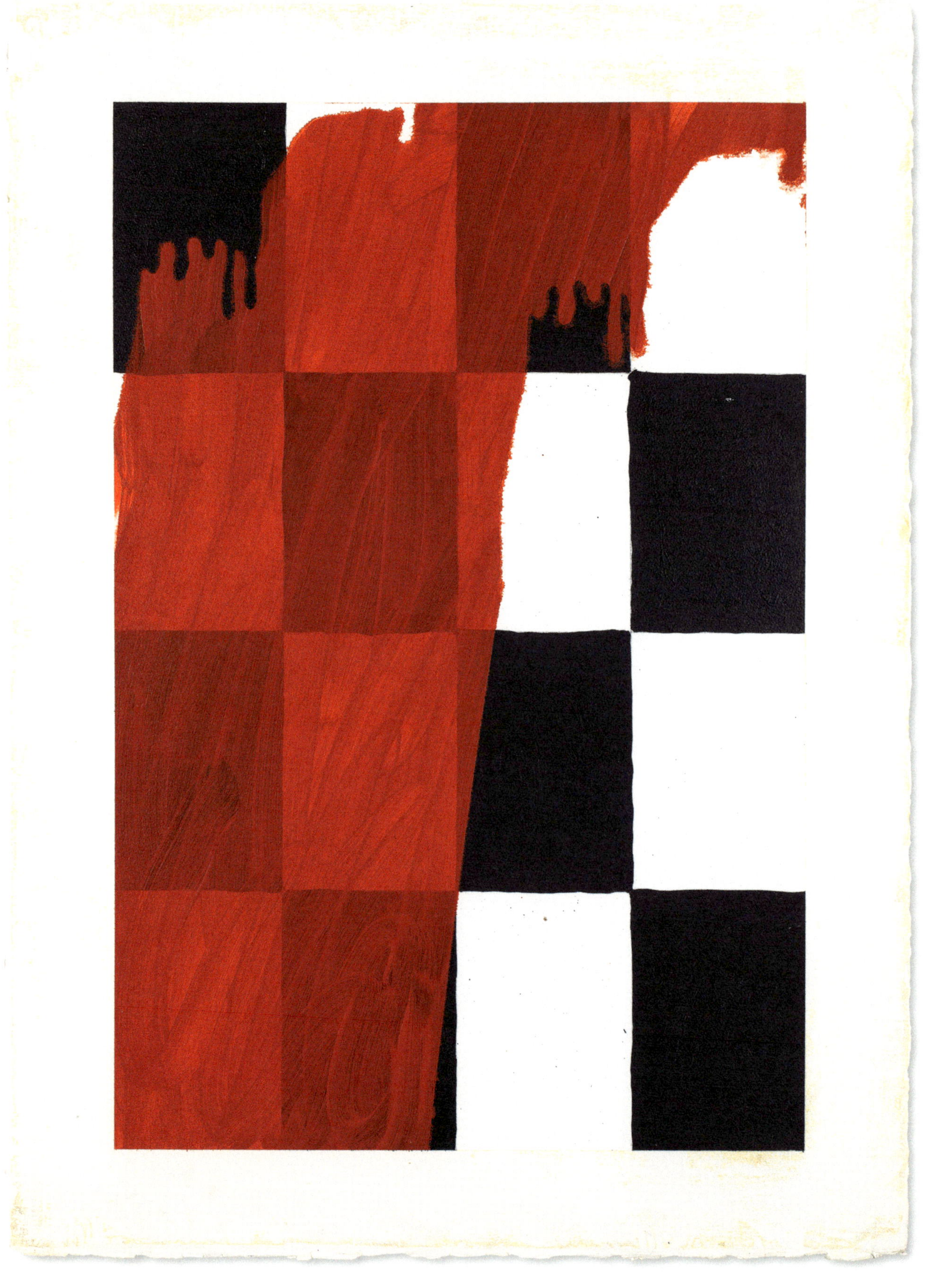

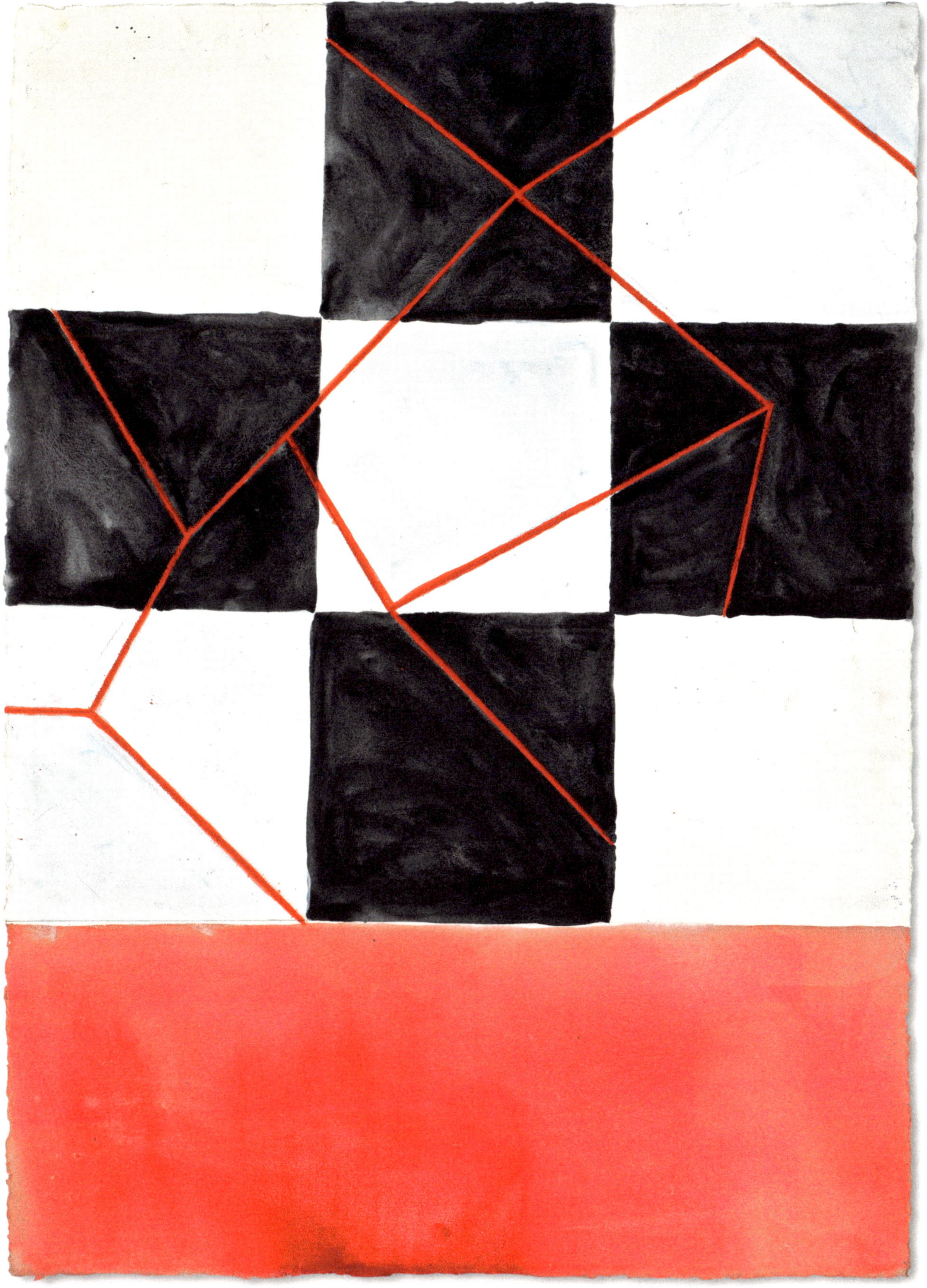

Broken Study, 2005. Oil on gessoed paper, 41 ½ × 29 ¼ in. (105.4 × 74.3 cm)

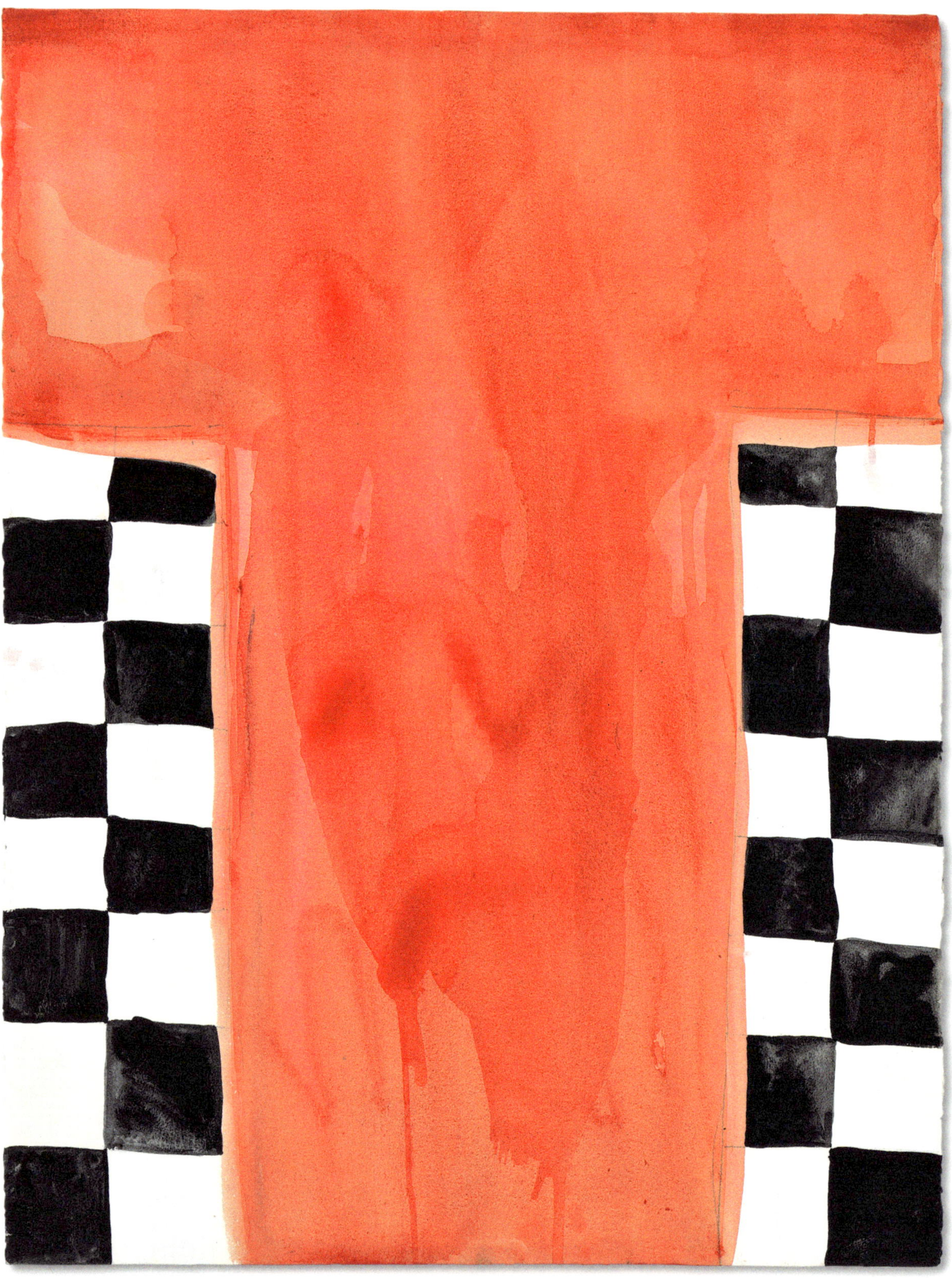

Kimono, 1984. Watercolor on paper, 30 × 22 in. (76.2 × 55.9 cm)

Negative Space One, 2014. Acrylic on handmade paper, 11 ½ × 11 ½ in.
(29.2 × 29.2 cm)

Negative Space Two, 2014. Acrylic on handmade paper, 12 × 15 in.
(30.5 × 38.1 cm)

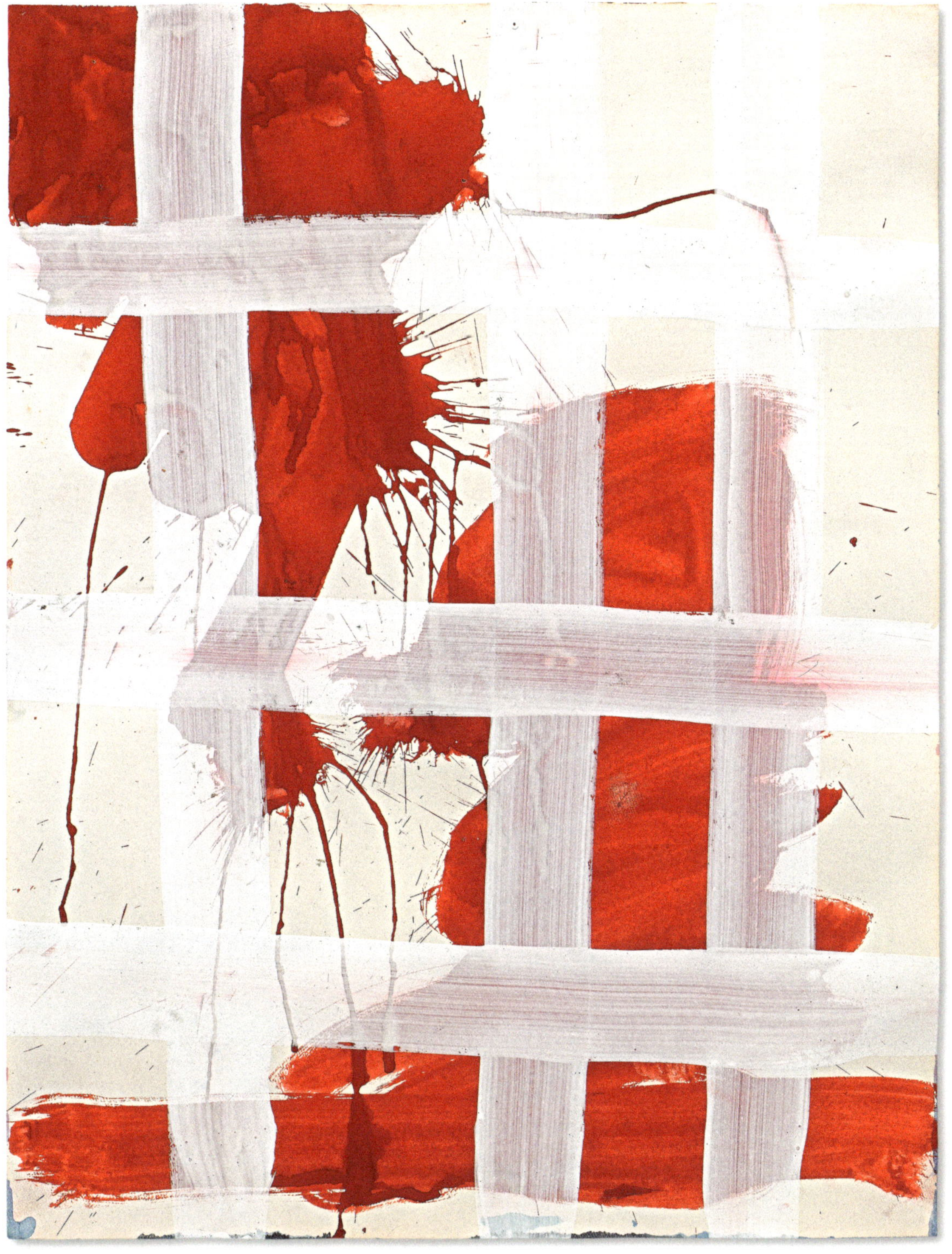

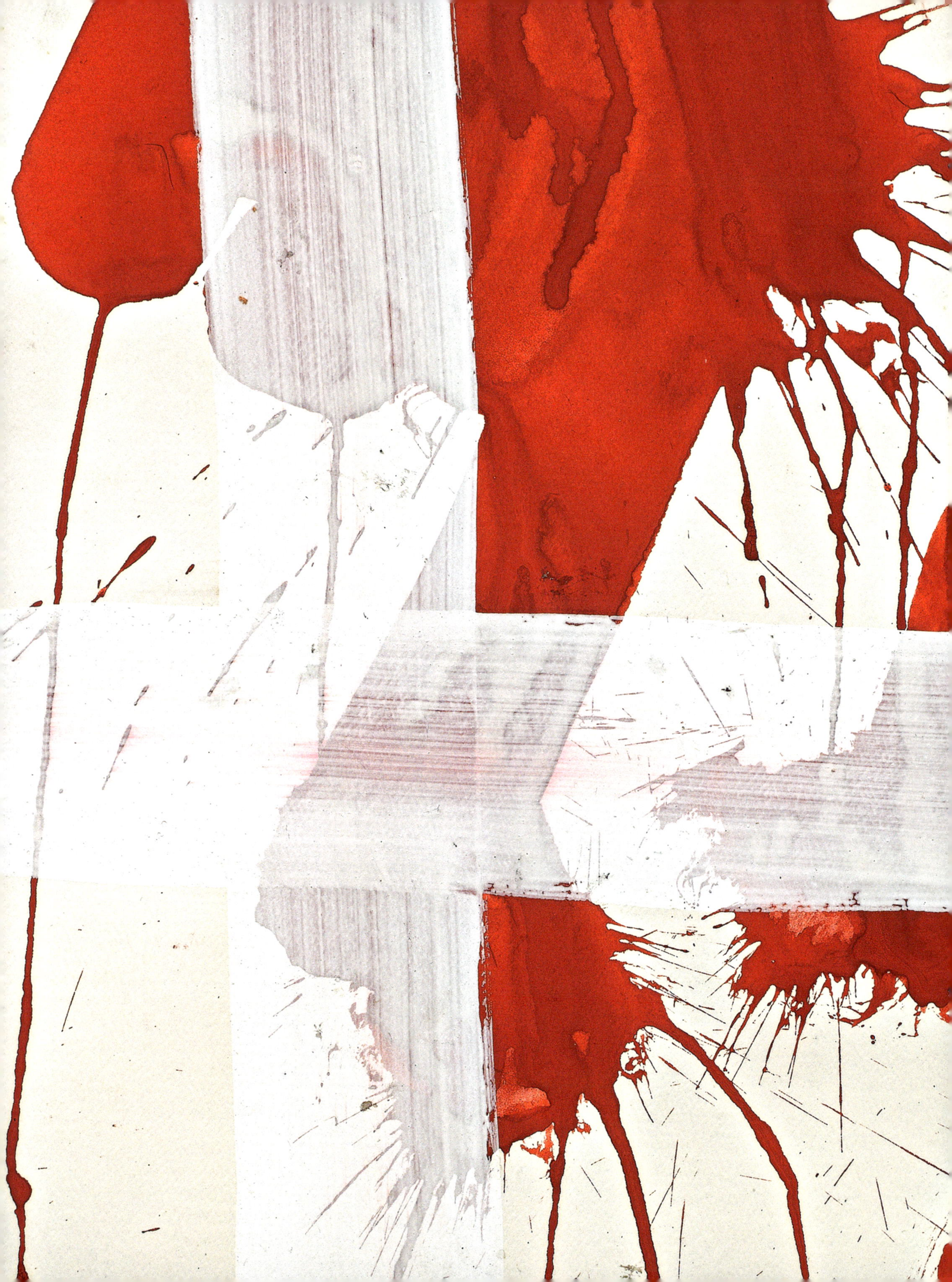

Maze, 1982. Watercolor on paper, 23 ¾ × 18 in. (60.3 × 45.7 cm)

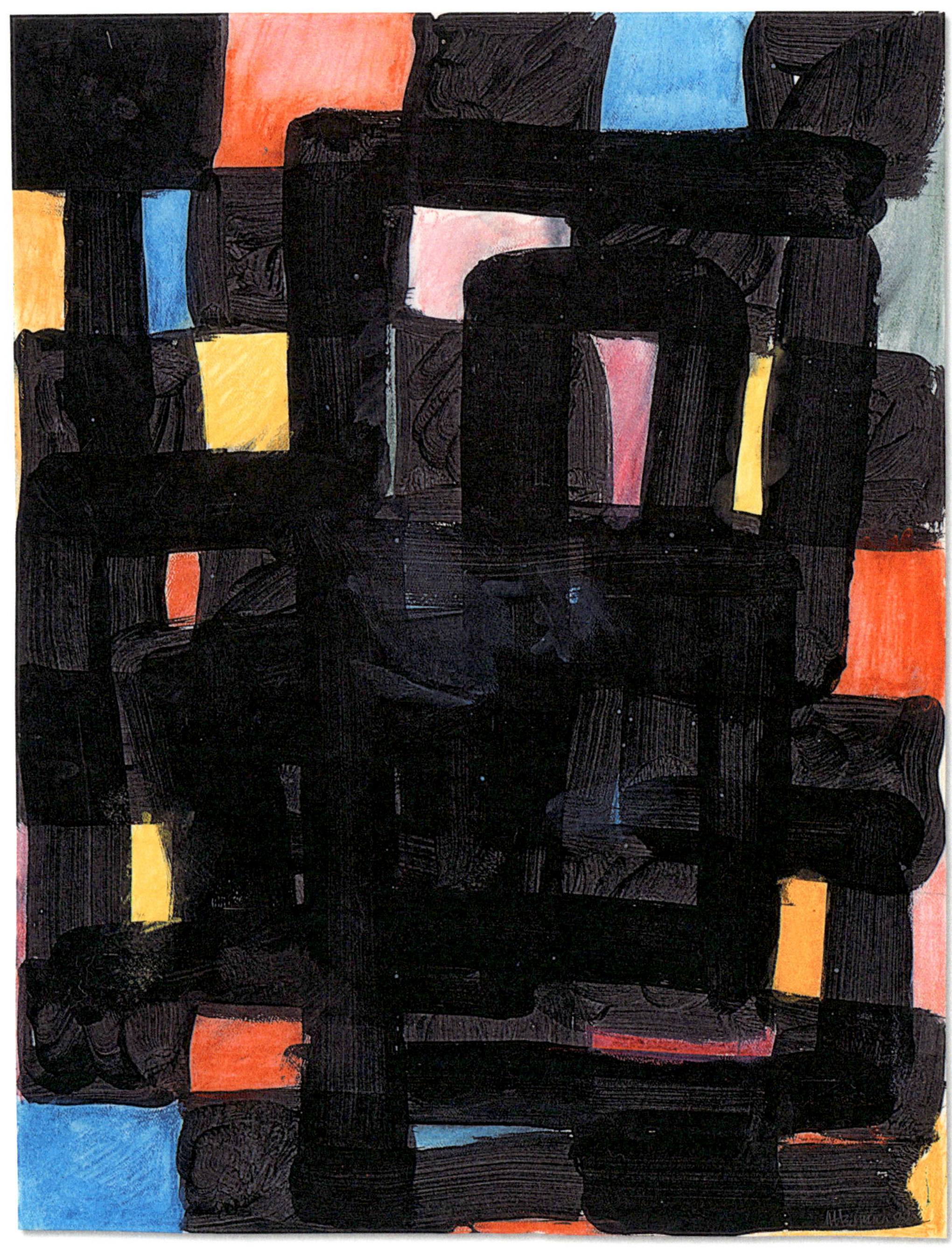

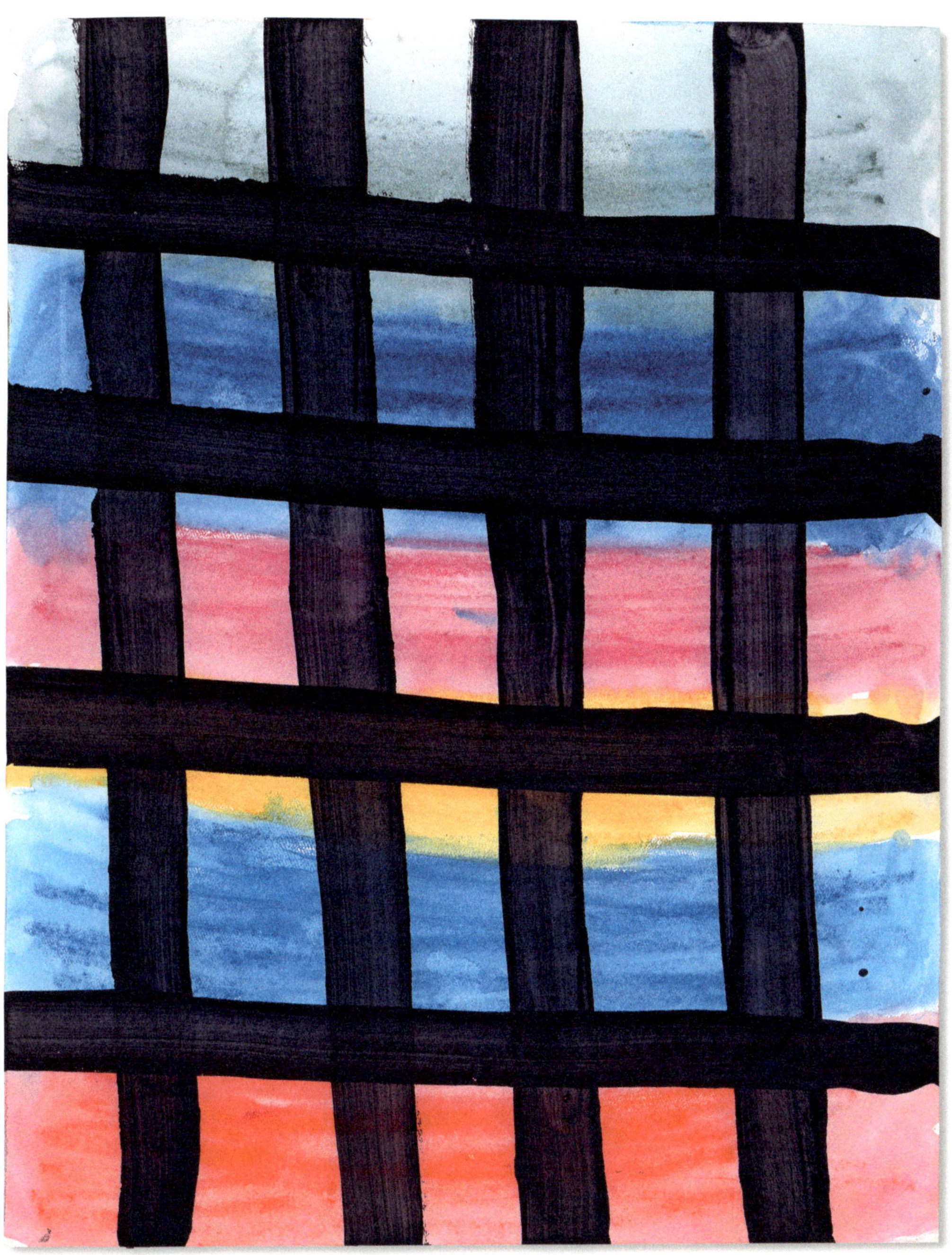

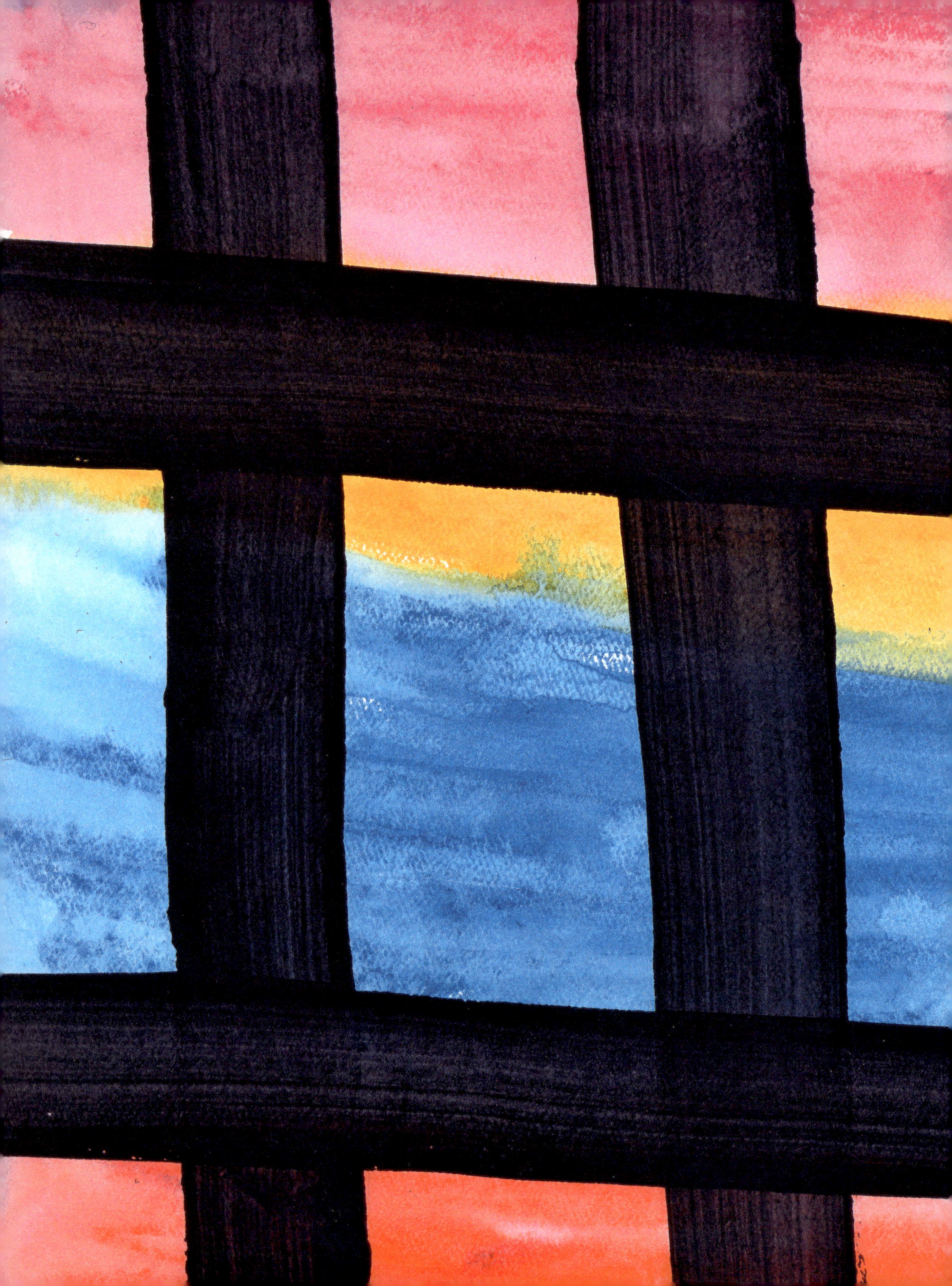

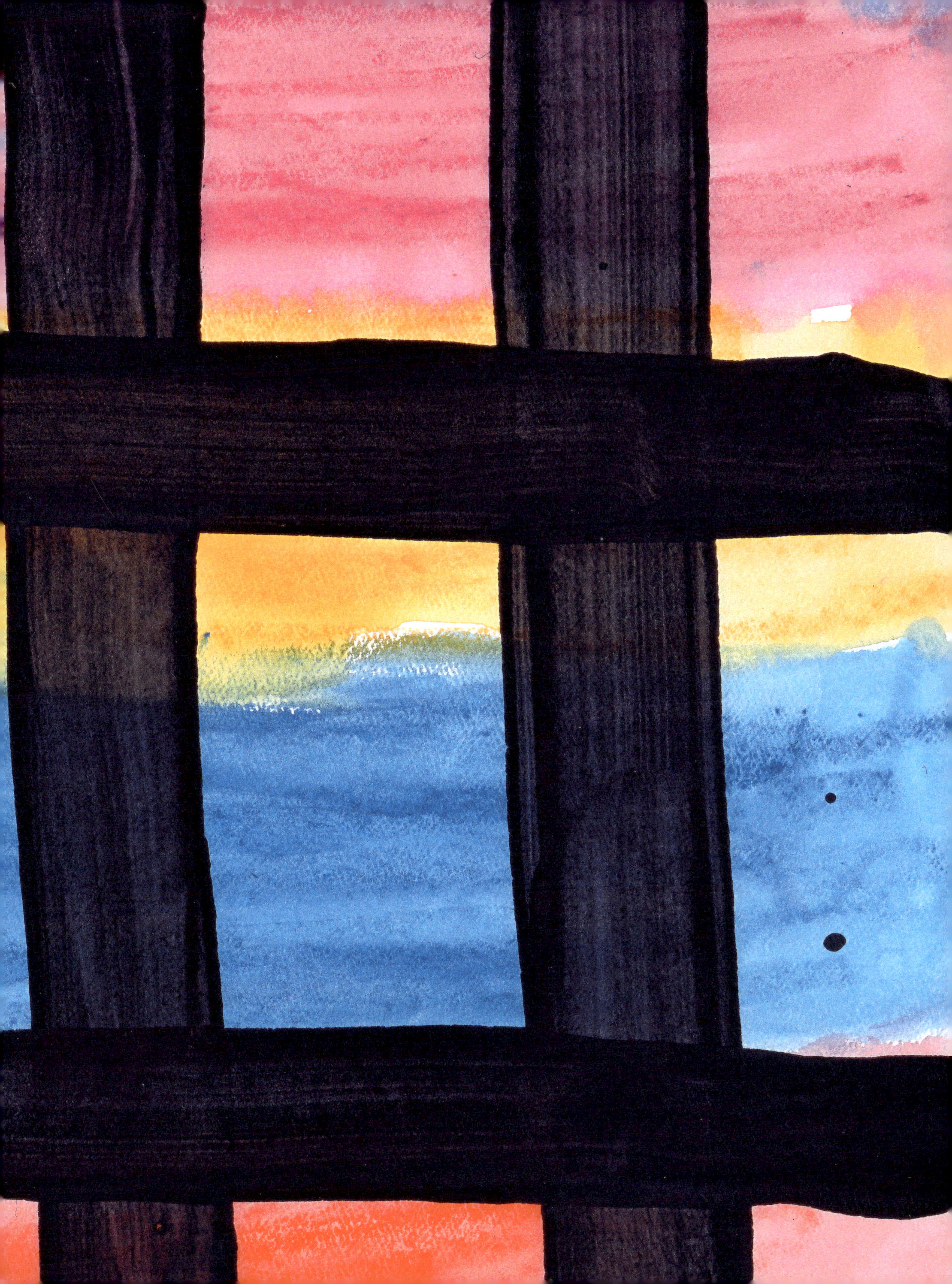

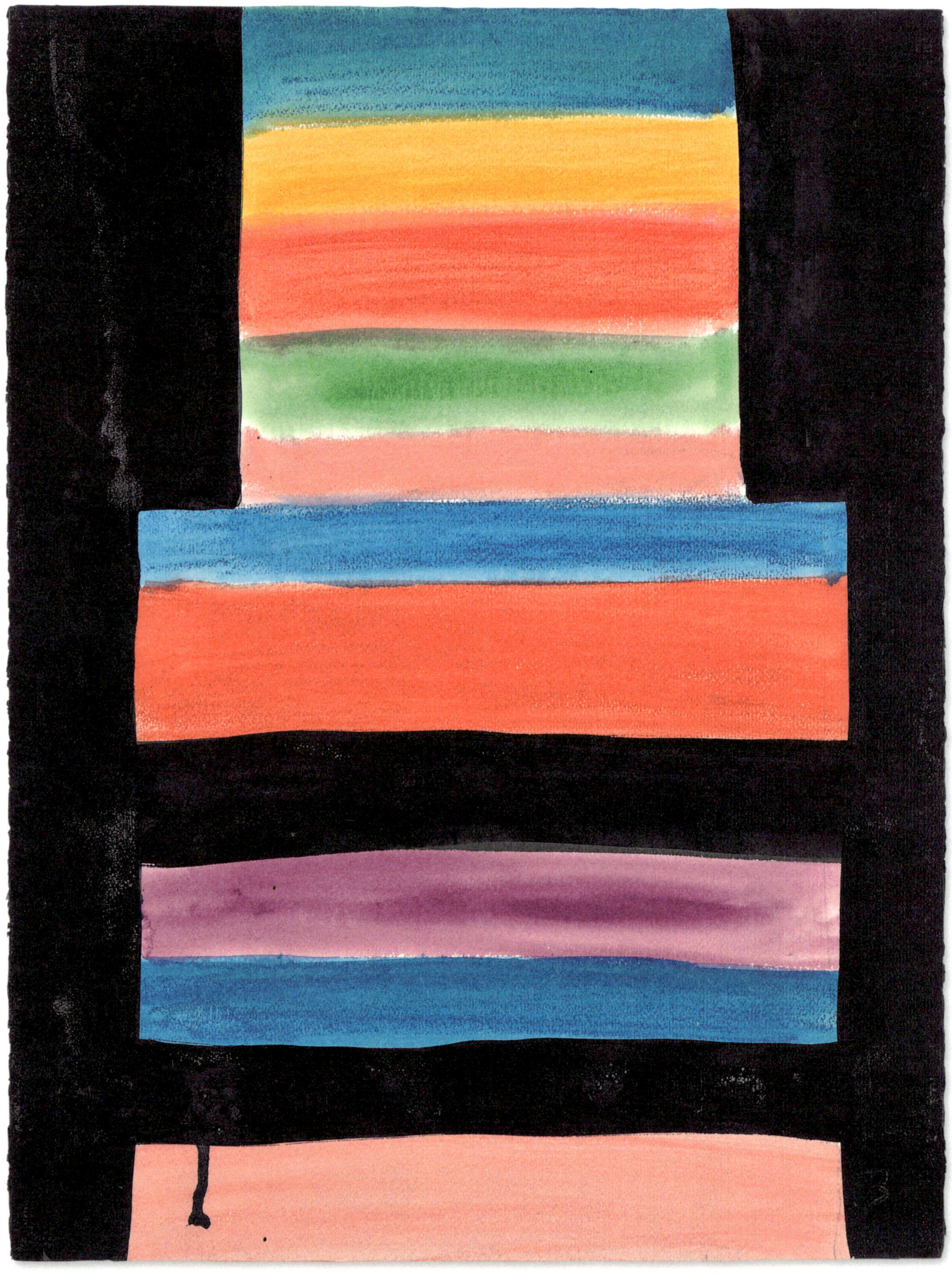

Rainbow Kachina, 1982. Watercolor on paper, 30 × 22 in. (76.2 × 55.9 cm)

Teapot, 1983. Watercolor on paper, 30 × 22 in. (76.2 × 55.9 cm)

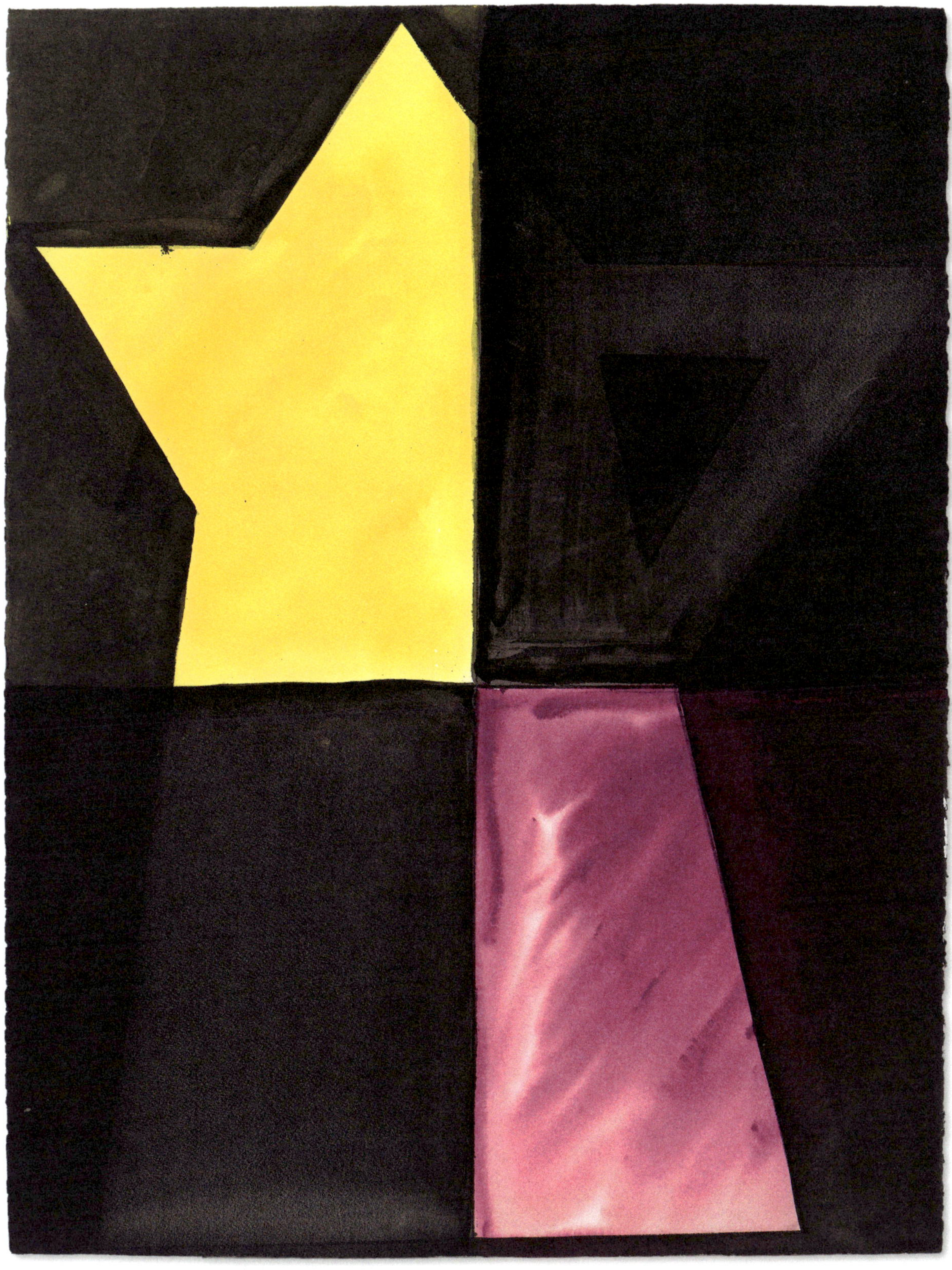

Untitled Study, *ca.* 2000s. Acrylic and pencil on paper, 12 × 9 in. (30.5 × 22.9 cm)

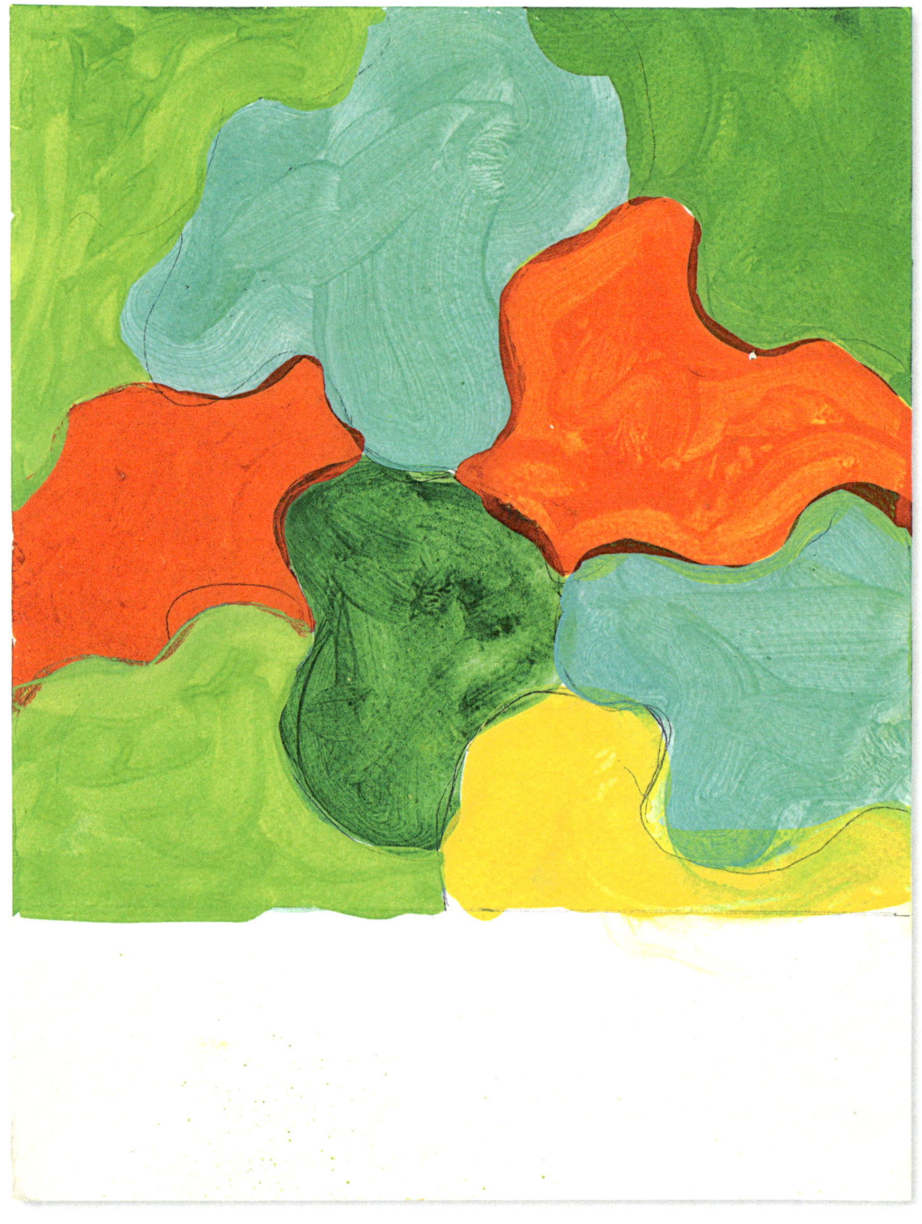

Untitled Watercolor Study, ca. 2000s. Acrylic and watercolor on paper,
10 ¼ × 7 ⅛ in. (26 × 18.1 cm)

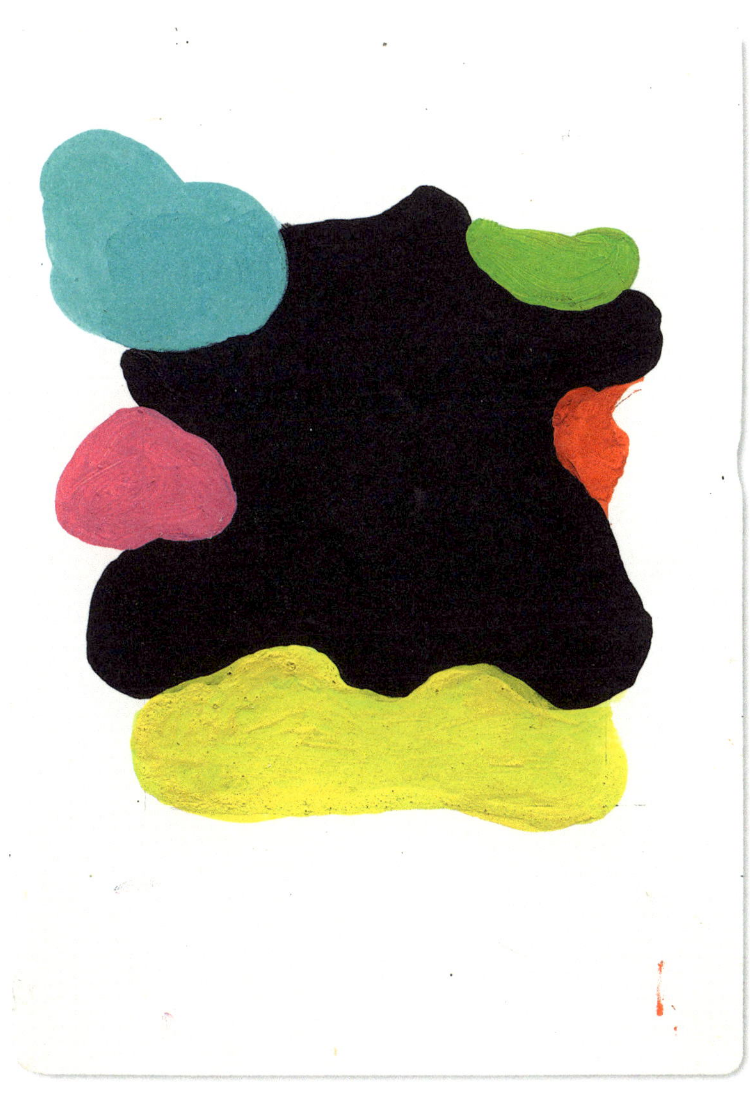

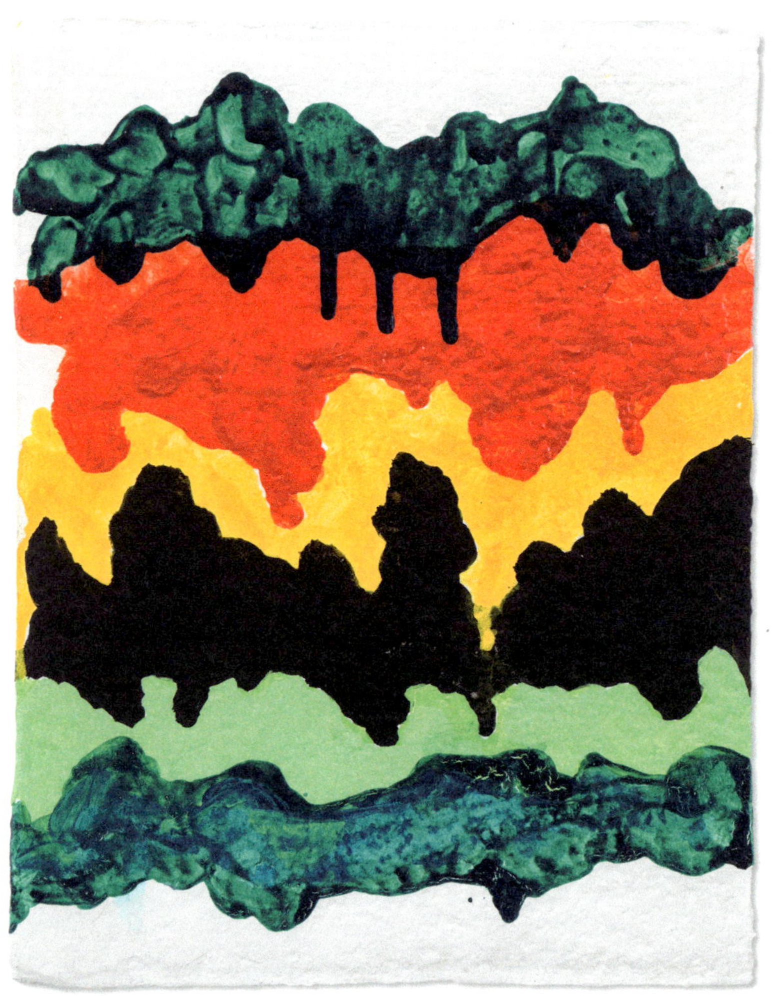

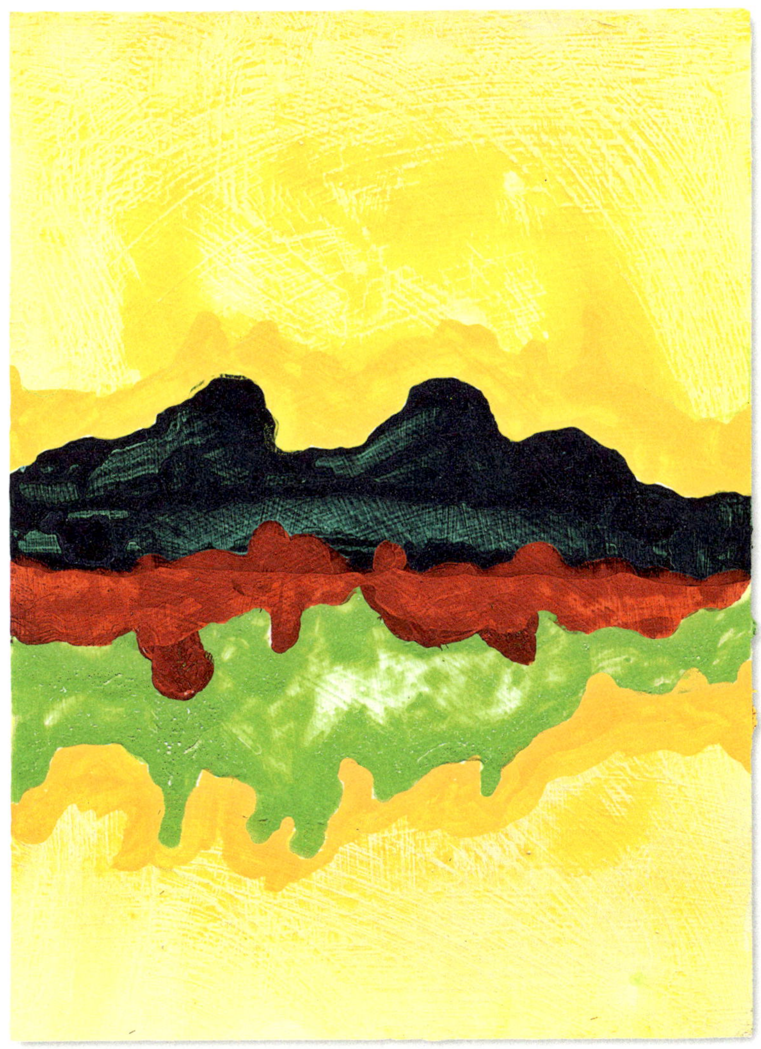

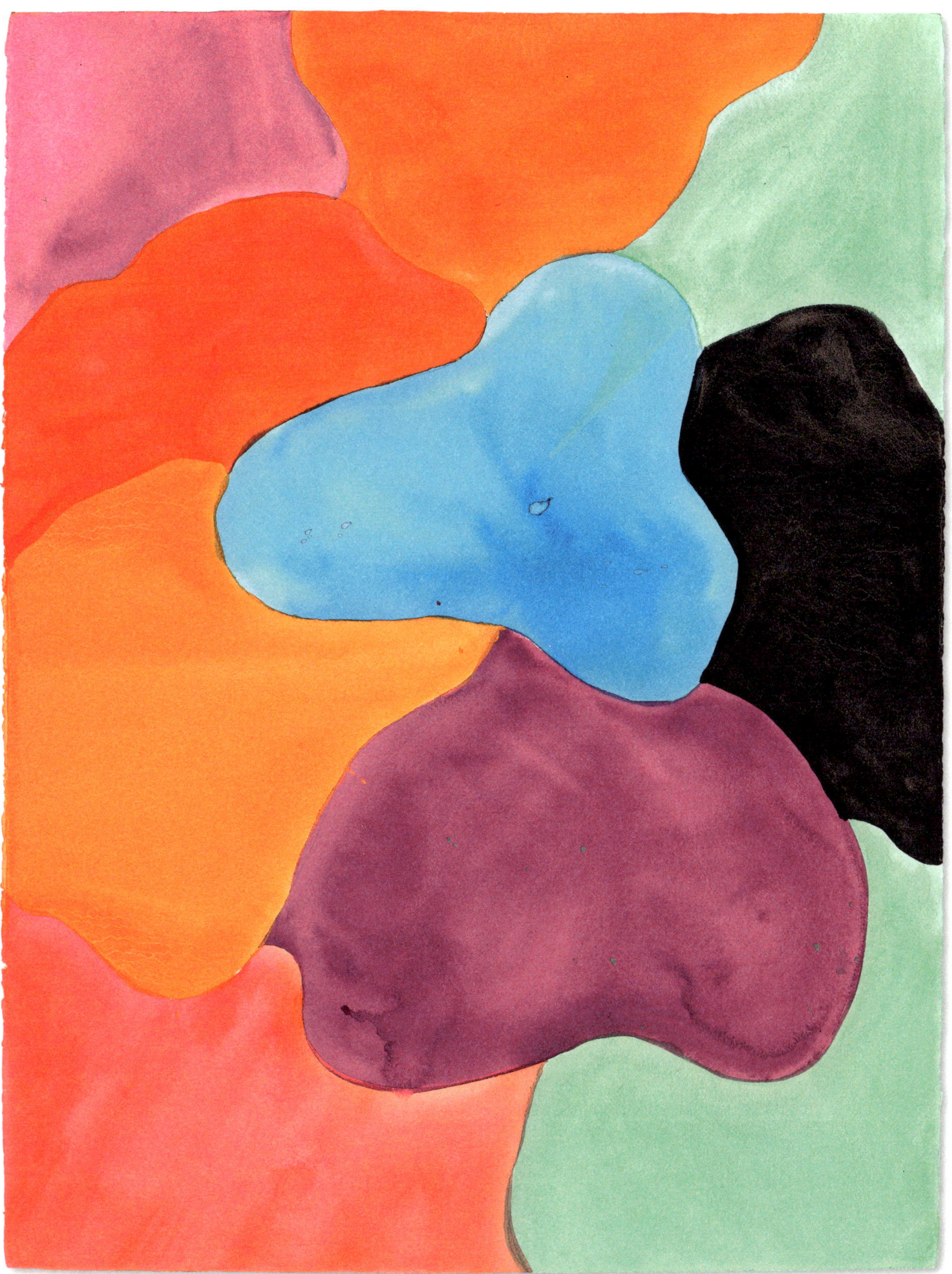

List of Works

The works reproduced in this book are listed below chronologically, including those with approximate dates. Unless otherwise noted as residing in a public or private collection, all works appear here courtesy the artist. Asterisks indicate works that were included in the exhibition *Mary Heilmann: Daydream Nation* at Hauser & Wirth, New York, 2024.

Pink Screen, 1973
Acrylic and spray paint on paper
22 × 28 in.
55.9 × 71.1 cm
Museum of Contemporary Art
Jacksonville, FL
pp. 10, 42

Hawaii, 1975
Ink and acrylic on gessoed paper
40 × 27 ½ in.
101.6 × 69.9 cm
p. 73

Untitled Study, ca. 1975*
Acrylic and marker on paper
7 × 5 in.
17.8 × 12.7 cm
pp. 30, 32–33

Red, Yellow, Blue Drawing, 1976
Acrylic on paper
30 × 22 in.
76.2 × 55.9 cm
Museum of Modern Art, New York
p. 31

Untitled, 1978
Acrylic on paper
44 × 29 in.
111.8 × 73.7 cm
Whereabouts unknown
p. 34

Orbit, ca. 1978
Acrylic on paper
30 × 22 ¼ in.
76.2 × 56.5 cm
pp. 35–37

Untitled Study, ca. 1978*
Gouache, colored pencil, and pencil on paper
8 × 6 in.
20.3 × 15.2 cm
p. 80

Descent, 1980
Acrylic and watercolor on paper
29 ⅞ × 22 ¼ in.
75.9 × 56.5 cm
Private collection
p. 81

Pink Embrace, 1980
Acrylic and watercolor on paper
29 ⅞ × 22 ⅛ in.
75.9 × 56.2 cm
Private collection
p. 82

Untitled Watercolor Study, ca. 1980s
Watercolor on paper
6 ¾ × 5 in.
17.1 × 12.7 cm
p. 47

Untitled Watercolor Study, ca. 1980s
Watercolor and pencil on paper
14 ⅛ × 10 ¾ in.
35.9 × 27.3 cm
p. 83

Untitled Watercolor Study, ca. 1980s
Watercolor on paper
6 ⅝ × 5 in.
16.8 × 12.7 cm
p. 60

Untitled Watercolor Study, ca. 1980s*
Watercolor on paper
6 ⅞ × 4 ⅞ in.
17.5 × 12.4 cm
Private collection
p. 110

Biomorph, 1982
Watercolor on paper
30 × 22 in.
76.2 × 55.9 cm
Museum Ludwig, Cologne
pp. 24–25, 141

Maze, 1982
Watercolor on paper
23 ¾ × 18 in.
60.3 × 45.7 cm
Private collection
p. 130

Psychedelic Serape #2, 1982
Watercolor on paper
23 ½ × 17 ½ in.
59.7 × 44.5 cm
Private collection
pp. 131–33

Rainbow Kachina, 1982
Watercolor on paper
30 × 22 in.
76.2 × 55.9 cm
Private collection
p. 134

Splash, 1982*
Acrylic and watercolor on paper
24 × 18 in.
61.0 × 45.7 cm
Private collection
pp. 127–29

The Diamond, 1982
Pastel and watercolor on paper
30 × 22 in.
76.2 × 55.9 cm
Private collection
p. 46

Untitled, 1982
Watercolor on paper
30 × 22 in.
76.2 × 55.9 cm
p. 107

Untitled Watercolor Study, ca. 1982–84
Watercolor and colored pencil on paper
3 ⅞ × 5 ⅝ in.
9.8 × 14.3 cm
pp. 85–87

Untitled Watercolor Study, ca. 1982–84
Watercolor and pencil on paper
12 ¼ × 10 in.
31.1 × 25.4 cm
Private collection
p. 112

Untitled Watercolor Study, ca. 1982–84*
Watercolor and pencil on paper
5 × 7 in.
12.7 × 17.8 cm
Private collection
p. 28

Teapot, 1983
Watercolor on paper
30 × 22 in.
76.2 × 55.9 cm
Museum Ludwig, Cologne
p. 135

Untitled, 1983
Pencil, crayon, and watercolor on paper
27 ½ × 39 ¼ in.
69.9 × 99.7 cm
p. 115

Red Flat Cup, ca. 1983
Watercolor on paper
Dimensions unknown
Whereabouts unknown
p. 116

Untitled Watercolor Study, ca. 1983–86*
Watercolor and pencil on paper
4 ½ × 3 ½ in.
11.4 × 8.9 cm
p. 27

Untitled Watercolor Study, ca. 1983–86*
Watercolor on paper
5 ⅝ × 3 ⅞ in.
14.3 × 9.8 cm
Private collection
p. 27

Kimono, 1984
Watercolor on paper
30 × 22 in.
76.2 × 55.9 cm
Private collection
p. 124

Tea Garden, 1984*
Watercolor on paper
30 × 22 in.
76.2 × 55.9 cm
p. 103

Aztec, 1985
Watercolor on paper
30 × 22 ¼ in.
76.2 × 56.5 cm
Private collection
p. 29

Mondrian, 1985
Watercolor on paper
30 × 22 ½ in.
76.2 × 57.2 cm
Private collection
p. 26

Lavender, 1986
Watercolor on paper
30 × 42 in.
76.2 × 106.7 cm
Private collection
pp. 88–89

Space Space, 1986
Watercolor on paper
5 × 7 in.
12.7 × 17.8 cm
p. 96

The Kiss (Saturday Nite), 1986
Watercolor on paper
30 × 22 in.
76.2 × 55.9 cm
Private collection
p. 91

Untitled Watercolor Study, ca. 1986
Watercolor on paper
5 × 6 ⅝ in.
12.7 × 16.8 cm
p. 92

Untitled Watercolor Study, ca. 1986–88*
Watercolor on paper
5 × 6 ½ in.
12.7 × 16.5 cm
Private collection
Cover, p. 93

Untitled Watercolor Study, ca. 1986–88
Watercolor and pencil on paper
5 × 6 ¾ in.
12.7 × 17.1 cm
p. 92

Untitled Watercolor Study, ca. 1986–88
Watercolor and pencil on paper
5 × 6 ¾ in.
12.7 × 17.1 cm
p. 93

Untitled Watercolor Study, ca. 1986–88*
Watercolor and pencil on paper
5 × 6 ⅞ in.
12.7 × 17.5 cm
pp. 93–95

Untitled Watercolor Study, ca. 1986–95*
Watercolor and colored pencil on paper
8 ¾ × 16 ½ in.
22.2 × 41.9 cm
p. 96

Untitled Watercolor Study, ca. 1987–89*
Watercolor and pencil on paper
11 × 8 ½ in.
27.9 × 21.6 cm
p. 98

Untitled Watercolor Study, ca. 1987–89*
Watercolor on paper
14 ⅜ × 10 ¼ in.
36.5 × 26.0 cm
p. 98

Islands, 1988*
Watercolor on paper
30 × 22 in.
76.2 × 55.9 cm
p. 84

Untitled Watercolor Study, ca. 1988
Watercolor and pencil on paper
6 × 3 ½ in.
15.2 × 8.9 cm
Private collection
p. 97

Untitled Watercolor Study, ca. 1988*
Watercolor and pencil on paper
6 ¼ × 3 ½ in.
15.9 × 8.9 cm
Private collection
p. 97

Untitled Watercolor Study, ca. 1988–90*
Watercolor, crayon, and pencil on paper
10 ¼ × 7 in.
26.0 × 17.8 cm
p. 58

Untitled Watercolor Study, ca. 1988–90
Watercolor, crayon, and pencil on paper
7 × 10 ¼ in.
17.8 × 26.0 cm
p. 58

Lifeline, 1989
Watercolor and colored pencil on paper
19 ½ × 19 ⅜ in.
49.5 × 49.2 cm
p. 117

Untitled Study, ca. 1989*
Gouache and pencil on paper
7 × 5 in.
17.8 × 12.7 cm
Private collection
p. 100

Untitled Watercolor Study (Self-Portrait),
ca. 1989*
Colored pencil and watercolor on paper
16 ⅜ × 12 ⅜ in.
41.6 × 31.4 cm
Private collection
p. 99

Untitled Watercolor Study (Self-Portrait),
ca. 1989
Watercolor on paper
16 ⅜ × 12 ⅜ in.
41.6 × 31.4 cm
p. 99

Untitled Watercolor Study, ca. 1989*
Watercolor on paper
6 ¾ × 5 in.
17.1 × 12.7 cm
p. 102

Blumoon, 1990
Watercolor on paper
30 ⅛ × 22 ¼ in.
76.5 × 56.5 cm
Private collection
p. 105

Untitled Watercolor Study, ca. 1990–92*
Watercolor and pencil on paper
5 ¼ × 4 in.
13.3 × 10.2 cm
p. 106

Untitled, ca. 1990–95*
Acrylic and watercolor on handmade paper
11 ½ × 11 ½ in.
29.2 × 29.2 cm
p. 101

Untitled, ca. 1990–95*
Acrylic on handmade paper
11 ½ × 11 ½ in.
29.2 × 29.2 cm
pp. 53–55

Untitled Watercolor Study, ca. 1990s*
Watercolor on paper
10 ⅞ × 14 ⅞ in.
27.6 × 37.8 cm
Private collection
p. 60

Chartreuse Web, 1991
Oil on handmade paper
19 × 19 in.
48.3 × 48.3 cm
Private collection
p. 52

Untitled Watercolor Study, ca. 1991–92*
Watercolor on paper
7 × 5 in.
17.8 × 12.7 cm
Private collection
pp. 69–71

Untitled Watercolor Study, ca. 1991–97*
Watercolor on paper
14 ⅞ × 10 ⅞ in.
37.8 × 27.6 cm
Private collection
pp. 106, 108–9

Little Chartreuse, 1993
Oil on gessoed handmade paper
27 ½ × 23 ¼ in.
69.9 × 59.1 cm
Private collection
p. 48

Untitled Study, ca. 1993–97*
Acrylic on handmade paper
15 ¼ × 10 ¼ in.
38.7 × 26.0 cm
p. 69

Garden of Allah #2, 1994
Watercolor on paper
41 × 29 ½ in.
104.1 × 74.9 cm
Private collection
p. 90

Au Go Go, 1995
Acrylic and pastel on paper
30 × 22 ½ in.
76.2 × 57.2 cm
Private collection
pp. 49–51

Close Out, 1995*
Oil on gessoed paper
41 × 29 ½ in.
104.1 × 74.9 cm
Private collection
pp. 62–64

Crimson & Clover, 1995
Oil on gessoed paper
30 × 22 in.
76.2 × 55.9 cm
Private collection
p. 28

Curl, 1995
Oil on gessoed paper
41 × 29 ½ in.
104.1 × 74.9 cm
p. 66

Hydrangia, 1995
Oil on gessoed paper
41 × 29 ½ in.
104.1 × 74.9 cm
Private collection
p. 111

Line Up, 1995*
Oil on gessoed paper
41 × 29 ½ in.
104.1 × 74.9 cm
Private collection
p. 65

Red Corner, 1995
Oil on gessoed paper
30 × 22 in.
76.2 × 55.9 cm
Private collection
p. 118

The Red Screen, 1995
Oil on gessoed paper
42 ⅛ × 29 ⅞ in.
107.0 × 75.9 cm
Private collection
p. 104

Tricky, 1995
Oil on gessoed paper
41 ½ × 29 ½ in.
105.4 × 74.9 cm
pp. 119–21

Untitled Watercolor Study, 1995*
Watercolor on paper
5 ⅝ × 4 in.
14.3 × 10.2 cm
Private collection
p. 77

Untitled Watercolor Study, 1995
Watercolor on paper
4 × 5 ⅝ in.
10.2 × 14.3 cm
Private collection
p. 77

Untitled Watercolor Study, 1995*
Watercolor on paper
4 × 5 ⅝ in.
10.2 × 14.3 cm
Private collection
p. 77

Untitled Watercolor Study, 1995*
Watercolor on paper
5 × 7 in.
12.7 × 17.8 cm
pp. 76, 78–79

Untitled Watercolor Study, 1995*
Watercolor on paper
5 × 7 in.
12.7 × 17.8 cm
Private collection
p. 76

White Screen, 1995
Oil on gessoed paper
41 × 29 ½ in.
104.1 × 74.9 cm
Whitney Museum of American Art, New York
p. 113

White Water, 1995
Oil on gessoed paper
41 × 29 ½ in.
104.1 × 74.9 cm
p. 61

Black Valentine, ca. 1995
Oil and pencil on handmade paper
12 × 11 ½ in.
30.5 × 29.2 cm
p. 53

Joe's Greens, 1996
Oil on gessoed paper
14 × 10 in.
35.6 × 25.4 cm
Private collection
p. 39

Palm Tree, ca. 1996*
Oil on gessoed paper
41 ½ × 29 ¼ in.
105.4 × 74.3 cm
Private collection
p. 74

Blue Line, 1997
Oil on gessoed paper
41 ½ × 29 ¼ in.
105.4 × 74.3 cm
Private collection
p. 59

Lovebird, 1997
Acrylic on paper
10 ⅜ × 10 in.
26.4 × 25.4 cm
Private collection
p. 40

Richie, 1997
Oil on gessoed paper
41 × 29 ½ in.
104.1 × 74.9 cm
Private collection
p. 41

Islands, 1999
Acrylic and watercolor on paper
29 ½ × 41 ½ in.
74.9 × 105.4 cm
Museum Ludwig, Cologne
p. 38

Charming Billy, 2000
Oil on paper
22 × 15 ⅝ in.
55.9 × 39.7 cm
p. 56

Charming Billy, ca. 2000
Watercolor and digital print on paper
7 ½ × 4 ⅞ in.
19.1 × 12.4 cm
p. 57

Untitled Study, ca. 2000s*
Acrylic and pencil on paper
12 × 9 in.
30.5 × 22.9 cm
Private collection
p. 136

Untitled Watercolor Study, ca. 2000s*
Acrylic and watercolor on paper
10 ¼ × 7 ⅛ in.
26.0 × 18.1 cm
Private collection
p. 137

Broken Study, 2005
Oil on gessoed paper
41 ½ × 29 ¼ in.
105.4 × 74.3 cm
Private collection
p. 123

Cloth Study, 2005
Oil on gessoed paper
41 ¾ × 29 ½ in.
106.0 × 74.9 cm
Private collection
p. 67

Half Jack, 2005
Oil on gessoed paper
41 ½ × 29 ¼ in.
105.4 × 74.3 cm
Private collection
p. 122

Mirage, ca. 2009*
Watercolor on paper
24 × 18 in.
61.0 × 45.7 cm
Private collection
p. 68

Negative Space One, 2014
Acrylic on handmade paper
11 ½ × 11 ½ in.
29.2 × 29.2 cm
Private collection
p. 125

Negative Space Two, 2014
Acrylic on handmade paper
12 × 15 in.
30.5 × 38.1 cm
Private collection
p. 125

Shore Break, 2014
Acrylic on handmade paper
13 ¾ × 10 ½ in.
34.9 × 26.7 cm
Private collection
p. 138

First Date, 2015
Oil on handmade paper
12 ½ × 15 ⅝ in.
31.8 × 39.7 cm
Private collection
pp. 2, 5, 57

Rainbow Crash, 2018
Acrylic on paper
14 × 10 in.
35.6 × 25.4 cm
p. 139

Yellow Right, 2018
Acrylic on paper
10 × 14 in.
25.4 × 35.6 cm
Private collection
pp. 43–45

6 Hot and Glassy, 2019
Acrylic on paper
4 × 6 ¼ in.
10.2 × 15.9 cm
p. 72

Mighty Right, 2019
Acrylic on paper
3 ¼ × 7 ¼ in.
8.3 × 18.4 cm
p. 72

Untitled Watercolor Study, ca. 2019*
Watercolor on paper
5 × 3 ⅜ in.
12.7 × 8.6 cm
Private collection
p. 110

Biography

Born 1940, San Francisco
Lives and works in New York and Bridgehampton, NY

EDUCATION

MA, Ceramics and Sculpture, University of California, Berkeley, 1967
Studies in Poetry and Ceramics, San Francisco State University, 1963
BA, Literature, University of California, Santa Barbara, 1962

This selected exhibition history and bibliography gathers the exhibitions, books, and articles in which Heilmann's works on paper have appeared.

SOLO AND TWO-PERSON EXHIBITIONS

2024
Mary Heilmann, Galleria Civica d'Arte Moderna e Contemporanea, Turin

Daydream Nation, curated by Gary Simmons, Hauser & Wirth, New York

2022
Squaring Davis, Jan Shrem and Maria Manetti Shrem Museum of Art, University of California, Davis

2021
Mary Heilmann, Pace Prints, New York

2020
Highway, Oceans, Daydreams, Hauser & Wirth, Southampton, NY

2018
Wavy: Sabra Moon Elliot and Mary Heilmann, Tripoli Gallery, Southampton, NY

2017
RYB: Mary Heilmann Paintings, 1975–78, Craig F. Starr Gallery, New York

2016
Looking at Pictures, Whitechapel Gallery, London

2015
Geometrics: Waves, Roads, etc., 303 Gallery, New York

2010
Home Sweet Home, Galerie Barbara Weiss, Berlin

Weather Report: Drawings and Prints, Museum Ludwig, Cologne

2008
Some Pretty Colors, Zwirner & Wirth, New York

2006
Saturday Night Kiss, Hauser & Wirth, Zurich

2001
Mary Heilmann, Galerie Meyer Kainer, Vienna

2000
Jessica Stockholder—Mary Heilmann (Gemälde aus der Sammlung Hauser & Wirth), Kunstmuseum St. Gallen, Switzerland

1997
This and That, Stiftung für konstruktive und konkrete Kunst, Zurich

Modern Art: Paintings and Papers, Wolfgang Häusler, Munich

Galerie Stadtpark, Krems, Austria

1995
New Works on Paper, Pat Hearn Gallery, New York

Mary Heilmann and Elizabeth Cannon, Cristinerose Gallery, New York

1994
Paintings, Drawings, Ceramics, Beaver College Art Gallery, Glenside, PA

Works, 1971–1994, Galerie m Bochum, Germany

1983
Paintings, Daniel Weinberg Gallery, San Francisco

1979
Paintings and Drawings, Daniel Weinberg Gallery, San Francisco

2023
A Walk on the Wild Side: '70s New York in the Norman E. Fisher Collection, Museum of Contemporary Art Jacksonville, FL

Small, Locks Gallery, Philadelphia

Two Pieces in the Shape of a Pear, curated by Pat Steir, Hauser & Wirth, Southampton, NY

Ecstatic: Selections from the Hammer Contemporary Collection, Hammer Museum, Los Angeles

On Paper: Gray at 60, Gray Chicago; Gray New York (traveling exhibition)

2022
18th Annual Thanksgiving Collective: A Paleolithic Age, Tripoli Gallery, Wainscott, NY

2021
There's There There, curated by Rashid Johnson, Hauser & Wirth, Southampton, NY

2020
The Backward Glance Can Be a Glimpse into the Future, curated by Beat Wismer, Von Bartha, Basel, Switzerland

2019
Material Actions, Hauser & Wirth, St. Moritz, Switzerland

2017
Lonely Planet, curated by Andrew Brischler, Gavlak, Palm Beach, FL

2015
Oceans Eleven, curated by Billy Sullivan, Ille Arts, Amagansett, NY

Works on Paper, Greene Naftali, New York

2014
Paintings on Paper, David Zwirner, New York

Eight Books Two Weeks, t.a.t. new talents powered by DEG, Cologne

Painting and Canvas in Conversation, Ille Arts, Amagansett, NY

Speaking Through Paint: Hans Hofmann's Legacy Today, curated by Stacey Gershon and Deborah Goodman Davis, Lori Bookstein Fine Art, New York

Hooray for Hollywood!, Pavel Zoubok Gallery in collaboration with Mixed Greens, New York

2013
40 Years at the Daniel Weinberg Gallery, Ambach & Rice, Los Angeles

2012
One Wish Always Remains Unfulfilled. Kasper König Takes Stock, Museum Ludwig, Cologne

Smile American Art – Kienbaum Collection, curated by Rolf Ricke, Galerie Thomas Zander, Cologne

Color Go-Lightly … An Homage to Color, Gallery Valentine, Bridgehampton, NY

Architectural Dispositions, Thomas Solomon Gallery, Los Angeles

Sidetracks: Painting in the Paramodern Continuum, Stavanger Art Museum, Norway

2010
For Your Eyes Only, De Markten, Brussels

2005
The Early Show, curated by Elysia Borowy-Reeder, Scott Reeder, and Tyson Reeder, White Columns, New York

1999
Free Coke, Greene Naftali, New York

Special Offer, Kasseler Kunstverein, Kassel, Germany

1996
Abstract Practice, Thaddaeus Ropac, Salzburg

1995
Works on Paper, Zeno X Gallery, Antwerp

Contemporary Drawing: Exploring the Territory, Aspen Art Museum, CO

"Made in the U.S.A." Original Paintings on Paper, Galerie Bob van Orsouw, Zurich

1994
Abstract Works on Paper, Robert Miller Gallery, New York

1993
The Return of the Cadavre Exquis, Drawing Center, New York; Corcoran Gallery of Art, Washington, D.C.; Santa Monica Museum of Art, CA; Forum for Contemporary Art, Saint Louis, MO; American Center, Paris (traveling exhibition)

New American Abstraction: The Conscious Gesture, Locks Gallery, Philadelphia

Watercolors, Nina Freudenheim Gallery, Buffalo, NY

1988
Sightings: Drawing with Color, Instituto de Estudios Norteamericanos, Barcelona; Pratt Institute, New York (traveling exhibition)

1984
Drawings: New Dimensions, Nina Freudenheim Gallery, Buffalo, NY

1983
National Drawing Invitational, Central Washington University Gallery, Ellensburg, WA

1980
The Norman Fisher Collection, Jacksonville Art Museum, FL

SELECTED BIBLIOGRAPHY

2024
Mary Heilmann. Turin: Allemandi. Exhibition catalogue.

Shana Dickler and Ylva Rouse (eds.). *A Walk on the Wild Side*. Jacksonville, FL: Museum of Contemporary Art Jacksonville. Exhibition catalogue.

"Best New York Exhibitions: Mary Heilmann, Turiya Adkins, and More." *Whitewall*, May 31. https://whitewall.art/art/best-new-york-exhibitions-mary-heilmann-turiya-adkins-and-more.

Benjamin Clifford. "Mary Heilmann: Daydream Nation." *Brooklyn Rail*, July/August. https://brooklynrail.org/2024/07/artseen/Mary-Heilmann-Daydream-Nation/

Natalie Haddad. "Five Art Shows to See in New York Before July Ends." *Hyperallergic*, July 16. https://hyperallergic.com/933742/five-art-shows-to-see-in-new-york-before-july-2024-ends

2023
Gray at 60. Chicago: Gray. Exhibition catalogue.

2019
303 Gallery: 35 Years. New York: 303inPrint.

2017
"Laura Hoptman: Condition of Good Painting." *Bijutsu Techo*, March.

Paul Laster. "Mary Heilmann talks about mixing geometry and pop culture in her work." *Time Out*, July 5. https://www.timeout.com/newyork/blog/mary-heilmann-talks-about-mixing-geometry-and-pop-culture-in-her-work-070517.

Paul Laster. "Living Color." *Time Out New York*, July 5–18: 74–75.

Brienne Walsh. "Mary Heilmann Wants to Make a Lot of Money so She Can Buy More Land in the Hamptons." *Forbes*, June 24. https://www.forbes.com/sites/briennewalsh/2017/07/24/mary-heilmann-wants-to-make-a-lot-of-money-so-she-can-buy-more-land-in-the-hamptons.

2016
Lydia Yee (ed.). *Mary Heilmann: Looking at Pictures*. London: Whitechapel Gallery. Exhibition catalogue.

2014
Thomas Micchelli. "Paintings on Paper, Abstract and Effervescent." *Hyperallergic*, August 9. http://hyperallergic.com/142624/paintings-on-paper-abstract-and-effervescent.

2012
Mary Heilmann. *Seeing Things — Visions, Waves and Roads*. Cologne: Snoeck.

Holly Williams. "Taken to the Max." *The New Review*, February 26: 38-41.

2008
Brice Brown and Trevor Winkfield (eds.). *Sienese Shredder*, New York: Distributed Art Publishers.

2007
Terry R. Myers. "Heil Mary." *Modern Painters*, April: 74.

1999
Mary Heilmann. *The All Night Movie*. Zurich: Offizin and Galerie Hauser & Wirth, 1999.

1997
"Space Craft." *Interview Magazine*, August: 114–15.

1996
Paul Mattick, Jr. "Review, Pat Hearn Gallery." *Art in America* 84, June: 99–101.

Roberta Smith. "The Gallery Doors Open to the Long Denied." *New York Times*, May 26.

1995
Howard Halle. "Mary Heilmann: New Works on Paper." *Time Out New York*, November 29–December 6: 24.

Mark Rosenthal. *Contemporary Drawing: Exploring the Territory*. Aspen: Aspen Art Museum. Exhibition catalogue.

Roberta Smith. "Heading West with Canvases." *New York Times*, November 17.

Time Out New York, November 29–December 6: 24. (Illustration only.)

1993
Richard Huntington. "Water Babies." *Buffalo News*, December 17.

Michael Kimmelman. "The Exquisite Corpse Rises From the Dead." *New York Times*, November 7.

Jane Philbrick (ed.). *The Return of the Cadavre Exquis*. New York: Drawing Center. Exhibition catalogue.

1989
New Yorker, October 30: 16. (Illustration only.)

1988
Sightings: Drawings with Color. New York: Pratt Institute; Barcelona: Instituto de Estudios Norteamericanos. Exhibition catalogue.

1983
"Mary Heilmann: Artist's Project." *Bomb*, no. 8: 63. (Illustration only.)

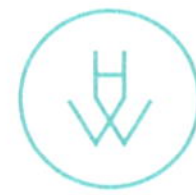

This book originates from and builds on the exhibition
Mary Heilmann: Daydream Nation, Hauser & Wirth New York,
22nd Street, May 2–July 26, 2024.

Editor: Alexis Lowry

Publisher: Michaela Unterdörfer

Managing editor: Jake Brodsky

Assistant editor: Susannah Faber

Editorial support: Liane Thatcher, Paul Gabrielli, and Philip Tan,
Mary Heilmann Studio; Emily Larson and Barbara Corti, Hauser &
Wirth

Proofreading: Anna Bane

Book design and typography: Polymode, Brian Johnson, Silas Munro,
and Randa Hadi, Los Angeles / Raleigh

Prepress: prints professional, Berlin

Production coordination: Christine Stäcker

Printing and binding: DZA Druckerei zu Altenburg

Cover paper: Fedrigoni Materica Gesso 360g

Interior paper: Lessebo Design Smooth Natural 150g

Typeface: Camelion designed by Sandrine Nugue for Oh No Type
Company

Mary Heilmann: Works on Paper, 1973–2019
© 2025 Hauser & Wirth Publishers

www.hauserwirth.com

Image credits
Cover, 2, 5, 28 top right, 47, 56, 57 bottom, 61–66, 69 right, 70–71,
74, 76 right, 77 top left, 84–87, 93 top, 93 bottom, 94–95, 97,
101, 103, 106 right, 107, 112, 115: Thomas Müller. 6, 9, 13, 73: Sarah
Muehlbauer. 10, 42: Museum of Contemporary Art Jacksonville, FL;
gift of Douglas W. Fisher and the Estate of Norman Fisher. 15, 46,
81–82, 90–91, 122–24, 134: Barbora Gerny. 15, 16 right: artwork ©
The Estate of Lee Lozano. 17 right: Peter McCourt. 18, 22, 27, 30,
32–33, 53–55, 57 top left, 58, 60, 68, 69 left, 76 left, 77 center
right, 77 bottom, 78–80, 83, 92, 93 center, 96 bottom, 98–100, 102,
106 left, 108–09, 110, 117, 119–21, 127–29, 136–37: Genevieve Hanson.
20: Jennifer DiSunno. 24–25, 38, 141: Tom Powel Imaging, courtesy
Museum Ludwig, Cologne. 26: Stefan Altenburger Photography
Zürich. 29: © 2017 Christie's Images Limited. 31: © The Museum of
Modern Art / licensed by SCALA / Art Resource, New York. 35–37,
43–45, 96 top, 139: Dan Bradica. 39, 48, 88–89: Peter Cox, courtesy
Zeno X Gallery, Antwerp. 41: Stephen White. 49–51, 72: Thomas
Barrat. 67: Courtesy 303 Gallery. 104: Jon Etter. 113: courtesy
Whitney Museum of American Art, New York. 125, 138: Adam
Reich. 130–33: Christopher Burke. All other images courtesy Mary
Heilmann.

Cover: Untitled Watercolor Study (detail), ca. 1986–88

Every effort has been made to trace copyright ownership and to
obtain reproduction permissions. Corrections brought to the
publisher's attention will be incorporated in future reprints or
editions of this book.

Distribution:

North and South America
ARTBOOK | D.A.P.
75 Broad Street, Suite 630
New York, NY 10004
artbook.com

All other territories
Thames & Hudson Ltd.
181A High Holborn
London WC1V 7QX
thamesandhudson.com

ISBN: 978-3-907493-18-2

Library of Congress Control Number: 2025930039

Printed and bound in Germany